Lifestyle Gurus

Lifestyle Gurus

Constructing Authority and Influence Online

STEPHANIE A. BAKER AND CHRIS ROJEK

polity

First published in 2020 by Polity Press

Polity Press
65 Bridge Street
Cambridge CB2 1UR, UK

Polity Press
101 Station Landing
Suite 300
Medford, MA 02155, USA

ISBN-13: 978-1-5095-3017-5 (hardback)
ISBN-13: 978-1-5095-3018-2 (paperback)

A catalogue record for this book is available from the British Library.

Library of Congress Cataloging-in-Publication Data
Names: Baker, Stephanie Alice, 1983- author. | Rojek, Chris, author.
Title: Lifestyle gurus : constructing authority and influence online /
  Stephanie Baker, Chris Rojek.
Description: Medford : Polity Press, [2019] | Includes bibliographical
  references and index. | Summary: "The rise of blogs and social media has
  facilitated an industry of self-appointed 'lifestyle gurus' who have
  become instrumental in the management of intimacy and social relations.
  Baker and Rojek trace the rise of lifestyle influencers in the digital
  age, relating this development to the erosion of trust in the
  expert-professional power bloc"-- Provided by publisher.
Identifiers: LCCN 2019020142 (print) | LCCN 2019980575 (ebook) | ISBN
  9781509530182 (paperback) | ISBN 9781509530175 (hardback) | ISBN
  9781509530205 (epub)
Subjects: LCSH: Social media. | Influence (Psychology) | Power (Social
  sciences) | Interpersonal relations. | Collective behavior.
Classification: LCC HM1206 .B354 2019 (print) | LCC HM1206 (ebook) | DDC
  302.23/1--dc23
LC record available at https://lccn.loc.gov/2019020142
LC ebook record available at https://lccn.loc.gov/2019980575

Typeset in 11.25 on 13 Dante
by Fakenham Prepress Solutions, Fakenham, Norfolk NR21 8NL
Printed and bound in the UK by by CPI Group (UK) Ltd, Croydon

For further information on Polity, visit our website: politybooks.com

Contents

Acknowledgements

Stephanie thanks Ian, Viola and Juliette, family and friends, who provided support at the time of writing this book.

City, University of London, have been generous in granting Stephanie a sabbatical, which assisted with the research for, and writing of, this book.

Chris would like to thank Luke, Kate, Amelie and Chloe, Eugene McLaughlin, Simon Susen, Barry Smart, Dan Cook, Maggie O'Neill, George and Sue Ritzer.

Stephanie and Chris would also like to thank the anonymous reviewers, who provided useful feedback on this manuscript, and the staff at Polity – including John Thompson, Mary Savigar and Ellen MacDonald-Kramer – for bringing this book into print.

Introduction

Our study of lifestyle gurus began in 2015 with the case of Belle Gibson. Gibson presented herself online as a cancer survivor. She claimed that she healed herself from terminal brain cancer by adhering to a healthy diet and lifestyle, rejecting conventional cancer treatments in favour of natural remedies. Using her blog and social media to document her experience, she created an online persona based around inspirational quotes, attractive selfies, healthy recipes and a general air of presumed intimacy. Gibson used these technologies to build an online community of over 200,000 followers. Her claims of self-recovery formed the basis of her online persona and successful global brand, with a bestselling app available on Apple, an international book deal with Penguin and series of public accolades built around her narrative of survival. Gibson's association with Apple and Penguin gave her story a sense of legitimacy and extended her global reach. Comprised of a collection of recipes, her book and app were about more than food; they were framed more broadly under the rubric of lifestyle philosophy as guides on 'how we should live, combating stress, achieving wellness and a healthy, wholesome lifestyle'. In short, Gibson's products were marketed to consumers as manuals filled with 'good advice on promoting better living' (Barker 2014).

The moral payload of Gibson's message was the unexamined assumption that most people do not live well and do not know how to acquire good advice to remedy the problem. Part of the appeal of Gibson's story was that she provided many of those suffering from cancer with hope. If Gibson was able to cure herself from cancer through nutrition and adopting a healthy lifestyle, perhaps others could do the same. Her audience was comprised of those who were ill, as well as health-conscious individuals seeking to optimise their well-being. Gibson, referred to on Instagram as @healing_belle, presented herself as a 'wellness guru' and an advocate of clean eating. She not only claimed to adhere to clean eating principles by restricting her consumption of coffee, gluten and dairy, she also rejected conventional cancer treatments, such as chemotherapy and radiotherapy.

In this respect she was distrustful of elite-professional interventions. She advocated alternative therapies, inspiring her followers to do the same.

In 2015, Gibson was exposed as a fraud. It was revealed that she never had cancer and failed to donate the $300,000.00AUD in proceeds from her book and app, *The Whole Pantry*, to charity, as promised. The scandal caused public outrage and prompted a series of questions: How was Gibson able to pull the wool over the eyes of so many people, including her followers and many branches of popular media? Why did the companies who promoted her products fail to verify whether she had cancer by fact-checking her claims? Why were people so willing to believe the advice of someone they followed online over established medical expertise? Our interest in exploring these questions was the impetus for writing this book. The more we considered this topic, the more we realised that the scandal spoke to a larger cultural phenomenon at play: the rise of lifestyle gurus in the digital age and, by extension, the crisis of confidence in the interventions of experts and professionals.

People go online to make sense of the world around them. Most of us use Google on a daily basis to search for mundane information: directions, transport times and weather updates. We also routinely use social media to connect with friends and social networks online. However, more than ever before, the internet is where we turn when we are lonely, concerned or afraid. Protected with the anonymity afforded by most forms of digital communication, the internet provides us with the capacity to explore many of life's most pressing questions in secret with those whom we perceive to be just like ourselves. Without doubt, this shared experience can be extremely rewarding, providing rich emotional connections in the form of online chat rooms, support groups and forums. The interactions enabled by these technologies can also foster meaning, identity and a sense of belonging. This is especially the case when individuals feel excluded and misunderstood by their immediate community, family and friends. Whereas in former times, one might have turned to a novel or film in times of need, the internet now provides a plethora of advice and solutions to life's eternal problems. What these media share in common is their capacity to facilitate a sense of 'mimetic vertigo', the recognition that the object represented also represents you (Taussig 1992). Their significance lies in the fact that they speak to the subject directly, while enabling them to reflect on their concerns at a safe aesthetic distance; achieving emotional pertinence through fusing the subject and object into a common narrative (Baker 2014). One of the key differences between novels, films and the stories documented online, is that the protagonist we read about online can speak back. The direct forms of communication afforded by social media enable users to engage in dialogic exchange with the protagonists they read about online. They can also communicate in visual form via images and videos, enhancing the feeling of proximity and intimate exchange.

Digital communication has changed the way in which people seek advice. In the twenty-first century, we are subject to more information than ever before as a result of the internet: 24-hour news channels, blogs, vlogs, forums, social network sites and a series of other online sources. One of the problems that users encounter when searching online is how to sift through the plethora of information. Much of the advice found online is conflicting and scientifically inaccurate, particularly in relation to health and well-being. Take coffee, for example. A quick Google search 'does coffee cause ...' provides the following results: cancer, bloating, constipation, acne and anxiety. Conversely, the search 'does coffee cure' provides the results: headaches, hangover, constipation, cancer and cold. The same is true of chocolate and wine, which are said to be both the cause and remedy for various ailments. With such contradictory advice found online, it is no surprise that people are confused about what health advice to follow. The average person is not an expert on these topics. Most of us have neither the time nor skills to explore these claims in detail. Moreover, much of the health and wellness marketing behind this content is deliberately designed to mislead and beguile. In light of these issues, the lifestyle dilemma becomes – who to believe?

In the saturated health and wellness market, celebrity advice reigns supreme. Celebrities exercise significant influence over our lives, how we view ourselves and who we aspire to be. This is particularly the case in relation to our ideas about our health and well-being due to their associations with beauty, dieting and fitness. The detox and cleanse market, for example, has been driven by celebrity endorsements. The same holds with respect to the lucrative wellness and beauty industries. Celebrities shape the concerns of consumers and feed on their insecurities by endorsing the products and services of weight-loss and anti-ageing industries. They promote products that are not only expensive but, in some cases, useless and harmful. Much has been written on this topic about celebrity culture as a source of pseudoscience and misinformation (Goldacre 2009; Caulfield 2015; Nichols 2017; Warner 2017). Books of this kind examine and debunk the claims and promises made by celebrities and pseudoscientists in relation to health, nutrition and beauty. In the book, *Is Gwyneth Paltrow Wrong about Everything?* (2015), Timothy Caulfield suggests that celebrity culture is 'one of our society's most pernicious forces', contributing to poor health decisions, wasted investments in useless products and services, a decreased understanding of how science works and dissatisfaction with our own lives and appearance (Caulfield 2015: xii). Tom Nichols (2017: 190) echoes this sentiment, highlighting the capacity for celebrity advocates of the anti-vaccine movement, such as the actress, Jenny McCarthy, a self-professed graduate of the 'University of Google', to influence people to avoid vaccinating their children, exposing them and others to serious illnesses and disease. Less has been written about health literacy and social media, specifically in relation to the dissemination of lifestyle advice by ordinary users who achieve influence online. Our study is a contribution to this topic. We explore the rise of lifestyle gurus in the digital age, examining the conditions that enable them to flourish and the methods they use to appear trustworthy, authentic and credible.

We situate our study in an historical framework. We make no claim to present a systematic historical perspective. Our discussion of nineteenth and twentieth-century contributions to lifestyle advice is intended as a corrective to the tacit assumption in much current writing that lifestyle gurus are a product of the digital age. The historical material also reveals that lifestyle advice today is generally shorn of the heavy emphasis upon Christianity that is redolent in nineteenth-century works. Our account of contemporary lifestyle gurus maintains that they offer consumers a version of 'salvation', but one that is mostly secularised and folk-based. More generally, our approach adopts an historical-comparative methodology. That is, we proceed on the basis that an historical understanding of context and social change is a prerequisite for understanding lifestyle gurus today, and we seek to cultivate an appreciation that the form and content of the advice that they impart is conditioned by national and cultural specificities.

A brief note on terminology. The term 'guru' traditionally referred to a spiritual master. This adjective is used more liberally now to refer to those with native experience, knowledge and skills associated with the domestic sphere and everyday life. The teacher–student relationship persists, but lifestyle gurus are presented as more accessible, collegial and less obviously religious, than in the past. The old distinction of hierarchy between the master and the follower, which was reproduced in most guru relationships, has been replaced by a more approachable and sustainable alternative. Despite the obvious fame and glamour enjoyed by successful lifestyle gurus, it is as if their lives are lived in co-partnership with their followers. Today's lifestyle gurus are mostly lifestyle bloggers, who share content on blogs and social media. In this book, we use the term 'lifestyle guru' to describe those lifestyle bloggers who have achieved authority and influence in the public domain. While much research has examined the role of the mass media (e.g. print, radio, television) on society and culture, today's lifestyle gurus mostly communicate using social media. As such, we often speak of social media (including blogs) in contrast to 'the media' (also referred to as traditional, conventional and the mass media) to signify the new forms of interactive media accessible to ordinary members of the public. We use the term 'native' to describe those lifestyle gurus who possess limited, or no certified qualifications, and hence, have no professional standing for claiming expertise in health and emotional management. Their skills and knowledge are those associated with ordinary people and everyday life; their perceived ordinariness itself part of their popular appeal. This description is not intended to be pejorative. Instead, it is used to highlight the forms of authority and influence based upon experience and folk wisdom rather than formal, certified training, which has given rise to an industry of lifestyle gurus increasingly placed in the same discursive category as trained doctors, psychologists and dieticians (Lewis 2008).

Although lifestyle gurus have emerged cross culturally, the examples in this book focus on the rise of lifestyle gurus in the modern Western world. There are several reasons for this. First, lifestyle gurus are ubiquitous in contemporary Western societies. This study is an attempt to examine the reasons for this, to demonstrate how the problems addressed in self-improvement literature (e.g. that on health, wealth, relationships and well-being) are enabled by living in certain economic and social conditions. Second, we contend that the rise of lifestyle gurus in the West is indebted to a specific understanding of the individual made possible by modernity, the Enlightenment and our Judeo-Christian heritage. While there are signs that the globalising effects of technology are bridging these differences, frameworks for understanding the self in the West are often a poor conceptual fit for developing and non-Western countries. Micki McGee (2012) cites an example from the feminist self-help classic, *Our Bodies, Ourselves* to demonstrate the point. Latin American editors of the volume critiqued the North American 'Anglo' notion of self-help for its emphasis on the individual, pointing out that this conceptual framework ignored the role of family, friends, and other community members in a woman's life. As a result, the editors replaced the term *auto ayuda* (self-help) with the term *ayuda mutal*, meaning mutual aid (Davis 2007: 180–1). Given that this book examines the rise of lifestyle gurus in modern Western societies, we build upon a body of literature concerned with the development of the self in the West. For this reason, there is specific emphasis on Anglo-American popular media and those social media sites most popular in English-speaking countries, such as North America, the United Kingdom and Australia (e.g. Facebook, Instagram, Twitter, Snapchat). With Instagram currently lifestyle gurus' preferred medium of choice, this book pays specific attention to the platform by noting how it affords specific forms of communication in comparison to other social media sites.

Blogs and social media have confounded issues around trust and credibility through altering how we seek advice and how we decide who we believe. The internet has not created lifestyle gurus, but it affords them a public platform on which to give advice and share their views. Most have a blog, an Instagram account and a YouTube channel on which to document their lives and lifestyles. People have shared lifestyle advice for centuries with their immediate families and friends. Claims about how to heal illness through diet and alternative therapies are far from novel. The established history of self-help literature points to the general need for obtaining comfort and wisdom from strangers with whom we associate a degree of success and achievement (McGee 2005). What is new is that these technologies enable lifestyle advice to be disseminated at an unprecedented speed and scale. These affordances make lifestyle blogging fundamentally different from previous forms of mediated exchange. Snake-oil merchants and charlatans have existed for centuries, taking advantage of the vulnerable. However, prior to the internet they had neither a global audience, nor the potential to go viral. Social media sites are infused with commercial interests, making it possible to profit from sharing advice. Affiliate marketing programmes have enabled bloggers to monetise their posts through advertising, with many turning blogging into a career.

While some lifestyle gurus claim to be personal trainers, yoga teachers or nutritionists, few have the certified credentials required to give health advice. Instead, they rely on narratives of self-transformation, providing anecdotal evidence, folklore and testimonies about how they have healed themselves and others during difficult times. These stories are supported by highly curated social media profiles featuring inspirational quotes, food imagery and before and after shots documenting their transformation into attractive, ostensibly happier and healthier subjects. The lifestyles presented online are designed to be inspiring, but they also serve as evidence of the possibilities of self-transformation – who you too could be – if you were to adhere to their lifestyle advice, purchase their books, products or services. Lifestyle gurus place the ultimate responsibility of problem solving upon the shoulders of the individual. Their advice is intended to be facilitative.

Personal solutions, however, are understood to be a matter of resetting your life by taking the guided, decisive act to change negative, sub-optimal behaviour, and renewing your new direction by online, top-up consultation. Social media has altered how we are influenced. Social media sites offer clear rewards for behaving in a certain way. Engineered around the quest for metric-driven status, influence is measured on social media by the number of followers one has, media recognition and the amount of comments, shares and 'likes' a post receives. An expert may have credentials and years of experience, but they are unlikely to be as compelling as a lifestyle guru who is 'Instafamous', with an attractive body and glowing skin to verify their lifestyle advice, together with a highly curated Instagram feed that conveys how widely admired and deeply approved of they are. The issue here is not merely about misinformation, but the methods we use to know what information to trust and who to believe.

In this book we aim to explore the phenomenon of lifestyle gurus in the twenty-first century. We move beyond examining the pseudoscientific claims of lifestyle gurus, to focus on the conditions that enable their emergence and the techniques they use to achieve authority and influence online. In Chapter 1 we outline the concept of a lifestyle guru. We provide a brief history of lifestyle gurus and discuss the cultural, economic and technological conditions that have enabled them to flourish. In Chapter 2 we examine the rise of lifestyle gurus in the digital age and how emergent technologies afford new forms of intimate online exchange. Chapter 3 focuses on the specific self-presentation techniques lifestyle gurus employ to achieve influence online. We examine how trust is fostered among different populations and how credibility is formed. We also reveal the emotional costs associated with lifestyle blogging. Chapter 4 explores the economic and technological conditions that have transformed lifestyle blogging into a commercial industry. We discuss the rise of influencers as global brands, how the self is commodified in the process of self-branding and how the path to purchase has changed in the digital age with specific emphasis on the creation of the wellness industry. Chapter 5 examines the rise of lifestyle gurus as unregulated advisers online. We focus specifically on the burgeoning public interest in diet and nutrition, contextualising our discussion in the current political climate of distrust towards governments and corporations. Chapter 6 introduces two cults of lifestyle perfectionism: 'assured perfectionism' and 'affirmative perfectionism'. The former is an historically significant iteration of lifestyle advice that was ascendant between the 1850s and 1970s. It often relied upon the authority of the Bible to offer followers 'the true way' in leading fulfilling, healthy, productive and rewarding lives. These historical precedents of lifestyle management and planning persist. But the internet has ushered in the age of 'affirmative perfectionism'. Under it, allure, acceptance, approval and success are not dependent upon following the Bible or some other, secular, doctrine for the good life. Rather, speaking precisely, they spring from the construction of a self that possesses the social capital of being instantly admired, automatically approved. The final chapter concludes by situating the rise of lifestyle gurus in low-trust societies. Rather than reducing the contemporary fascination with lifestyle gurus to secularism or a culture of narcissism (Lasch 1979), we argue that the turn to lifestyle gurus for advice is symptomatic of new conceptions of selfhood and the growing distrust of experts and elites. Having dedicated most of the book to exploring the conditions that have enabled lifestyle gurus to flourish and the methods lifestyle gurus use to achieve authority and influence online, we conclude by reflecting on the implications of living in a 'low-trust society'.

While we approach the phenomenon of lifestyle gurus from a critical standpoint, this book is not a rejection of the internet. Like all new technologies, there are many cultural anxieties around the internet, especially regarding its use and impact on younger generations. The role of the internet in how we navigate lifestyle advice is more complex and nuanced than reductionist critiques about causes and necessities. The ubiquity of mobile broadband and digital devices offers incomparable benefits, providing new opportunities to share health information and experiences with others. But despite discourse about the democratic potential for social media to give everyone a voice, and the opportunity to access health advice and share knowledge at an unprecedented scale, these relations are not without their risks, not least because of the potential for information to mislead. While some internet sites are credible and well moderated, many are not. There are concerns over the quality of information found online, how to differentiate credible from bogus advice and how to recognise when advice is compromised by commercial interests. This is not because people are stupid, but because it has become increasingly difficult to know what lifestyle advice to trust online. These concerns become more pressing as scientific and medical issues become incorporated into the wellness industry. The internet is a growing source of health information and lifestyle advice that aligns with broader goals of self-improvement and personal life management. As more of us turn to the internet for answers, there is a need to become more informed about the sources we use online.

Most would agree that you cannot believe everything you read online, yet it is not always clear what and whom to believe. There is a tendency to overestimate our capacity to discern quality information online, assuming that only others are fooled by pseudoscience and quackery. The Belle Gibson scandal encourages us to rethink this proposition. Gibson had over 200,000 followers on Instagram, 200,000 downloads of her app in the first two weeks of its release, and sold thousands of copies of her book. Her following enabled her to make close to half a million dollars from sales of the app and book in just eighteen months. Gibson's rise to fame and the success of her global brand indicates how compelling her narrative was to the general public. Those duped were not confined to cancer patients in search of a miracle cure, they were health-conscious individuals, informed consumers, media pundits, nutritionists and dieticians bound by a common interest in health and well-being. It is only by understanding how lifestyle gurus like Gibson achieve authority and influence online that we are able to be better informed as consumers.

1

What is a Lifestyle Guru?

How to be *among*, and what to expect from, and rely upon, Others? These questions occur to every child, and are repeated, over and over again, in countless different settings, by every adult, for a lifetime. In part, the rise of today's lifestyle gurus may be conceived as a response to these imperatives in the digital age. In this book, we use the term 'lifestyle guru' to refer to unlicensed native agents of awareness, positioned in conventional and social media, to offer emotional support, an identity matrix and pedagogy for self-discovery and well-being. By the term 'unlicensed native' we aim to highlight that lifestyle gurus are ordinary members of society, who possess limited, or no certified qualifications, and hence, no professional standing to claim expertise in emotional management, health, constitutional law and licensing matters. Lifestyle gurus employ a mixture of selective scientific knowledge, folk tradition and personal experience to offer alternative advice and guidance on medical, psychological and social problems afflicting others. The stance that they adopt is often dismissive of professional, elite knowledge and practice on the grounds that it under-values lay traditions and ordinary experience. While lifestyle gurus typically present themselves as anti-establishment, it would be an overstatement to propose that they are part of an anti-scientific movement. A sounder way of looking at things would be to describe them as generally adopting a *selective, instrumental approach* to science. Given that much scientific knowledge about lifestyle issues is conflicted, and often turns out on inspection to be tainted, lifestyle gurus cherry pick information to advance the profile and appeal of their own views. The media often collude in making these views newsworthy in an attempt to capture public attention. Lifestyle gurus embrace a broad range of editorial newsroom concerns from health to beauty, fitness, fashion, food, wealth, relationships and travel. They provide practical advice that people can apply in order to function more optimally and effectively under the guise of well-being. Against the implied remoteness of scientific and professional authority, with its lofty jargon that bespeaks insinuated superiority, and the uncomfortable rituals of privilege that distinguish it from habitual, mundane experience, lifestyle gurus propagate knowledge and applications that are a mixture of science, ordinary life experience, plain speaking and marginalised, discarded, or forgotten, ways and means of coping and wellness.

Lifestyle gurus typically portray themselves as offering practical, no-nonsense advice on life issues. Using psychological concepts, they propagate a cult of perfectionism that mostly celebrates and affirms middle-class values. Although there are manifold inflections of this cult, at its core are four life goals:

1. Acceptance
   The attainment of recognition and access in social groups and society at large.
2. Approval
   The achievement of positive reactions from individuals, groups and society that reinforce a sense of self worth.
3. Social impact
   The acknowledgement by individuals, groups and society of bearing markers of elevated status associated with achievement, significance and attention value.
4. Self-validation
   The affirmation by individuals and groups of valued personal characteristics of the self that contribute to a sense of positive self-worth.

The cult of perfection is part of the wider culture of achievement and high-status differentiation. It treats the goals of acceptance, approval, social impact and self-validation as universally desirable. This is manifest in the exceptionally high number of lifestyle platforms dedicated to techniques of self-improvement and self-transformation, covering the topics of beauty, fitness, fashion, relationships, wellness, wealth and business success. It might be thought that questions of improving lifestyle immediately raise related social and economic questions of inclusion, equality, justice and social engineering. Be that as it may, the vast majority of lifestyle guru sites pass over these questions in seraphic silence. Instead, their typical approach is determinedly person-centred. They address an audience for whom the complexities of life have proved challenging with practical, plain speaking, oracular, non-hierarchical remedies. Gaining practical, positive self-knowledge is the bugle call rallying audiences to lifestyle communicators. Although most lifestyle gurus regularly participate in conferences, symposia and teach-ins, digital communication is the overwhelming and decisive point of exchange.

Despite the strong ethos of non-hierarchy, and the deliberate emphasis upon empathy (co-partnership), accessibility (friendship) and complicity (against 'the system') between *Communicators* (gurus) and *Communicants* (audiences), the latent power dynamics typically privilege the former over the latter. The paradox of these lifestyle sites is that they generally claim to solve various challenges of complexity in life with *simplicity*. This is communicated to followers in three main ways:

1. Lifestyle gurus present themselves as having faced, and vanquished, the same or analogous life traumas that their audience encounters. Among the most common traumas are serious physical illness, depression, anxiety, low self-esteem, career disappointment, relationship troubles and chronic self-dislike. Emotional disturbance may derive from continuing concrete health issues and their consequences, or more general anxieties about not possessing desired levels of acceptance, attraction and approval, or just not 'fitting in' with others. The persuasive power of lifestyle gurus is directly related to their apparent ordinariness and receptivity. The first rule of effective on-site contact is to create a culture of exchange in which audiences trust that communicators genuinely understand, and feel, their pain. A compelling narrative of self-transformation, articulated by those who have already successfully made the journey, is key.

2. They advance a step-by-step programme to enable people to improve themselves and, in doing so, to extract themselves from the negative thinking that prevents them from optimal conduct and reaching their full potential. This programme is typically supported by products and services of commercial benefit to the lifestyle guru in question. From a psychological standpoint, positive thinking, celebrating inner strength and the need to love oneself are the most common remedies.

3. Programmes of intervention may draw on selected strands of scientific knowledge to appear credible and true. However, although lifestyle gurus commonly appeal to scientific knowledge, they are generally defined in antithesis to professional expertise and elite diagnosis and treatment. While lacking any objectively adequate certification of probity, and with surprisingly low responsibilities to subject themselves to independent regulatory discipline, the

lifestyle solutions and motivational programmes advanced by lifestyle gurus carry the enamel ring of common-sense. Virtue signalling is the means to achieve the end of life satisfaction. The power of positive thinking, self-knowledge and level-headed acceptance of one's limits along with consciousness of one's potential, prevail over all other proposed solutions to lifestyle dilemmas and problems. Although much online advice wears its 'alternative' credentials with pride, solutions to life's problems are generally exclusively focused on the individual. Testimonials to the value of collective mobilisation, organisation and protest are thin on the ground. Complicity against the domination and power of professionals is a crucial resource in social bonding and trust building. Lifestyle gurus offer lifestyle solutions that are crucially, *outside of the system*. Remedies are usually presented in a ludic way, involving escapism and fun. In the country of wounded *amour propre*, the smiley solution set by the lifestyle guru is king.

The Generalised Other and the Looking-Glass Self

The rise of lifestyle gurus as a component in the lives of ordinary people reflects a change in the ratio of inter-personal relations in society. For over a century, sociologists have studied how spatially segregated relationships influence self-formation. In doing so they have devised a variety of concepts to investigate and clarify the issue. For example, George Herbert Mead (1934) developed the concept of the 'Generalised Other' to refer to the assembly of roles and attitudes of others that provide role models of behaviour. Integral to the concept is the nuance that this assembly includes 'Significant Others' – those who play a major role in providing direct and indirect advice and guidance. They may take the form of family relations, friends, artists, scientists, politicians, religious leaders and other types of celebrity, whose example is internalised and pursued as a lodestar of personal well-being. Lifestyle gurus are unequivocally 'significant others' for their subscribers and followers. Earlier, Charles Horton Cooley (1902) had already introduced the famous concept of the 'Looking-Glass Self'. The term refers to the construction of a self-image through the reading of how we imagine ourselves to appear to others, based on their reactions to our behaviour. Our judgement of what motivates their reactions, and the feelings of pride or shame that result, either reinforce or undermine our self-image. The result is a social self based on co-presence, imagination and reflection: 'each to each a looking-glass reflects the other that doth pass'

(Cooley 1902: 93). While Mead included indirect relations in the formation of the self, for the greater part Cooley concentrates on the direct, interpersonal relationships that individuals have with others. Mead was a great advocate of the value of Cooley's social psychology. As he notes approvingly, Cooley's definition of society is 'the contact and reciprocal influence of certain ideas named "I" ... I do not see how anyone can hold that we know persons directly except as imaginative ideas in the mind' (Mead 1930: 694). Not surprisingly, Mead's view of the Generalised Other echoes the basic tenets of Cooley's concept of the Looking-Glass Self. It holds that one has an idea of oneself through interaction with others and the perceived impressions of others that one attributes to them. At the heart of the self is self-reflectivity and self-feeling. However, the content of this private, inner reserve is largely a product of the observable emotional, rational and imaginary relationships that one forges with others.

Mead and Cooley wrote before the age of modern mass communications. It is generally accepted that the rise of modern mass communications, particularly television, has altered the ratio between the influence of direct and indirect relationships in the construction of self-feeling and self-knowledge. A key concept here is 'para-social relationships'. Coined at the dawn of the television age, the term refers to the affective and imaginary relationships that audiences form with figures transmitted to them through the media of film and television (Horton and Wohl 1956). On-screen Others became significant affective resources for modifying the Looking-Glass Self. These para-social relationships were understood to challenge the primacy of kith and kin networks, especially in the lives of vulnerable and isolated people (Horton and Wohl 1956). In general, the discussion accepted that it was the fate of para-social relationships to loom larger in the field of interpersonal contact. Horton and Wohl did not speculate upon the form and content of imaginary and fantasy relationships in the para-social field. However, it is clear that these matters are integral to the concept.

Today, the ubiquity of digital technologies in the West means that the concept of para-social relationships needs to be radically recast. Horton and Wohl took it for granted that para-social transactions are located within the *organised* system of media transmission. In contrast, online transactions in social media are conducted *outside of the system*. Emotionally speaking, the internet has enabled vlogging sites, political platforms, chat rooms and crowdsourcing, in which interaction is founded upon an alternative sense of complicity rather than obedience to hierarchy. Transactions on social media sites, such as Facebook, Snapchat, Twitter, Instagram, carry the ring of authentic co-existence, because they are essentially understood to be beyond the control of corporations and the other media giants (although, as discussed in Chapter 2, commercial and corporate hierarchies persist on these platforms). Psychologically speaking, to dip into these conduits of data exchange is ultimately to swim free of the transmission belts of organised media culture and its corporate paymasters. Some commentators refer to an increasing ratio of 'micro-celebrities' (Senft 2008; Marwick 2013) or 'influencers' (Trammell and Keshelashvili 2005; Gillin 2008) in the texture of online life with others. If you feel that your parents and siblings are not listening to you, or your friends fail to understand your point of view, there are now forums, chat-rooms, blogs and social media sites organised around what we refer to categorically as online *awareness agents*, with whom relations of intimacy and complicity can, in theory, evolve and lead to sustaining affective balances of acceptance, approval, social impact and self-validation. Lifestyle gurus are part of this general upheaval in the dynamics of para-social relationships. They constitute new Significant Others in the lives of ordinary people. Their *raison d'etre* as accessible, non-hierarchical, plain-speaking sources of advice and guidance about life issues represents a genuine challenge to the knowledge, hegemony and status of professionals. In creating new Looking-Glass Selves for the modern world they offer new imaginary standards and relationships for bringing out the best in oneself.

De-Traditionalisation and its Discontents

The view that we have escaped the myths and superstitions of the past is at the heart of what is understood by the term 'de-traditionalisation'. In late modernity, individuals have learned to cultivate the self-image of escaping the burden and behavioural scripts of tradition (Giddens 1991). The decline of traditional religious and political structures has been accompanied in the public domain by the widespread conviction that there is little to be achieved by trying to revive them. In a word, their day has gone. It has become fashionable, as Frank Furedi (2013) notes, to treat traditional forms of authority – the monarchy, church and parliament – with ridicule and scepticism. The challenge to authority, and the preoccupation with the individual, has its origins in the Judeo-Christian tradition as personified by Christ. The emphasis on the rational individual to which this tradition subscribed reached its pinnacle in the Enlightenment, notably in the writings of John Locke, Adam Smith and Immanuel Kant. However, there are grounds for holding that the so-called escape from tradition is a hand overplayed by Enlightenment supporters. Since the late-1970s, the revival of Islamic fundamentalism, culminating in the project by ISIS to establish a new 'caliphate' of eternal certainties in Arabia, has dramatically called into question the belief in the inevitable superiority of Western Reason. Westerner's rightly abhor the fundamentalist moral system, and particularly the use of violence by ISIS against individuals and heritage. Conversely, there was also grudging envy that the leader of the so-called caliphate, Abu Bakr Al-Baghdadi, was able to inspire levels of mass passion and certitude that some felt were absent in the West. This reaction among Westerners suggested two things. Firstly, wherever its hand had touched, the Enlightenment revolution of Reason had produced a bloodless quality in everyday life. As Weber (1905) argued, it has let predictability, routine, regimentation and standardisation out of the traps and contributed to feelings of disenchantment. Judged on an emotional level, the tolerance, mutuality and respect generated by the Enlightenment were no match for the passion and exultation produced by magic, myth and religion. Second, disquiet with the bloodless character of political life in the West provoked the insight that the Enlightenment may have been over-confident in holding that Science and Reason must necessarily diminish magic, myth and religion.

This should not be a surprise. From the very beginning, de-traditionalisation inevitably precipitated a counter-reaction. Science and technology saw no place for traditional philosophical and religious questions having to do with the meaning, purpose and the mystery of existence. The Enlightenment assumed that these questions would gradually wither and die to be universally replaced by the secular, verifiable benefits of Reason. This has not turned out to be the path that history actually followed. Despite being dismissed by strict Enlightenment values, religious belief, and various forms of myth and magic, survive. Collective emotion, thought and identity continue to be organised around the sacred and profane. This was an outcome observed by Émile Durkheim (1912) in his analysis of the religious dimensions that bind social life. The sacred is not confined to religion or tradition. It refers to the idealisation of group beliefs as manifest in the social movements, scandals and political events that characterise modern life. The non-rational factors driving these events highlight that belief in the sacred persists, contemporary social life continues to be infused with symbolic meaning, morality, affective 'ritual-like' practices and storytelling (Alexander et al. 2006; Baker 2014; Alexander 2017). These characteristics, together with the revolt against scientific expertise, are hallmarks of lifestyle guru sites.

The Weberian conception of modernity as governed by rationality is limiting. Today, the Enlightenment's ethos of progress and rationality is itself subject to cynicism and distrust. A side effect of this is that the authority of professionals and scientists is questioned (Furedi 2013; Nichols 2017). Modern life is suspended between a conception of the autonomous individual emancipated from the dogmas and superstitions of tradition, domination and control, and an understanding of the individual as plagued by uncertainty, ambivalence and doubt, for which religion, myth and magic supply both comfort and a sense of purpose. Poststructuralism and postmodernism with their relativistic and deconstructivist approaches to reality have encouraged a loss of faith in Truth and grand narratives (Lyotard 1984). Societies have become more complex, differentiated and fragmented, but the need for meaning persists. In post-traditional societies, religious sects and New Age practitioners, many of whom describe themselves collectively as 'spiritual', have emerged, while the universal rule of Reason remains elusive. De-traditionalisation has resulted in a greater ability to construct the self through the reflexive shaping of personal biographical narratives and selecting the collectives with whom we identify. Life ceases to be understood as 'fate'. Instead, it becomes an accumulation of changing resources designed to achieve the self-determined pursuit of living well. Lifestyle gurus assist in this process by helping people to navigate the uncertainties of life through reflexive life planning, identity reconstruction and the ongoing management of the self. Their prominence in modernity as a new alternative system of expertise is the direct result of the fluidity of the authoritative structures that traditionally characterised social life and the search for meaning and purpose that science and technology seem unable to deliver.

The challenge to authority in late modernity is also due to shifting understandings of our relationship to risk. While society is not necessarily more risky than in the past, scholars have argued that people are increasingly preoccupied with safety and mitigating risk (Giddens 1991; Beck 1992). Scientific and technological innovations have introduced unknowable and unanticipated consequences that cannot be easily calculated or assessed. To some extent, the complexity of these systems mean that there is a greater reliance on experts for knowledge and understanding of risk (Giddens 1991; Beck 1992: 1). At the same time, the increased appreciation of risk in modernity is part of what Ulrich Beck terms 'reflexive modernisation' where, in contrast to Industrial society's belief in progress, a more critical perspective on science and technology is adopted (Beck 1994: 5–6). Here scepticism is extended to 'the foundations and hazards of scientific work' and as a result 'science is thus both *generalised* and *demystified*' (Beck 1992: 14 [emphasis in original]).

The source of this demystification is not only the inability of experts to calculate and control risk, but the failure of key institutions of modernity (e.g. science, business and politics) to take responsibility for them. History reveals multiple examples of corporations and governments acting unethically, succumbing to corruption and commercial interests. The Beech-Nut Fake Apple Juice Scandal in the US (1979), the emergence of Bovine Spongiform Encephalopathy ('Mad Cow Disease') scandal in Britain (1980s), the Melamine Milk Scandal in China (2008), and the Horsemeat Scandal in Europe (2013) are just a few of the scandals that have eroded trust in science and caused public disquiet (Baker and Rojek 2019). Public distrust of food corporations is particularly high in the US, where lobbyists exercise the power to influence government policies. In *Risk Society* (1992), Beck cites government oversight during the Chernobyl and Bhopal disasters as noteworthy incidents that lowered public trust of politicians, science and technology. Scandals involving pharmaceutical companies buying the opinions of doctors and scientists to endorse particular drugs further erodes trust relations between professionals and the public (Goldacre 2012). In these circumstances, experts themselves are condemned as a risk and hazard to well-being (Beck 2006: 336). The result is growing public scepticism of professionals that undermines the legitimacy of the institutions they represent, often referred to as 'Big Business', 'Big Food' and 'Big Pharma'. It manifests in general feelings of distrust towards experts and elites, providing a space for alternative religious and secular voices to claim authority in opposition to received fiat. This attitude was forcefully expressed during the 2016 United States presidential election and United Kingdom European Union membership referendum in 2016 when both the Republican candidate, Donald Trump and Michael Gove, the former British Justice Secretary, attacked the sanctity of expert knowledge and practice. Late modern life, then, is characterised by a distinct set of attitudes towards professional expertise. On the one hand, we rely more on experts to help ameliorate the complexities and uncertainties of modern life; on the other, distrust of authority and expertise is part of the scepticism that characterises 'reflexive modernity'.

Lifestyle gurus have exploited and developed these contradictions. They have emerged, with little or no formal training, to afford authoritative help to enable people to navigate their life trajectories to avoid the rock of failure. It is not that authority and expertise has altogether eroded; deference to expertise has been replaced by deference to the celebrity lifestyle guru and social media influencer. The various life courses set by professional helmsmen, have been rivalled, and in some cases outflanked, by folk heroes. The current prominence of the latter appears to negate the Enlightenment conviction that the destiny of society was to be ruled by a new priesthood organised around Reason and Science (Comte 1998). Contrarily, they also suggest that the Enlightenment was right about one thing: the crisis of trust that characterises contemporary institutions (religious, political, media institutions and even social media with the rise of 'fake news'). Trust is socially manufactured and easily broken. When we are disillusioned, we simply seek a new celebrity influencer or lifestyle guru to follow.

Traditionally, the word *expert* was assigned to a narrow range of professionals. The term was typically applied to describe a person who acquired knowledge or skills in a specific area through formal training and approved certification. These credentials were a sign of quality and achievement that distinguished trustworthy knowledge from lay experience. Qualifications took the form of an apprenticeship or tertiary education, such as a law or medical degree. Conversely, what constitutes expertise in lifestyle matters has historically been more liberal and unclear. To be a good cook, a thorough cleaner, or a competent parent, is increasingly valued as expertise, particularly following the mass entrance of women into the workforce, the outsourcing of many of these traditionally 'feminine' practices and the rise of the middle class. The shift from credentialled knowledge to lay knowledge has been conceived as part of the growing 'informalisation' of everyday life, where access to advice and expertise became relatively democratised and presented in increasingly accessible, digestible forms (Lewis 2008; Wouters 2007). Informalisation teaches that you are the master of your own destiny. However, because modern life is complex, and subject to change, every master needs an authoritative compass. Lifestyle gurus fulfil this role. They are 'information providers' who offer advice and guidance about how to manage oneself and navigate personal problems in everyday life (Hanusch 2013). The online ethos in which this is nurtured is one of non-hierarchical, alternative, co-operative labour. Most lifestyle gurus make a virtue of rejecting the 'master–servant' relationships of professional life as bad practice. Instead, in line with Enlightenment precedents, they cultivate an ethos of mutuality, informality, tolerance and openness. Getting the most out of yourself is typically presented as a ludic experience rather than a draft of medicine. The play form of self-motivation and self-construction allows life lessons to be learned in a non-hierarchical, enjoyable fashion. However, concomitant with this is the commodification of lifestyle, whereby ordinary life skills have become packaged and monetised (Fürsich 2012). True to their commercial roots, lifestyle gurus generally take it for granted that the best things in life do not come free. To be an optimal individual requires the cultivation and practice of positive 'self-feeling'. The positive thinking strategies and methods of practice developed by online lifestyle gurus are commercially packaged to bring this within the reach of their subscribers.

The History of Lifestyle Gurus

Today lifestyle gurus are often thought of as an adjunct of social media. This is a mistake. The phenomenon of virtue signalling and using positive thinking to achieve self-fulfilment and make a meaningful contribution to society pre-dates digital technology. What is commonly regarded as the first self-help book in English, *Self-help with Illustrations of Character and Conduct (1859),* was written by Samuel Smiles. The book was concerned with cultivating various human qualities in personal life and business and perseverance to the duty of 'becoming a better person'. Smiles advised that people should learn from the Christian good example in history and society of people who would act as role models in the rational duty of self-improvement. In his later book, *Character* (1908), he comments on what readers of his own day could profitably learn from men and women of the past with respect to topics like 'Companionship', 'Work', 'Courage', 'Self-Control', 'Duty', 'Truthfulness' and 'Temper'. These virtues are presented as lifestyle resources calculated to pay a dividend in – to borrow a phrase that he repeatedly returns to in the book – 'the school life'. For Smiles, it is the will of God for each individual to work out the end of one's being to the best of one's power (Smiles 1908). However, charting a course without a proper life-compass to life runs the risk of shipping water. The principles of self-help are intended to be an exhaustive guide to the most effective methods for solving life's problems and maximising one's potential. It defines life, not merely as a passage, but as a project.

Smiles' work was part of the industrialisation of self-help. This was a process that respected the wisdom of the past. The prime mover, however, was the principle that motivation comes from within, by rote learning and application of what can be rationally extracted from significant others in history, culture and society. Other influential writers were swept up in the same moment. For example, the American feminist and household management guru, Catharine Beecher's influential book, *A Treatise on Domestic Economy* (1841), advised 'women to perfect themselves as Christian wives and mothers, adhering to quite traditional New England values, so as to master the economic logic of modern time' (Allen 2005: 68). Effective time management and the cult of perfectionism was the nucleus of her household management system. What she took from science and professional management in the marketplace was selectively mediated through the local folk values, imbricated with Christian teaching, with which she was raised. The regime of self-help that she advocated was class based and asserted fixed, rigid principles of perfection. For example, she regarded domestic virtue to lie in the punctually regulated standardisation of behaviour in the home. Family members were urged to rise together at the same hour, eat together at the same hour and take to their rest at the same hour. This was presented not only as the right choice for modern individual families but the best course for the future of society. In Beecher, the middle-class notion that self-improvement is the key to social progress is accentuated. Time management is expounded as a tool to master the economic and moral ambiguities of the market (Allen 2005: 74). It is worth noting that this is the inverse of the arguments made by subsequent generations of historians concerning the project of modern industrial development. For example, in a justly celebrated study, Edward Thompson (1967) maintained that the introduction of the mechanical clock into factories in England inscribed upon workers not only the notion of time–work discipline, but the logic of using time optimally that followed from the operation of the quantifiable price mechanism in the market. Thompson presented time management in the workplace as the foundation of order in the market place. Conversely, Beecher's *Treatise* insists that it is in the *home* that the lessons of doing things at the proper time and in the proper place are most deeply learned.

The lessons absorbed at the hearth about how to be, and how to live with others, are the keystones of moral perfectionism. Equivalent respect for the virtues of time management is to be found in Isabella Beeton's, *Book of Household Management* (1861). For example, in her advice to the 'Mistress of the Household', she writes:

> Early rising is one of the most essential qualities which enter into good Household Management, as it is not only the parent of health, but of innumerable other advantages. Indeed, when a mistress is an early riser, it is almost certain that her house will be orderly and well managed. On the contrary, if she remains in bed till a late hour, then the domestics who, as we have before observed, invariably partake somewhat of their mistress's character, will surely become sluggards. (Beeton 1861: 2)

The authority in Beeton's system of moral perfectionism plainly rests in the hands of 'the mistress'. She assumes a clear divide between the physical and moral cleanliness of the middle-class household and the implied disorder of peasant and proletarian family conditions in the external world. Again, the intertwining of self-improvement with social progress is evident. The foundations of her system rest upon three principles of good management, which both Smiles and Beecher would have enthusiastically concurred:

1. Setting a good example and giving clear instructions to household staff as to their duties and what is expected of their moral bearing and behaviour;
2. Controlling household finances (treating the home as a 'cost centre');
3. Applying cleanliness, punctuality and order and time management consistently in the domestic sphere. (Wensley 2004: 67)

Beeton presents the strictly regulated consumption of meals and the management of the domestic sphere as a measure of rank. The course of progress that she sets faith by is middle class in every significant co-ordinate. Her bourgeois values and practice were set as role models against both the implied ostentatious waste of the aristocracy and the distemper of conditions on the lower ranks. 'A place for everything, and everything in its place' was her celebrated, endlessly adaptable, maxim (Beeton 1861: 42). The habits of household management naturally translate into the customs of bodily management and self-presentation (Beetham 2008: 393–5). As with Beecher, this is mediated through a mixture of folklore and instrumentally selected elements drawn from science, management and public life. Hence, cleanliness in the kitchen, and in one's person, is a precondition for presenting oneself in the most favourable light in society; order and time management are the tools for success in the external world. The motivation of keeping an efficient, household that is a source of pride and admiration, is to learn and apply the characteristics required to be an effective, successful, progressive agent in general life. The immediate focus of Beecher's work, as with Beeton's manual of life, is self-revelation and self-transformation. However, this is also understood to be the first step in the greater goal of social progress. Already, the bourgeois philosophy of getting the most out of yourself in order to get the most out of the world is present, albeit in embryonic form. Beecher and Beeton follow on the heels of Utilitarianism in proposing that the aristocracy and the lower ranks have much to learn from them, and little to teach.

At this time it is easy to see how, and why, these interventions were so readily analysed in a framework of class struggle. The ideas of Marx and Engels emerged and developed as a sort of counter life to the monological side of bourgeois progress. For them, class struggle was the determinant of human history. They proposed that the struggle between the bourgeoisie and the proletariat should end in the transcendence of class by virtue of the attainment of communism. In contrast to common perceptions today, they understood the communist society to be one that guarantees and nurtures the full and free development of the individual. However, as it turned out, the class model proved to be of limited value. It was persuasive when applied to the rising power of the bourgeoisie in the nineteenth century. Thus, Smiles, Beecher and Beeton all fit snugly into a framework that explains the methods of self-help as tools in the mission of social mobility and class domination. The model is less helpful, however, when applied to the means of persuasion and ends of lifestyle gurus today. The goals of acceptance, approval, social impact and self-validation are not strictly speaking means of controlling people. Today's lifestyle gurus do not peddle the line that lifestyle makeovers will result in a fully and finally realised individual or, still less, that they will produce a superior society (McGee 2005; Raisborough 2011). Instead, they typically operate upon a just-in-time principle that techniques of marshalling acceptance, approval, social impact and self-validation are only as good as the challenges presented by the present moment. Hence, the resort to 'update packages' and subscriptions as part of their lifestyle programme. Integral to today's form of lifestyle management is the idea that the 'journey' of self-discovery is continuous and without end. The pace of social change makes life a permanent race with no final finishing line. Lifestyle management and improvement is in perpetual motion. One is only as good as one's last makeover.

The Globalisation of Self-help

The writings of Smiles, Beecher and Beeton were immensely influential. Still, in terms of what was to come, they were more in the nature of being first runs in the territory of lifestyle architecture and engineering positive intimacy. The period from 1875 to 1914 was the epoch in which the household management and cookery book came into its own as a genuinely global phenomenon (Driver 1989: 13–14). It was also the period when women's magazines and problem pages, in which journalists acted as counsellors for anguished individuals seeking advice, began to cater for a mass, global consumer market concerned with intimate life (Bingham 2012: 51). The first 'Agony Aunt' is thought to have been Annie Swan, in *Women At Home* (1892–1920). At the outset, these pages were coy about intimate questions. They drew upon reserves of folk 'common sense' to address the marital difficulties, child-rearing challenges and the veiled desires of their readers. Sexual matters were seldom referred to directly. This changed after the 1920s. Partly under the influence of the emergence of the mass sex survey and psychology, the Victorian moralism and strictures against what could be imparted in 'problem pages' was relaxed. In the UK during the 1930s, journalists, such as the American agony aunt 'Dorothy Dix' (the working name of Elizabeth Meriweather Gilmer) in *The Daily Mirror,* and Anne Temple, in her 'Human Case-Book' column in *The Daily Mail,* began to adopt a more open attitude to issues of carnal desire, sexual problems and related topics of an intimate nature, sent in by readers (Bingham 2012; Bingham and Conboy 2015: 139–40). It was not that morals were abandoned and an 'anything goes' climate on sexual, emotional and other intimate matters was initiated. On the contrary, the advice given by journalists tended to reinforce moral rectitude based on the class based stereotype of behaviour appropriate to women, drawing upon inviolable Christian precepts and parable. All the same, the new media frankness about intimate and lifestyle matters signalled the growing power of women in the public sphere. This carried over into book-length works dealing with intimacy and lifestyle. For example, *The Marriage Book* (Various 1930), a 766-page manual published in 1930 by the Amalgamated Press included chapters on 'Happiness in Marriage', 'The Love Art of the Husband', 'The Love Art of the Wife', 'Choosing a Career', alongside more traditional chapters on 'The Healthy Family', 'Cookery' and 'Home Dressmaking'. Interestingly, *The Marriage Book* was published without an identified author, as if it were a folk oracle of common sense and wisdom, liberated from the shackles of Victorian prudery.

The agony aunt, recipe aunt or marriage advice aunt, perpetuated in magazines of the interwar period established a culture of presumed intimacy and informality (Rojek 2016). It saw itself as part of what we now call, *the informalisation process,* loosening the reserve and hierarchy while, of course, at the same time holding true to the template of respectable society (Wouters 2007). The rise of lifestyle journalism emerged in the 1950s and 1960s when the emergence of consumer culture, coupled with increased periods of leisure time, led to a demand for information about optimal time use, not only in the area of household management, but also in respect to the general presentation of the self. During this period newspapers and magazines introduced sections dedicated to health, food and travel. This new journalistic field addressed its audiences as consumers, providing them with information and advice about goods and services that they could use in their daily lives (Hanusch 2013: 4). As a precursor to the self-improvement movement, lifestyle media provided practical advice that people could apply to improve their lives from recommendations about what to eat and where to travel, to tips about how to live a healthier, more fulfilling life. As print media and television developed so too did lifestyle journalism, providing content to fill the growing number of pages in newspapers and channels on satellite and cable television (Cole 2005: 33). Though criticised by some for being frivolous in comparison to 'hard' political reporting, lifestyle journalism is now mainstream. Prestigious journalistic institutions, such as the *BBC* and the *Guardian*, regularly feature lifestyle media and advice columns where anonymous readers seek advice from an experienced individual, who emulates the agony aunt method of counselling, about how to navigate personal problems. A case in point is the British newspaper, the *Guardian*, which features a weekly column entitled, 'Dear Mariella' in which Mariella Frostrup, a self-described agony aunt, 'offers words of wisdom' to readers (*Guardian* 2018). Departing from the more generic concerns of lifestyle media, much of this content focuses on intimacy, including sex and relationship troubles of various kinds (e.g. familial, marriage, lovers and friends). There has also been a rise in 'how to' articles dispensing practical lifestyle advice on a range of editorial concerns from health to beauty, fitness, fashion, food and travel. Lifestyle gurus tell us what to eat, what to wear, who to love and where to travel. Though generally lacking certified credentials, these popular experts present themselves as user-friendly 'information providers', providing information and advice about the management of the self and everyday life (Hanusch 2013).

Lifestyle media is instructive, but it is also marked by commercialisation, having a strong market-orientation and connection to advertising (Fürsich 2012). This raises ethical issues about the impartiality and objectivity of lifestyle advice and 'expert' reviews; it also reflects a time when the boundary between commercial and private spheres have become more intertwined. Market values, such as rationality and cost-benefit analysis, are increasingly applied to the management of intimate relations. Eva Illouz (2007) terms this process 'emotional capitalism'. Here, the intimate sphere is subject to commercial principles as a site of ongoing production, a place for reinventing a 'marketable self' (McGee 2005: 22). The emphasis on reinvention has been theorised as a new form of 'immaterial labour' (mental, social, emotional) required for participation in an insecure world and labour market (McGee 2005: 24). In twentieth-century America, for example, the market for self-improvement products (e.g. books, videos, seminars and the like) rose following women's mass entry into the paid workforce, which generated competition and challenged traditional gender roles and cultural expectations of men and women. This period was coupled with economic uncertainty as a result of reduced wages, outsourcing and downsizing. Scholars have shown how following the breakdown of tradition, intimate relations are characterised by both choice and an increased sense of fragility (Giddens 1992; Beck and Beck-Gernsheim 1995; Hochschild 1983; Bauman 2003). Just as advertising relies on insecurity by promising to solve an array of social problems, the self-improvement industry thrives during periods of social and economic uncertainty. From this standpoint, self-improvement is essential to remaining employable in a volatile and competitive labour market where job security and life in general is less predictable and controllable than it had been in the past. It is also part of remaining desirable at a time when divorce is rising and marriage is less certain and secure: 'It is no longer sufficient to be married or employed; rather, it is imperative that one remains marriageable and employable' to stay ahead in an uncertain world (McGee 2005: 12).

The consumer of self-help is conceived as what McGee (2005) terms the 'belaboured self', undergoing constant self-improvement in their quest to remain socially and economically viable. Hence, the rise in makeover programmes designed at reinventing the self by improving one's skills, confidence and physical appearance. Makeover programmes, and lifestyle media more broadly, are predicated on solving ordinary problems through specialist knowledge ('know how') and practical advice. Makeovers in the form of a new wardrobe, kitchen, garden, face or fitness regime are designed at solving larger lifestyle issues: marriage, divorce, employment, raising children and boosting self-esteem. They find their expression in the popular lifestyle programmes *Queer Eye for the Straight Guy*, *What Not to Wear* and *10 Years Younger*, to name a few. Much of this advice is highly gendered, priming masculine courage and feminine beauty. However, following the increased participation of women in the workforce and the introduction of no fault divorce in the late-twentieth century, lifestyle media increasingly caters to both genders on the topics of health, wealth and relationships (Lewis 2008). The idea of the 'ambush' – friends and family members nominating a contestant for a makeover – highlights that no-one is immune from society's critical gaze (McGee 2005: 17–18). What self-improvement literature shares in common is the idea of the individual as uncertain and insufficient, in need of development with the assistance of those gurus who have mastered lifestyle issues.

The self-help movement, which achieved tremendous growth in the late-twentieth century, was part of this process (McGee 2005: 11). The movement's basic principle was that we create the world through our thoughts. While this idea can be traced back to Stoic philosophy, the rise of self-help was largely due to psychological understandings of the self as autonomous and the idea of self-actualisation: the notion that the self is something to be discovered, realised and improved upon (Goldstein 1940; Maslow 1950, 1954; Rogers 1961). The rise of self-improvement culture in the West has been framed as a corollary of individualism in so far as the challenge to traditional religious, political and civic structures in late modern society was marked by an emphasis on the individual. This move towards the individual was evident in the growth of psychoanalysis in the mid-twentieth century – what was termed 'the triumph of the thera-peutic' (Rieff 1966) – but it was also part of a culture that emphasised self-fulfilment and self-actualisation over determinism. In contrast to the doctrine of essentialism, which saw the essence of the self as determined by a set of biological or social characteristics (e.g. gender, race, ethnicity), self-actualisation conceives of the self as autonomous and a 'reflexive project' in need of perpetual development and fine tuning (Giddens 1991). These models of selfhood emphasise the role of reflexive awareness and choice in decision-making processes. From this standpoint, lifestyle choices, and the self more generally, are an individual undertaking arrived at through considered reflection and weighing up alternatives. Feeding into mythology of the 'self-made man' and the American Dream, the appeal of self-help literature is that it emphasises the individual's capacity to achieve success and social mobility; although the barometer for achievement is more amorphous with self-help characterised by subjective understandings of success (e.g. feelings and well-being) rather than external, measurable achievements, such as buying a house or receiving a promotion, as was typically the case with the ethos of the American Dream (McGee 2005: 19).

The common thread weaving these ideals is one of empowerment. By empowering readers with the belief that they have the capacity to change their lives, self-help literature achieved global and commercial success in a series of bestsellers including *Think and Grow Rich* (1937), *The Power of*

Positive Thinking (1952) and *The Secret* (2006). These texts present the idea that 'self-concept is destiny' (Branden 1995). As Hill writes, 'You are the master of your destiny. You can influence, direct and control your own environment. You can make your life what you want it to be' (1937: 185). Or, as Peale (1952) explains, 'When you expect the best, you release a magnetic force in your mind, which by a law of attraction tends to bring the best to you'. Self-help takes the basic truth – that our mind shapes our reality – and exaggerates it by attributing relationship, career and financial success to 'positive thinking' (Peale 1952) and the 'law of attraction' (Byrne 2006). What this literature overlooks is the role of luck, habitus and positional power relating to class, status and group membership in co-creating your life's trajectory. We have the capacity to influence our thoughts and actions, yet we are also situated in society and constituted in relation to others, as Mead and Cooley's theories so convincingly point out. Despite this, the industrialisation of lifestyle saw few barriers to spreading its message. In principle, the notion that motivation comes from within rather than through relations with others, and is not impeded by boundaries of class, race, ethnicity, age or nation. The aim is to join the adventure of self-discovery and create 'lifestyle citizens' who can move fluidly and confidently, through various spatial and social settings, with the same, singular poise and effortless aplomb (Raisborough 2011). Lifestyle citizens have the psychological confidence and civic know-how to enter most conceivable life situations and adapt to all ranks and walks of life. They are not restricted by national boundaries or personal hang-ups. Indeed, they are most accurately defined as citizens of the world.

Attention, Capital and Celebrity

While advice manuals have existed for hundreds of years prescribing how to live 'the good life', today's lifestyle gurus offer advice on how to achieve acceptance, approval, social impact and self-validation as made manifest in happiness, financial success and well-being. There is a shift in orientation here from 'being good' to feeling good. The Ancient Greeks' concern with moral virtue is replaced by a type of moral emotivism in which feeling is perceived to be the barometer of success. The primary cause of this doctrine – which reduces all moral judgements to 'expressions of preference, expressions of attitude or feeling' – is liberalism with its emphasis on individual rights and freedom over a determinate conception of the human good (MacIntyre 1981: 11–12). The central idea driving this doctrine is that it is our individual right to select moral values that accord with our feelings. The self-help movement develops this doctrine further. Here, our moral values are based on the pursuit of subjective self-esteem and validated by having meaningful social value in the sight of others and one's capacity to generate attention capital.

The term 'attention capital' was coined by van Krieken (2012). It emerged in relation to an investigation of celebrity and refers to 'the accumulation, distribution and circulation of the abstract form of capital that is attention' (van Krieken 2012: 10). The clear parallel is with money. As with monetary value, attention is desired, subject to variation in value (inflation/deflation) and the laws of demand and supply. The analogy helps us to think of lifestyle citizenship as a type of coinage. By the term lifestyle citizenship we mean a deterritorialised form of social belonging based around shared values of openness, tolerance of difference, recognition of personal vulnerability, planetary responsibility and devotion to personal well-being. The analogy also usefully reiterates the importance of the just-in-time principle that underlies lifestyle management today. The internalisation and display of lifestyle attributes that convey acceptance and approval, which translate into the attainment of impact, are means of exchange that can fluctuate in value. Although lifestyle gurus typically urge that motivation must come from within, their position as guides and role models confirms the continuing importance of significant others in learning how to succeed in the school of life.

It is by no means an accident that many of the most popular and influential advocates of lifestyle citizenship are celebrities. Super-stars such as Oprah Winfrey, Martha Stewart and Gwyneth Paltrow present themselves, and are widely regarded as, lifestyle polymaths. The attention capital they have generated in the sphere of entertainment carries over into wider realms of self-engineering and virtue signalling in which ordinary people participate and innovate. There is a reason for this. Super-stars are at the top of the tree of attention capital because the rewards assigned to them are valued as public confirmation that they possess talents and people skills that are in short supply, and therefore highly valued. Since 'people skills' are indispensable for nearly every walk of life, from successful family relationships to achievement in the labour market, celebrities are readily absorbed as role models for upgrading and polishing lifestyle. Like celebrities, lifestyle gurus exploit and develop techniques and conventions of 'informal life coaching' (Rojek 2012, 2016). That is, a sphere of dedicated knowledge combing the spectrum of intimate relations, and expressing insights regarding behaviour, self-presentation and social impact. Revealingly, sharing experience, and offering accessible practical solutions to life problems and life opportunities, is often presented with conspiratorial overtones. When Oprah Winfrey advises her audience about how to deal with weight issues, we forget that in 2015 she bought a ten per cent stake in 'Weight Watchers' and joined its board of directors or that her net worth in 2018 was estimated to be $3 billion (Wiener-Bronner 2018). Instead, she communicates with the audience as if she were outside of the system and living on equal terms with them, traversing the ostensibly contradictory values of religious piety and consumer capitalism (Lofton 2011). For the most part, social and economic distance is a requirement for the attention capital of celebrity status. However, when celebrities present themselves as lifestyle advisers they take care to step off their pedestal and espouse the philosophy of being accessible and on a level playing field, not only with ordinary people, but in the case of celebrities who advocate environmental responsibility, with the Earth itself.

Celebrities who engage in expanding lifestyle consciousness generally do so on the presumption that they are, in the end, just 'one of us'. The marginalisation or absence of recognisable party political affiliations is a crucial part in this process. In privileging 'humanity' over 'race' and 'party politics', celebrity lifestyle campaigners boost their apparent integrity and, in doing so, have an easier job of bringing people 'into confidence'. Additionally, while claiming to have real and relevant knowledge about the human and environmental issues that they address, they are at pains to avoid being labelled as 'experts'. In cultivating informality, the apparatus of celebrity life coaching is defined as offering an alternative route to the 'us and them' polarity that is often thought to mar transactions with professionals and experts. Lifestyle gurus also make a virtue of being non-judgemental. They appear to offer a world that is beyond 'us and them'. Informal coaching fetishises the value of 'native' knowledge drawn from lay experience rather than training or professional expertise (Keen 2008). The race to win in life is the final arbiter of trust and useful knowledge. Lifestyle gurus appeal directly to 'common sense' and 'plain speaking' and contrast this with the 'abstraction', 'aloofness' and 'insensitivity' of the professional canon.

Digitally 'Sitting Next to Nellie'

We can perhaps illustrate the point with an example from work relations. Lifestyle gurus frequently offer a variation of what is known in human relations management as the 'sitting next to Nellie' phenomenon. The notion developed from the nineteenth-century factory system. According to the *Oxford English Dictionary* it refers to on-the-job training by unqualified instructors (fellow workmen and women) who have been doing the job for years. Instruction is unplanned and unsystematic. While trainees may learn the nuts and bolts of the job, they may also acquire the good and bad work habits of the instructor. All of this can be extended to apply to lifestyle gurus. For them, lifestyle issues, rather than work practice, are the crux of online transaction. Lifestyle gurus offer the chance to copy and learn from receptive strangers who position and advance themselves as significant others. The passport of their attention capital is the claim either to have directly experienced identical lifestyle challenges that perplex the audience, or to have devised resources to overcome them. They appear not just as knowledgeable practitioners, but as successful role models in overcoming life's hazards and hurdles. Following the rise of reflexive modernisation, a series of ordinary people with 'know-how' today claim the authority to advise people on how to live. The example of 'sitting next to Nellie', also helps to consolidate another important point about the character of lifestyle guru dynamics. The apparatus of self-improvement is often presented as the basis for play, self-discovery and self-revelation. Whatever truth rests in these perceptions must not be permitted to obscure the equivalent characteristic that lifestyle gurus provide people with an additional form of work. Acceptance, approval, social impact and self-validation are not achieved at the drop of a hat. They require planning and labour. It might be said that the original lifestyle advisers and guides such as Smiles, Beecher and Beeton in the nineteenth century also understood this. Smiles' *Self-help*, Beecher's *Treatise* and Beeton's *Household Management* are paeans to hard, muscular, organised work and the moral superiority of Christian values. They led readers to believe that being faithful to the enunciated principles of self-help will result in full graduation from 'the school of life' – entry to heaven. This implies that, once learning is complete, successful life management will simply consist in the robust application of the same learned principles that are fit to match any occasion until the end of one's days. Today's lifestyle gurus offer not so finite a scheme in their compass of advice. They make the same pledge that successful inculcation of the lifestyle values and strategies that they enunciate will produce personal fulfilment. However, when one explores the various multitude of online sites, one finds that a common part of their message is that we live in a rapidly changing world. Successful lifestyle planning and application is not just adaptive, it is presented as eternally evolving. The type of labour that today's lifestyle gurus offer, therefore, is not a once-and-for-all undertaking. On the contrary, in the race to achieve acceptance, approval, social impact and self-validation, the discipline that lifestyle gurus preach is cultivating attention capital by continuous labour. If you want to make the most of yourself in life, which changes in rapid and often unpredicted ways, you must make a lifelong commitment to work without end (Crary 2014).

2

The Rise of Lifestyle Gurus in the Digital Age

The lifestyle guru phenomenon is born of the media. Oprah Winfrey and Martha Stewart are two lifestyle polymaths who achieved lifestyle guru status by virtue of the media. Having achieved success hosting the talk show, *A. M. Chicago,* in 1986 Winfrey launched *The Oprah Winfrey Show* (1986–2011), using the programme to canvass the struggles of everyday life. The show explored a range of personal predicaments: dilemmas about our purpose, moral commitments and how best to relate to ourselves and others. Winfrey's cultural appeal stems from her ability to address questions about identity and personal relationships in late modern society (Illouz 1999: 111). Her authority reflects a profound transformation in conceptions of the self in modernity (Giddens 1991), characterised by the 'affirmation of ordinary life' as the site within which conceptions of identity and 'the good' are articulated, realised and 'discovered' (Taylor 1989). Oprah speaks to the mundane, addressing everyday struggles from weight loss and relationships to self-esteem. Her brand was built around sharing these everyday life problems and providing pragmatic solutions to them as encapsulated by her magazine's mission statement, 'Live Your Best Life'. In this regard, Oprah's brand as a lifestyle guru shares much in common with the self-help movement. Both address an audience for whom life is perceived to be lacking, transforming problems into solutions by evoking empowering therapeutic discourse about acceptance, self-discovery and self-realisation that resonate with contemporary conceptions of the self (Carbraugh 1994).

Despite branching into radio and print media, it was television that formed the basis of Oprah's fame and influence. The *Oprah Winfrey Show* was built upon a tradition of female talk-show hosts on American television. Since the mid-1950s, talk shows hosted by women appealed to the familiar, domestic, folksy feel popularised by Oprah (Haag 1993). In the 1950s, Virginia Graham hosted *Food for Thought* (1953–1957), followed by *Girl Talk* (1963–1970) and *The Virginia Graham Show* (1970–1972), combining wit, charm and gossip to attract audiences. In the early 1970s,

Dinah Shore invited viewers to *Dinah's Place* to cook and talk with guests. Staged on a set replicating her home kitchen and living room, Shore represented a conventional portrayal of woman as hostess and homemaker (Timberg and Erler 2010). Winfrey rose to fame in the 1980s and 1990s at a time when talk shows dominated the ratings. But Winfrey captured the popular imagination and differentiated herself from her competition, most of whom were men (e.g. Gerlado Rivera and Phil Donahue), through her touching emotional displays, appearing more compassionate and better attuned to her audience than her contemporaries.

It was in the mid-1990s that Winfrey achieved lifestyle guru status. During this period, Oprah's talk show evolved into what she termed, 'Change Your Life Television' (Lofton 2006). What we later call the lifestyle 'Reset' is fully unveiled here (134–6). Her goal was no longer merely to enlighten and entertain, but to *transform* people's lives (Winfrey 2019). There was a religious dimension to Oprah's new format. Discussions of 'souls', 'spirits', 'truth' and 'miracles' infused her vocabulary with psychological problems recast as 'spiritual struggles' (Illouz 2003; Lofton 2006), 'I believe beneath the surface of all physical problems is a spiritual solution', Oprah explained in her *Life Class* (Oprah Winfrey Network 2012). This theological language was all the more compelling to viewers in that it seemed to answer to an urgent need for meaning by involving forces that are themselves, ineffable and inscrutable. Whereas *The Oprah Winfrey Show* had originally focused on personal and relationship dramas characteristic of the talk-show genre in the 1980s and 1990s, her new format was oriented towards the spiritual salvation of the individual.

Although she identifies as Christian, Oprah's popular appeal is predicated on the way she distances herself from traditional dogmas and institutionalised religion. Commensurate with an era of New Age spirituality, individual awakening was the hallmark of her show – the idea that spirituality is 'found' from within. Drawing upon the contemporary preoccupation with self-realisation, the show became an educational platform for self-discovery and self-improvement canvassing a range of inspirational stories under the guidance of celebrities and self-help gurus. For those with problems, Winfrey had solutions. All you needed was a willingness to change in order to start your 'inner revolution'. Oprah presented spirituality as a practical undertaking. She offered spiritual and moral counsel with her personal prescriptions ('Stop wishing, start doing'; 'Live in the space of Spirit'; 'Live your life in an open heart through love'), instructing audiences how to live a better life. Her various media enterprises (i.e. television, radio, magazine) operated as 'how-to' manuals for these prescriptions, with each segment devoted to a different mode of self-improvement (Lofton 2006). While Oprah shared her own beliefs and daily spiritual practices on the show, she also conveyed self-improvement as inhabiting the mundane aspects of the everyday. Through disclosing her own habits and proclivities, Oprah used her personal lifestyle choices – what she ate for breakfast, her favourite book, exercise regime and piece of clothing – to model the 'good' life. The motif of being co-present and equal in facing life's dilemmas, sometimes rendered by the cliché that 'we are all in it together', is strongly accentuated in this material. Her magazine categoried these lifestyle pursuits into topics (beauty, style, health and food), making self-improvement a manageable exercise. This message of self-improvement was manifest in her own narrative of spiritual awakening as well as those of guests and celebrities she interviewed. Her show popularised what has become a successful lifestyle guru formula: present a common problem and list a series of practical steps and products you can use to change it in order to achieve happiness and success in life (see Chapter 1). But while the process of discovery, for Oprah, is found from within, self-realisation is also tangibly found from without through consuming various lifestyle products and services.

Despite Oprah's allegiance to the masses, her program advocates high levels of consumption (Lofton 2006). She combines spiritual counsel with consumerist practices, dedicating entire episodes towards lifestyle change via consumption. For example, 'Oprah's Favorite Things', one of the highest rating annual segments of the show, featured Oprah sharing a curated list of her favourite products with her audience, gift ideas including brand endorsements for specific foods, beauty products, music, books and homeware. Audience members present during the filming of the episode received free items from the list adding to the hype and allure of the products. This consumerist logic infiltrates her other media enterprises with her monthly *O Magazine* including the 'O List', a list of products her editors think are 'just great'. Each monthly issue curates a list of products – teas, slippers, throws – designed to invoke a specific mood whether it be feeling a little more 'festive' (February 2019) or 'relaxed' (January 2019). Purchasing a new lipstick, bag or set of pyjamas is conceived as more than a way to feel good, buying into Oprah's brand and lifestyle is a step towards spiritual salvation.

Television has been instrumental in Winfrey's revered stature. In 2011, *The Oprah Winfrey Show* was replaced by *Super Soul Sunday*, a daytime series that in Oprah's own words 'delivers insight and inspiration from renowned thought leaders to awaken viewers to their best selves and discover a deeper connection to the world around them' (Harpo Productions 2018). The programme covers conversations between Oprah and 'top thinkers', authors, celebrities and 'spiritual luminaries' as well as health and wellness experts. In Oprah's own words, it is designed to help viewers awaken, 'discover' and connect to the world around them and in line with the self-help ethos 'guide you through life's big questions and help bring you one step closer to your best self' (Harpo Productions 2018). While Oprah has recently distanced herself from the prescriptive ethos of 'change your life television', her programme continues to use the naturalistic style of television as a way to document 'real life' in her quest to promote change, responsibility and empowerment. Oprah is a confessional subject, disclosing her own history of sexual abuse, tumultuous relationships, drug and weight struggles to relate to her audience. When interviewed in 2018 about the intention of her talk show, Oprah explained, 'The intention was to let people know that they were not alone. I wanted everyone watching to know that there is a story just like yours and there's a way you fit into the story of the world' (Winfrey 2018b). In an interview with *Time Magazine,* she described her shows as 'hour-long life lessons' (Zoglin 1988), drawing on the 'commonality of human experience' as a way to connect with her audience. Her confessional communication style conveys the impression of friendship, tolerance and accessibility, enabling her to appear empathetic, likeable and approachable and, thus, able to overcome the distance engendered by her wealth and celebrity status (Haag 1993). She draws on the affordances of television as a para-social medium to foster intimacy and connection with her fans with the ritual practice of watching television enabling her to feature as a regular fixture in their daily lives (Horton and Wohl 1956); the placement of the television in the home further blurring the boundary between public and private space (Spigel 1989). It is these technologies that enabled Oprah to access mass audiences and to communicate as our friend and equal.

Whereas Oprah achieved fame using the talk-show genre, Stewart followed a more conventional trajectory as a lifestyle guru, producing lifestyle advice on traditional domestic pursuits including cooking, sewing, gardening, renovating and entertaining. In this regard, Stewart can be seen to continue the emphasis that nineteenth-century female lifestyle gurus placed on the home and family, strengthening the connection between women and the domestic sphere (Leavitt 2002). Stewart forms part of a resurgence of lifestyle gurus in the late-twentieth century, most of whom are women (Brunsdon 2005). Regardless of the changing role of women in society, the authors of domestic advice manuals have remained remarkably consistent across the centuries (Leavitt 2002). Criticised for promoting unrealistic standards of perfection and a return to domesticity (Golec 2006), Stewart and her contemporaries emphasise the centrality of the home as a site for the cultivation of the self and a specific kind of class ideology. Like her predecessors, Stewart represents particular cultural ideals of 'good taste' drawn from an idealised white, upper-middle-class lifestyle (Davies 2004). But rather than convey the kitchen as a reductive space confined to domestic duty, cooking and lifestyle pursuits are presented as a 'gateway to the world' of affluence, privilege and lifestyle citizenship (LeBesco and Naccarato 2008: 233). The language that infuses Stewart's texts is overtly positive. Everything associated with her brand is 'good', 'beautiful', 'wonderful', 'luxurious' and 'fantastic', with food and lifestyle practices employed as a vehicle to affirm class identity (LeBesco and Naccarato 2008: 234). Although Stewart does not dwell on her humble origins, her media texts function as handbooks for social mobility that mirror her personal transcendence from working-class, New Jersey, to become America's first 'self-made' female billionaire. Like Oprah, Stewart's display of affluence as a lifestyle worthy of 'aspiration' and 'emulation' has been criticised for encouraging a preoccupation with consumerism (Mason and Meyers 2001) and for offering illusory access to class mobility (LeBesco and Naccarato 2008). The key difference between Stewart and those who came before her, is how she uses the media to achieve fame and communicate with the masses.

Stewart's rise to fame as a lifestyle guru is the result of media saturation. In 1982, her bestselling book, *Entertaining*, earned her the title, the 'domestic goddess'. This was followed by other popular books, a quarterly magazine and the *Martha Stewart Living* television show, a weekly series that Stewart hosted, where she presented segments on lifestyle topics such as cooking, gardening, craft making and decorating. Her television show was so popular that it expanded to weekdays and became an hour-long program, supplemented by radio (*Martha Stewart Living Radio*). In the lifestyle genre, media leads to merchandising, and the popularity of Stewart's books, magazines, television and radio show enabled her to commodify her influence by selling homeware and product lines in various department stores: Kmart, Macy's and the Home Depot. In 1997, she created *Martha Stewart Living Omnimedia Inc.*, consolidating her various media ventures: publishing, internet, broadcasting media platforms and merchandising product lines to solidify the Martha Stewart brand. These platforms have enabled Stewart to popularise the domestic education previously formalised by Beecher in the Victorian era by making lifestyle advice accessible to the masses, and self-transformation the key to social progress (Leavitt 2002). In 2000, Martha Stewart became America's first self-made female billionaire (later joined by Oprah), feeding into the ethos of empowerment popularised in the late modern West by the self-help movement. Like her contemporaries (e.g. Oprah Winfrey, Delia Smith, Nigella Lawson), Stewart's commercial success and visibility in the public domain was a product of the mass media with television making her accessible to the masses.

Migrating Online

Much has changed in how knowledge is produced and consumed in the digital age. The ubiquity of the internet, smartphones and mobile devices has allowed people to create and share information at an unprecedented rate. The lifestyle gurus that once dominated the mass media have begun to migrate online, changing how we access advice and information in the twenty-first century. Rather than see a doctor when one is ill, it is now common for people to use the internet to self-diagnose and search for health and lifestyle advice. In 2013, Pew Research Center reported that 72 per cent of internet users had searched online for health information within the past year (Fox and Duggan 2013). Searches included those pertaining to general medical information, serious conditions and minor health problems both for oneself and on behalf of others.

The rise in people using the internet to seek information and advice has led to debates about the social consequences of technology. These debates tend to centre around the opportunities for democratisation and fears about the quality and reliability of the information that people access online. Tech enthusiasts emphasise the democratic potential of technology with the internet allowing a greater number of people to access information from a variety of online sources. The result is said to be a democratisation of knowledge where power is decentralised from the authority of experts and ordinary users can contribute to the formation of knowledge. Critics, conversely, have raised concerns about the quality of information online. They emphasise that more data is not synonymous with better knowledge. In *The Death of Expertise* (2017), Thomas Nichols argues that rejection of experts has been facilitated by the internet. While the internet has enabled more people to access a greater volume and variety of information online, he argues that the sheer sum of information available has given people the illusion of knowledge when in fact most are cherry-picking information that conforms to their pre-existing views rather than accepting new information (what is referred to as confirmation bias). Many people use social network sites to access their news. In most cases people network online, as they do offline, with those like themselves. This tendency has been explained by the principle of *homophily* (translated as 'love of the same'). As a result, the views that people are exposed to online tend to conform to their own, with social media sites operating as homogeneous echo chambers, rather than challenging preconceived beliefs and opinions. There are also concerns about the quality of information produced online. The barriers to entry have decreased in the digital age. In principle, anyone with access to the internet can post advice on a blog, social media site or forum with critics pointing to the risks associated with user generated content. Whereas books and articles are generally subject to a rigorous peer-review process, the internet is subject to relatively low levels of regulation. Lifestyle bloggers have the freedom to post advice about topics in which they have no knowledge and expertise that may misinform those who read them.

The hopes and fears that surround the new media used by lifestyle gurus today are far from novel. At the time of their emergence, 'new' media commonly inspired awe and fear (Marvin 1988). There were fears following the arrival of Gutenberg's printing press in the fifteenth century that cheaply printed books and broadsheets would undermine religious authority, demean the work of scholars, and encourage 'debauchery' and 'sedition' (Carr 2008). The nineteenth century witnessed the expansion of the print industry giving rise to a large volume and variety of printed material that could be distributed at an unprecedented speed and scale. Improved literacy rates meant that this material could reach a wider audience. Despite the promise of these technologies, the mass production of books was criticised for undermining the quality of knowledge by promoting superficial reading practices and discouraging thoughtful immersion (Mill 1836).

In addition to concerns about the quality of print media, in the Victorian era people were cautioned that reading fiction could atrophy the mind (Gettelman 2011). Numerous books were banned as a consequence of their content: Gustave Flaubert's *Madame Bovary* (1856) and D. H. Lawrence's novel, *Lady Chatterley's Lover* (1928) on the grounds of obscenity and Ernest Hemingway's, *For Whom The Bell Tolls* (1940) on accusations of being pro-Communist and pro-Republican. By the nineteenth century, the issue was the speed of transmission with the telegram accused of undermining 'Truth' (LaFrance 2014), triggering isolation and mental illness (Lehrer 2010). The invention of the radio and television in the nineteenth century brought with them accusations that these new technologies sullied the mind by turning active readers into passive audiences (van Dijck 2009). More recently, concerns have been raised with regard to internet addiction and the psychological impact of the information that people consume online. Critics suggest that, while people are now exposed to more information than ever before, online practices of clicking, surfing and scanning diminish our capacity for concentration and contemplation (Carr 2010; Turkle 2011; Alter 2017), thereby echoing earlier critiques of the print industry. What is threatened in all of these cases is not only the minds of the audience, but established standards of authority and expertise.

New media is a relative term, yet the hopes and fears that new media evoke repeat themselves over time. There is a tendency for critics to associate emergent technologies with social decline and the degradation of moral values. These fears are often coupled with nostalgia about an idealised past when life was perceived to be better and safer (Pearson 1983; Marvin 1988, boyd 2014). Since the time of the Ancient Greeks, there are records documenting people's nostalgia for a Golden Age. Plato expressed these concerns in *The Republic* when he suggested that poetry ought to be banned because it aroused intense emotions that left audiences in a potentially harmful state – impressionable, emotionally incontinent, and unable to discern appearance from 'knowledge of its real nature' (Plato [1935] 2006: 419). Views of this kind focus on the harmful effects of technology, particularly in relation to youth, who are thought to be impressionable and susceptible to misinformation, lacking the discernment to judge information critically. There is also a strong utopian ideology associated with the concept of 'new' that invokes ideas around progress and improvement. Utopian views assume that technology is the solution to social problems. In the case of the internet, it was expected to be the great 'equaliser' by facilitating user engagement, participation and democracy (boyd 2014). Both utopian and dystopian views succumb to technological determinism, assuming that technology determines human behaviour by producing the same outcome regardless of context and how it is used by various groups. In both cases, there is a tendency to focus on causes – how technology 'causes' people to act – as though a technology's impact on human behaviour were universal and predetermined.

The approach taken in this book is different. Although lifestyle gurus have been subject to scrutiny in the digital age, our contention is not that online communication renders a universal outcome. Rather, we focus on the social practices afforded as a result of these applications. The term 'affordance' is useful here (Norman 1988; Hutchby 2001). Affordances are the possible actions that arise from the material functionalities of a technology (Bucher and Helmond 2018). In short, what a technology enables a user to do and what it precludes. With regard to lifestyle gurus, the affordances of social media configure how authority and influence is constructed online. Instagram, for example, which affords users the ability to document the self in photo and video form, places an emphasis on aesthetics. In this context, lifestyle gurus are usually attractive people who display success and achievement in visual form (e.g. a toned body, a desirable meal or a beautiful home), due to the platform's emphasis on the image. Conversely, Twitter, which is characterised by brief, text-based communication, affords more opinionated, impulsive forms of discursive online exchange. The specific features on these sites – the 'like' button, @ replies and favourites – are powerful symbols. They configure the communication practices and social interactions that various technologies afford. Although these affordances do not determine social practice, they are engineered in such a way that they shape how people interact online.

Technologies are symbolic, but they also enable certain opportunities and facilitate social interaction. The emphasis here is on possibilities rather than pre-determined outcomes. While the properties of a technology do not determine how they will be used, they open up new possibilities and encourage certain uses. For example, mobile communication enables communication across vast distal settings through the use of voice and text-based interaction (Ling 2010); the introduction of the camera phone extends the possibilities for mobile, visual, interactive communication in real time. These affordances can result in tangible consequences with photographic imagery contributing to particular beliefs and narratives by validating or discrediting certain narratives and points of view (Baker 2012, 2014). The media play a significant role in how we perceive and experience the world. Rather than focusing on causes, we explore the role media technologies play in social interactions and cultural practices. This shift in focus enables us to examine how the technologies used by lifestyle gurus to communicate today influences how we come to know and relate to others.

Establishing Native Knowledge and Expertise Online

The internet has permitted new, deterritorialised encounters with others. Increased internet access, together with the ubiquity of smartphones and social media, has provided lifestyle bloggers with global platforms on which to share their views, participate in social networks, and establish authority and influence online. Whereas knowledge was traditionally disseminated via those who controlled the means of production (e.g. the printing press, broadcasting licenses), the rise of user-generated content means that ordinary users can access public audiences and inhabit the same public platforms as celebrities, experts and elites. Previously, one might have had an opinion that one wished to share, but it would be difficult to access an audience beyond those people one knew and with whom one physically interacted. Social media has extended audience reach by providing greater access to publics. While there is no guarantee that a user will be seen and heard online, the potential is there to be viewed, recognised and listened to by others. Native knowledge, which was often scorned by professional experts, has a revitalised global platform of articulation and exchange. This general trend towards user-generated content has been conceived as a process of democratisation by enabling the free movement of ideas and making visible the knowledge and opinions of ordinary users. While new media have contributed to changes in media production, distribution and use, the rise of lifestyle gurus is less about technological innovation than the internet's domestic diffusion and appropriation into pre-existing social practices as a mass-market phenomenon (Livingstone 2011).

The pervasiveness of the internet in everyday social life has played a significant role in the rise of lifestyle gurus and native expertise. When the internet was first created in the late 1990s, its use was confined to early adopters and subgroups (unrepresentative of the population). The internet is now mainstream. In North America the proportion of people with high-speed broadband service at home increased rapidly between 2000 and 2010. In 2017, roughly nine-in-ten American adults used the internet (Pew Research Center: Internet, Science & Tech 2018a). Usage rates in North America correspond to internet use in Great Britain. In 2017, 90 per cent of households in Great Britain had internet access – an increase from 57 per cent in 2006. Mobile access has also increased, with 73 per cent of adults accessing the internet 'on the go' using a mobile phone or smartphone; more than double the 2011 rate of 36 per cent (Office for National Statistics 2017). Blogs and forums, which were once reserved for a minority of early internet adopters, are now ubiquitous. WordPress, the largest self-hosted blogging tool in the world, is accessed by tens of millions of people every day and the microblogging service, Twitter, averages 321 million monthly active users (Statista 2018). Social media use has also increased at a significant rate. In 2010, there were 0.97 billion social media users worldwide. This figure increased to over two billion users in 2019 (Statista 2019c). Social media are now familiar technologies, with around seven-in-ten Americans using social media to connect with one another, engage with news content and share information online (Pew Research Center: Internet, Science & Tech. 2018b).

Unsurprisingly, many of the audiences that consume lifestyle advice online are youth (Khamis et al. 2017). Those under the age of twenty-five have grown up with the internet. At the same time, not all youth experience these technologies in the same way. There is an assumption that those generations that have been exposed to the internet in their youth have a natural aptitude for technology, possessing knowledge and skills that set them apart from older generations because of the contemporary web culture in which they live. The terms 'digital immigrants' and 'digital natives' have been used to describe this phenomenon. Many teenagers are not as technically proficient as these terms suggest. In her study of technology and youth, danah boyd (2014: 22) found that the teenagers she interviewed knew how to use Google, but had little understanding about how to construct a query to get reliable information from the search engine. People have neither the same access, nor the same skills to navigate the internet. Their usage is constrained by their ability to access the internet, whether their access is filtered (as is the case with many public computers) and their technological abilities, as the terms 'digital divide' and 'second-level digital divide' suggest (Hargittai 2002). Barbrook and Cameron contend that ideals of democratic participation overlook the mostly non-white underclass who cannot afford computers or access the internet; internet adoption varies across demographic groups, with racial minorities, older adults, rural residents, and those with lower levels of education and income less likely to have broadband service (Pew Research Center: Internet, Science & Tech 2018a).

Just as internet usage varies across demographic groups, platform use varies among populations. The demographic that use Reddit, for example, tends to differ from those that use Instagram due to the affordances of these technologies (Reddit designed for text-based discussions while Instagram privileges the visual, therefore appealing to brands, celebrities and youth). Moreover, how people use technology is dynamic and subject to change. A case in point is Twitter. Whereas early usage was satirised for the trend of posting banal updates in the third person about what one ate for breakfast, this type of communication is no longer common with the platform used primarily to share updates and opinions about news, politics and current affairs. In this book, we account for these nuances rather than applying a fixed understanding of social media. Though new media technologies vary in their design and use, there are a series of tools that have led to the proliferation of lifestyle gurus in the digital age. These tools have been instrumental in the rise of lifestyle gurus as native experts online.

The Tools of Lifestyle Gurus in the Digital Age

The main tools of lifestyle gurus in the twenty-first century are blogs and social media. Both presuppose the internet. In recent years blogs have replaced the homepage as one of the primary media of self-expression. By documenting personal thoughts, observations and opinions on topics of interest, they mirror the informal and conversational style of a diary or journal; the key difference being that blogs are made public online for others to read. The intended audience is the point of demarcation between the two forms. Whereas documentation is the end result of journal writing, documentation is the means of self-expression on blogs and social media. It is precisely because blogs are public that they facil-itate engagement and familiarity with an audience, providing personal updates on one's life or subject of interest in textual and visual form. The documentary style of blogging mimics the medium of television by invoking the intimate, friendly feel popularised by Oprah and Martha Stewart on their lifestyle shows. But whereas television is a one-to-many broadcast medium, blogging software encourages readers to comment on blog posts, lending itself to interactive, direct forms of communication between the blogger and their audience. This brings a community element to blogs often only imagined by television audiences.

While blogs were first created in the mid-1990s, their popularity in the last decade is largely due to the pervasiveness of the internet and a range of free, easy to use, open-source blogging software. The original blogs were updated manually, often linked from a central home page or archive. This was inefficient, but there were few options to customise your blog unless you were a computer programmer. The introduction of a series of new blogging services meant that very limited technical knowledge was required to start a blog. Blogging platforms, such as Blogger (1999) and WordPress (2003), enabled users with basic technical abilities to share content online and to customise their blogs. The rise of microblogs, such as Twitter (2006) and Tumblr (2007), in the mid-2000s encouraged brief, frequent engagement in the form of updates and opinions on a specific topic due to their restricted word limit. The usability of these platforms is largely responsible for making lifestyle bloggers mainstream with the proliferation of smartphones and mobile broadband extending audience reach by making it possible for public audiences to interact with blogs anytime and from (almost) any place.

Social media is the primary mode of communication for lifestyle gurus. We use the term 'social media' to refer to the collection of sites and services used to create and share content, to socialise and interact. While blogs are not technically social media, we include blogs in our description because most lifestyle gurus are lifestyle bloggers who publicise their blog posts on social media, so that the two media become merged in a feedback loop. Emerging during the early 2000s, Facebook (2004), YouTube (2005), Reddit (2005), Twitter (2006), Pinterest (2010), Instagram (2010) and Snapchat (2011) are the primary sites used to access lifestyle advice in the West. Similar to blogging, by the mid-2000s social media became mainstream with participation on social media routine and expected. Founded in 2004, by 2012 Facebook had over one billion active users, rising in 2018 to 2.32 billion monthly active users worldwide (Statista 2019b). Although Facebook is the most widely used social media platform, and its user base most representative of the population (Pew Research Center: Internet, Science & Tech. 2018b), Instagram is currently lifestyle gurus preferred medium due to its popularity among brands and younger consumers. As a social network site, Instagram allows users to construct a public or semi-public profile to be shared with 'friends' and 'followers' on that platform. The emphasis on friendship distinguishes the social network site from other social media platforms, such as the video-sharing site, YouTube, which is typically consumed by anonymous viewers. While blogging attracts audiences with shared interests, social network sites are built around friendship enabling lifestyle gurus to establish a sense of intimacy with their followers. What makes these sites popular among lifestyle gurus is that they provide a shared space to connect with fans as friends (although friendship is applied broadly to include acquaintances, friends of friends and strangers). This idea of friendship, although broadly applied on many social network sites, is one of the primary ways in which intimacy is established online.

There are a plethora of digital tools to support meaningful interaction online (e.g. email, instant messaging, forums). What is significant about social media is that they allow lifestyle gurus to access public audiences on an unprecedented scale. Danah boyd (2014) notes four key affordances of social media: *persistence* (the durability of online content); *visibility* (the potential for content to be seen); *spreadability* (the ease with which context can be shared); and *searchability* (the ability to access content through search functions). These affordances have altered the ways in which lifestyle gurus achieve influence online. It is also why lifestyle gurus who promote pseudoscience and misinformation are more problematic today than they were in the past. The capacity to generate pseudoscience and misinformation is far from novel. What has changed is the speed and scale with which this information can be disseminated. A quack promoting alternative cancer treatments using social media has the potential to shape the decisions and practices of people on an unprecedented scale. Social media make this content persistent and increase its potential to be seen, shared and found. Whether this potential is realised depends on a combination of skill, fashion (the public's appetite for certain information), chance and performance.

Social media afford new possibilities for people to make themselves visible and to connect with a wider public, referred to as 'networked publics'. The term refers to the social space constructed by networked technologies and the imagined community that emerges as a result (boyd 2010). The space exists because of the intersection of people, technology and practice. When this communication occurs across social media sites, it is referred to as a 'networked audience' (Marwick 2013: 213). The internet has altered the media's role in society. People are increasingly networked with, and through, media. Yochai Benkler (2006) employs the term 'the networked public sphere' to describe a series of technological developments and emergent social practices that created new opportunities for how information is produced, exchanged and consumed. The term is often understood in contradistinction to the mass media that characterised public discourse throughout much of the twentieth century; a time when to speak required a platform and the owner of the platform was a commercial entity that could determine what was published. The networked public sphere points to the ways in which digital technologies decentralise power structures by allowing ordinary users to participate and influence public discourse. The term networked publics is employed as an alternative to terms such as audience and consumer. It emphasises the ways in which the internet and new media enable publics to produce and distribute information and knowledge to complex networks, via what is commonly referred to as 'Web 2.0'.

Web 2.0, the Active User and Participatory Culture

Web 2.0 is commonly used to describe the second stage of development of the internet, characterised by user-generated content and social media.

The term was popularised by Tim O'Reilly as part of a conversation he had with Dale Dougherty at the O'Reilly Media Web 2.0 Conference in 2004. O'Reilly used the term as a way to resurrect the internet economy after the dot.com crash in 2000. One of the ways he sought to attract potential investors was by highlighting that these second-generation web applications were radically different from those that had failed. For O'Reilly, 'Web 2.0 is the network as platform, spanning all connected devices', creating network effects through an 'architecture of participation' (O'Reilly 2005b). As this definition implies, Web 2.0 does not refer to an update to any single technical specification, but rather to changes in the way web pages are designed and used. These functions and uses include the following characteristics: 'the web as platform', participation instead of publishing, users as contributors, data control, improved software, rich user experience, radical trust in users as co-developers, and 'collective intelligence' (O'Reilly 2005a). The 'new Web', as O'Reilly described it, was also characterised by decentralisation.

Although there is disagreement about how novel Web 2.0 technologies are, the technology associated with Web 2.0 has had a significant impact on the dissemination of lifestyle advice. While there is some overlap between Web 1.0 and Web 2.0, the latter is characterised by the rise of user-generated content, usability (ease of use by non-experts) and the growth of social media. This development has been conceived as a shift from provider-driven content to user-generated content: 'Web 2.0 is a more locally conceived, bottom-up system while Web 1.0 is more centrally conceived and top-down' (Ritzer and Jurgenson 2011: 627). While Web 2.0 has become synonymous with user-generated content and social media, the emphasis is not on the technological specifications of second-generation web applications (e.g. blogs were part of Web 1.0), but rather their use by non-experts and the discourses that accompany these applications.

One of the defining discourses around Web 2.0 is the idea of the active user participating in online culture. Traditionally, media scholars have theorised the agency of media recipients in close connection to the type of medium; television and film are said to produce 'passive' spectators that merely consume content (van Dijck 2009). In contrast to the passive consumption that was said to characterise engagement with earlier media forms, Web 2.0 and user-generated content emphasise the role of the active 'user' (Livingstone 2004). Web 2.0's many-to-many model of communication is often contrasted with the one-to-many broadcast models of communication, characteristic of radio and television, where a sender (typically in a position of power, such as Oprah or Stewart) transmits a message to many recipients. Web 2.0 decentralises knowledge and information by allowing ordinary users to generate content that can be shared with others. One of the ideals that has accompanied Web 2.0 is the belief that the decentralisation of the internet would challenge the monopoly of Big Media by giving users equal access to broadcast and distribution technologies as content creators.

This shift towards content creation has been conceptualised by the notion of 'the prosumer'. Coined by Alvin Toffler in the late-twentieth century, the term is used to describe how agency traverses between both producer and consumer, 'blurring' the line that separates the two (Toffler 1980: 267). Web 2.0 technologies are seen to give prosumption greater centrality with new hybrid terms such as 'produser' and 'co-creator' used to describe user agency as inherently productive (Bruns 2007). Examples of produsage include open-source software development, citizen journalism and Wikipedia, where 'collaborative knowledge' is generated and revised by a collection of users (in contrast to traditional encyclopaedias, which are generally confined to experts). The emphasis here is on the creative collaboration that characterises user agency in networked spaces and enables all participants to be users as well as producers of information and knowledge. The result is said to be a 'participatory culture' comprised of active users with the web conceived as a site of 'consumer participation' (Jenkins 2006).

There is a utopian ideology associated with Web 2.0 that emphasises the democratic potential for these technologies to liberate ordinary users from established power hierarchies. The cachet of the net is to comment and have influence *from outside of the system*. The proliferation of ordinary users generating and sharing information online has been conceived as part of the democratisation of everyday life where knowledge is viewed as a collective enterprise rather than the result of 'a few great men'. Terms such as 'crowd sourcing' (Howe 2006), 'wikinomics' (Tapscott and Williams 2008), 'citizen journalism' (Bruns and Highfield 2012) and the 'cult of the amateur' (Keen 2008) have been used to describe the user-led knowledge that characterise Web 2.0 environments. These terms point to a paradigm shift in the way media content is produced with the internet conceived as a democratic development because it is egalitarian and allows more people to participate online. Testifying to the popular conception of the internet as a liberating force, in 2006 *Time Magazine* declared their 'Person of the Year' as 'you'. In contrast to the 'great men' who typically achieved such recognition on the cover of the magazine, the emphasis was on the 'everyman' (and woman) as creators of knowledge. Lev Grossman (2006), the author of the article, explained:

> It's a story about community and collaboration on a scale never seen before. It's about the cosmic compendium of knowledge Wikipedia and the million-channel people's network YouTube and the online metropolis MySpace. It's about the many wresting power from the few and helping one another for nothing and how that will not only change the world, but also change the way the world changes.

While there was a strong cyber-libertarian ideology present during the creation of the internet (early users of the web sought to keep information and services free), this change was largely perceived to be the result of Web 2.0 technologies. This is because Web 2.0 is seen to privilege participation, democracy (the free movement of knowledge and ideas) and the millions of ordinary users who contribute to online culture:

> The tool that makes this possible is the World Wide Web. Not the Web that Tim Berners-Lee hacked together (15 years ago, according to Wikipedia) as a way for scientists to share research. It's not even the overhyped dotcom Web of the late 1990s. The new Web is a very different thing. It's a tool for bringing together the small contributions of millions of people and making them matter. Silicon Valley consultants call it Web 2.0, as if it were a new version of some old software. But it's really a revolution ...The answer is, you do. And for seizing the reins of the global media, for founding and framing the new digital democracy, for working for nothing and beating the pros at their own game, TIME's Person of the Year for 2006 is *you*. (Grossman 2006 [emphasis added])

This utopian vision of Web 2.0 as central to a new digital democracy was strengthened by the various social movements and political protests that occurred from late 2010 and continued throughout much of 2011–2012: Anonymous' defence of WikiLeaks, the Arab Spring, the 2011 English riots, and the Occupy movement, to name a few (Baker 2014). Many of these events were organised and enacted on social media, giving credence to the popular narrative about 'the many' wresting power from 'the few' and using Web 2.0 technologies to bring about collective change for the greater good. In this context, social media was linked to new models of organisation and radical social change as popular terms such as the 'Twitter revolution' and the 'Facebook riots' suggest. Lifestyle gurus have drawn upon these utopian discourses by framing their advice as part of the democratisation of information where information is free and everybody's message can be voiced and heard. Co-presence and equality in facing life's problems are powerful and strongly stressed motifs.

The suggestion that Web 2.0 platforms stimulate a democratic, participatory culture dominated by creative amateurs has come under scrutiny (Keen 2008; Fuchs 2014). The concept of the active user draws upon a false dichotomy with earlier forms of 'passive' spectatorship (van Dijck 2009). Just as radio and television audiences were never solely defined by passive spectatorship (e.g. watching television involved subjective interpretation and listeners had the opportunity to engage with hosts on talk-back radio), Web 2.0's notion of the active user assumes many forms. User agency is comprised of different levels of participation. These can include content creator, respondent and viewer with the majority of internet users consisting of passive spectators that merely consume content (Dijck 2009: 44–5). Moreover, the assumption that users have equal participation, skills, resources and access overlooks the inequalities and context of online users. A case in point is *Wikipedia*. Knowledge production on *Wikipedia* may be trackable and more dialogic than the authoritative style of traditional encyclopaedias, which typically presented knowledge as fact. However, a minority of dedicated users are still responsible for making most of the edits on Wikipedia, highlighting that user agency is more complex than the phrase 'participatory culture' implies.

Despite the democratic potential of Web 2.0 technologies to decentralise information and lifestyle advice, the internet has not been able to resist corporate hierarchy and commercialisation. The idea that Web 2.0 engenders a participatory culture overlooks the role that platform providers play in steering agency (van Dijck 2009). The video-sharing site, YouTube, is a case in point. While YouTube was created to revolutionise the dominance highly consolidated media companies had over video content by providing a space for unconventional and marginalised voices of amateurs, interaction on the platform has become heavily commercialised and engineered. Those who use YouTube are steered towards consuming certain videos by means of algorithms that rely heavily on promotion and ranking tactics, such as the measuring of downloads and the promotion of popular favourites. Algorithms do not simply reflect users' behaviour, they actively encourage users to engage and interact on the platform in specific ways by recommending certain content as suggested viewing (Amazon and Spotify do the same by encouraging certain shopping and music practices). While users creatively produce content on their profiles, they 'lose their grip on their agency' as a result of technological algorithms tracking their behaviour and refining their profile (van Dijck 2009: 49). The vulnerabilities of these platforms – their architecture, business models and algorithms – allow savvy users to influence public discourse and knowledge by strategically producing content that will be recommended to viewers. Many user-generated sites are transforming from commons-like structures towards commercially driven platforms. In these environments, the user's role as data provider surpasses their role as content creator due to the revenue companies make from targeted advertising with data commodified and transformed into currency (van Dijck 2009: 52). Web 2.0 thrives off free labour (Terranova 2004). As a result, online advertising has been conceived as a mechanism by which corporations exploit internet users; internet 'prosumers' and 'produsers' viewed as part of a surplus-value generating class whose labour and time is exploited by capital (Fuchs 2007). These critiques indicate that while the Web 2.0 technologies used by lifestyle gurus today are associated with ideals of creativity, democracy and participation, a more critical approach of Web 2.0 and its relationship to knowledge and information is required.

Celebrity and the Power of Visibility on Social Media

One of the major ways in which social media have contributed to the rise of lifestyle gurus in the twenty-first century is by increasing people's visibility in the public domain. A case in point is celebrity. While fame has existed for centuries, celebrity culture was multiplied prolifically by the media. The development of communication media in the nineteenth and twentieth centuries made famous figures more visible than they were in the past. Until the early twenty-first century, the public personas that people projected onto celebrities were mostly formed through the mass media. The close-up shot, the photograph, interviews, radio, television and film were some of the ways in which celebrities were made visible to the public and a sense of connection fostered with their fans. As communication media evolves, so too does the concept of celebrity. Prior to the advent of social media, celebrities relied heavily on television producers and magazine editors to promote their image. These content producers controlled what programmes and articles were produced and, in turn, consumed by audiences. In short, because the media were highly centralised, media executives decided who was seen and heard. The mass media also played a significant role in shaping a celebrity's public persona. Having a good relationship with an editor, for example, could determine whether a celebrity was portrayed or perceived in a popular light.

Celebrities no longer merely feature in the news, they co-create it through sharing parts of their lives with the public on social media. It is now common for aspiring television stars, models and athletes to have social media accounts, with many encouraged to do so by their agents and managers. In most cases, these include Instagram, Facebook and Twitter with sites used slightly differently depending on their affordances (e.g. models tend to favour the photo and video sharing app, Instagram, because the platform prioritises visual communication; whereas politicians aiming to intervene in public discourse mostly use Twitter since the social media site allows brief updates via text-based communication). This is not to say that celebrities rely solely on social media for their status or that traditional forms of media are redundant to celebrity culture. On the contrary, the mass media continues to play a significant role in establishing and maintaining the fame of celebrities and many of the most well-regarded actors and actresses do not have social media accounts. The celebrities who use social media tend to be relatively young, reflecting the demographic of social media users in general. They also tend to be those that are popular with youth given that social media use is widespread among younger demographics. The most popular social media users are celebrities whose fame is conferred by the mainstream media. On Instagram, for example, the most followed accounts are comprised of musicians and reality-television stars, such as the Jenners and the Kardashians. The popularity of social media among celebrities is largely because these tools facilitate self-promotion and can be used to manage public perception.

Social media has given lifestyle gurus more control over their image. Like blogs, these sites allow celebrities to form direct relationships with fans and followers (although these relationships remain mediated in the sense that they are configured around platform interfaces and algorithmic structures, as well as being bound by the rules and regulations of internet service providers and in many cases monitored by agents and managers). As actress, Sienna Miller explains,

> … with social media, I look at young girls who are friends of mine, who are of a similar nature, and they're so in control of their own image that the media has lost its power. In those days, you were what they said you were, and that was frustrating. (Miller in Aitkenhead 2017)

The Harvey Weinstein scandal illustrates the power of social media. In October 2017 a series of actresses accused the film producer of rape and sexual assault. While many victims had previously reported his crimes to journalists and agents, Weinstein's influence over the news and popular press meant that he was able to prevent the stories from being published and adequately investigated. In his memoir, *Moguls, Monsters and Madmen: An Uncensored Life in Show Business* (2016), filmmaker Barry Avrich recalls how Weinstein used a combination of charm, coercion and threats to sabotage his film about the producer. When that failed, Weinstein secretly conspired with IFC Films to buy the distribution rights to turn *Unauthorised: The Harvey Weinstein Story* into a semi-authorised story. It was Weinstein's influence over the traditional channels of media production that prevented many of his victims from having their stories published. Social media provided Weinstein's victims with a platform on which to express their views. When these were echoed by others on social media, the story of Weinstein as a serial sexual predator acquired credibility and momentum. The point here is not that traditional media is redundant – newspapers and television networks played a significant role in publicising the scandal – rather social media provided a public platform for people to share their views publicly, one in which powerful figures (such as Weinstein) could not intervene. The power of social media in this context is not just about power in the traditional sense of authority and control, social media gives people a platform on which to influence public discourse through putting forward a particular point of view. When these views are shared publicly, they have the opportunity to shape collective beliefs and perceptions.

The Making of Micro-Celebrities

The shift from broadcast to participatory media, and the ubiquity of social media technologies, have two consequences for celebrity culture. In addition to enabling celebrities to form direct relationships with fans and followers, social media create the conditions for micro-celebrity (Marwick 2015). The term refers to 'a new style of online performance that involves people "amping up" their popularity over the Web using technologies like video, blogs and social networking sites' (Senft 2008: 25). At the heart of micro-celebrity is visibility. In contrast to conventional celebrities, their visibility is achieved on social media through self-broadcasting about niche topics to a small community of followers. Micro-celebrities may have a relatively small following compared to mainstream celebrities, but they typically share in-depth information about their personal lives online from what they eat, to where they shop and how they feel. These revelations facilitate the perception of intimacy with their followers. The emergence of micro-celebrity has contributed to the rapid rise in lifestyle gurus in the twenty-first century with social media users having a platform for knowledge creation and exchange. Micro-celebrities traverse a broad range of topics and interests. They include singers, actors, children and even animals (e.g. *Doug the Pug, Grumpy Cat, Manny The Frenchie* and *Tuna Melts my Heart*, each of whom have millions of followers on Instagram), who create content on social media that captures public attention. Their fame may increase over time or be short lived in the case of a viral video. They are defined not by the duration of their status, but by their visibility in the public eye.

Those micro-celebrities perceived as lifestyle gurus are mostly lifestyle bloggers who use their everyday experiences and knowledge about a particular lifestyle topic to achieve fame online. By sharing tips and recommendations on social media in the form of blog posts, photos, videos and online tutorials (i.e. 'how to' videos that deconstruct lifestyle advice into first principles), micro-celebrities are able to attract and inspire followers previously restricted to the mass media. The rise of micro-celebrity can be seen as part of the trajectory of conferring fame on ordinary individuals (see Chapter 3). In the 1990s and early 2000s, there was a rise in the featuring of ordinary people in the media. Lifestyle media focused on lifestyle pursuits, bringing together expert advice and voicing the perspectives of lay people. It featured ordinary people in partially scripted situations. This content seemed more accessible by revealing 'behind the scenes' footage and insight into their personal lives. Similar to reality television stars on lifestyle media programmes (e.g. the fashion makeover show, *What Not to Wear* or the home renovation show, *The Block*), lifestyle bloggers are mostly ordinary individuals celebrated for their knowledge and experience in a particular lifestyle area. It is the perception that they have mastered a particular lifestyle domain that gives them guru status. The celebration of the ordinary user as a micro-celebrity marks a key difference between the lifestyle gurus who achieve fame online and those who use the mass media. Whereas most celebrities and reality-television stars achieve fame with the assistance of managers, agents and directors, social media enables micro-celebrities to self-broadcast and achieve fame by participating online (Marwick 2013). The shift from broadcast to participatory media allows micro-celebrities to access and share information with a broad public audience, it also enables them to present themselves as celebrities, regardless of who might be paying attention. In this context, micro-celebrity is performative. Unlike the fame conferred on celebrities by virtue of their skills, talents or qualities, micro-celebrity is a set of practices, a way of perceiving of oneself as a celebrity, that can be performed *in principle* by anyone with internet access and a computer or mobile device (Marwick 2015).

Intimate Strangers

While lifestyle gurus have existed for centuries, a new group of native experts concerned with lifestyle and self-improvement has emerged online in the twenty-first century. Expertise, which was traditionally confined to those with authority or professional training in a specific area, has been replaced by knowledge formed through experience, what we refer to as 'native expertise'. Several technological conditions have facilitated this development. Firstly, the diffusion of the internet as a mass market phenomenon and the proliferation of mobile smartphones and digital devices. The internet and smartphones are integrated into many people's lives. These technologies enable individuals to access a large volume and variety of information online and to participate in instant, textual and visual communication that can be disseminated en masse. Secondly, the rise of accessible and affordable blogging platforms and social media sites that give ordinary users the capacity to create and share content with a broad social network. Thirdly, because much of this communication is visual, transmitted by the user directly in photo or video form, there is a veracity and sense of familiarity bestowed onto the image that is not as easily transferred onto text-based communication or the manufactured images produced by the mass media.

Despite the ideals that accompany Web 2.0 (creation, participation, transparency and democracy), the availability of these technologies does not automatically turn every user into an active participant. The capacity for dialogue on these sites is seldom realised, asymmetrically tilted towards high status users who broadcast information to their followers. As a result, the vast majority of users remain content consumers on these sites. What is novel about digital technologies is that they give lifestyle bloggers better access to social networks, enabling them to acquire a broad public following. The capacity for bloggers to generate content on these sites provides new opportunities for visibility, publicity, interaction and self-promotion formerly limited to celebrities, media organisations and powerful elites. Occupying these social platforms does not guarantee fame or celebrity, but it does provide greater potential for visibility and a capacity for users to communicate directly with a broad public audience.

The history of media is the history of its uses (Marvin 1988). Understanding how digital technologies have contributed to the rise of lifestyle gurus is less about technical efficiencies in speed and performance than the meanings and actions afforded by these modes of communication: Who has the authority to speak? Who can be seen and heard? Who is believed and trusted and, thus, able to shape ideas, thoughts and actions? These questions move away from reductionist discourses of causality, to an examination of how these technologies are designed, by whom and for what (both their intended and unintended consequences). It draws attention to issues of power, positioning and inequality both in terms of how we produce knowledge and how we come to understand the social world. In this regard, digital communication opens up considerable potential for lifestyle gurus in the twenty-first century by challenging knowledge hierarchies, reframing the dynamic between public and private life and creating the conditions for trust and intimacy among those with whom they interact.

3

'Be Authentic': Lifestyle Gurus as Trusted Companions

In 2009, Anna Saccone Joly created a popular YouTube channel, the *SacconeJolys*, with her husband, Jonathan. He was struggling to find a job after graduating from university, so the couple began to experiment with vlogging (video blogging), documenting their daily lives and relationship milestones in videos uploaded on YouTube. The couple have amassed a huge public following with over 1.9 million subscribers to their YouTube channel, whom they address as 'friends'. In 2016, so many fans showed up during their annual trip to Sorrento, knowing they would be there to celebrate their anniversary, that they no longer make the journey: 'There was like a convention of fans, and we couldn't go anywhere, walking down the high street, no matter what we did', Jonathan said. 'There were constantly boats coming over. We were just like, okay we're not the *Kardashians*, calm down people'. Anna also has a blog where she shares, 'bits and pieces of her life from motherhood, babies and toddlers to beauty, fashion and lifestyle!' (Saccone Joly 2018). Her blog posts feature regular updates of her four children, six dogs, pregnancies and diet; including a weekly post called, 'What I Ate Wednesday' that lists everything she ate in a day and weekly pregnancy updates, which enables pregnant viewers to compare symptoms. Her blog also features beauty and fashion tutorials. Anna Saccone Joly is an example of a successful micro-celebrity in so far as her fame is conferred by a niche community of followers on social media. In addition to the couple's 1.9 million YouTube subscribers, Anna has over 1.4 million followers on Instagram. She also has profiles on Facebook, Snapchat, Pinterest and Twitter with large public followings.

Since the mid-2000s, there has been a rise in ordinary people using social media to create micro-celebrity personas. As discussed in Chapter 2, micro-celebrity is about visibility and attention. Users achieve micro-celebrity status through self-broadcasting online to a niche community of followers. Micro-celebrity is a self-presentation technique designed to achieve fame online. It allows users to present themselves as a celebrity to others, regardless of who is actually paying attention, by virtue of the fact that they occupy the same social media platforms as celebrities and can perform to a similar audience (Marwick 2015). In *Camgirls* (2008), Theresa Senft, who coined the term micro-celebrity, explored the practices of 'camgirls', women who achieved fame online by broadcasting themselves via webcams to public audiences. In *Status Update* (2013), Alice Marwick developed this concept, exploring how technology entrepreneurs in San Francisco used social media to enhance their status following the *dot.com* crash. This was achieved, she argued, using a set of techniques including, micro-celebrity, self-branding and lifestreaming. From this perspective, micro-celebrity is not only a mindset, but a series of practices and self-presentation techniques designed to foster the feeling of intimacy with others.

In this chapter we explore the self-presentation techniques that lifestyle gurus employ to achieve micro-celebrity status online. Micro-celebrity is achieved using social media. There are many ordinary people with knowledge and experience on lifestyle issues. One may seek relationship advice from a mother, an uncle, a colleague or friend. Without social media, however, these ordinary experts are unable to achieve the same volume and velocity of attention in the public domain. This highlights an important point about the role of the audience. To achieve lifestyle guru status depends upon an audience. They must be visible in the public eye and perceived as one worthy of giving advice. An individual may write a book or self-brand themselves as a lifestyle blogger, but if they are not followed by a public audience they would not be described as a lifestyle guru.

Creating a Compelling Narrative and Persona

Lifestyle gurus achieve fame through promoting a carefully constructed persona. Fame is inextricably bound to the media. Without the media to promote their persona publicly, lifestyle gurus would only have access to a limited audience (typically those within spatial or temporal reach). There is a qualitative shift in how lifestyle gurus achieve public recognition from being promoted by the media (e.g. television, print and radio) to self-promotion on social media. Social media encourages self-promotion because it is centred on the individual. It allows people to self-consciously construct a persona. Most social media sites require individual users to create an online profile comprised of a username and profile picture. Individual profiles can be elaborated using brief descriptions. For example, Facebook asks users to 'describe who you are' and Instagram enables users to add a brief 'bio' to their profile (e.g. mum, wife, philanthropist, friend). Users can also add a collection of photographs to supplement their profile picture. The way lifestyle gurus perform micro-celebrity is configured around the technological affordances of the platform. While Facebook encourages users to add biographical details about their work and education, where they have lived, their family relationships and major life events, Instagram focuses on the visual representation of the self, curating the self visually in photo and video form. These sites differ from Twitter where the user is represented primarily textually in relation to their thoughts and opinions (e.g. 'tweets' and 're-tweets'). Given the way Twitter is configured (i.e. limited to 140–280 characters per tweet), the platform encourages brevity, wit and debate (one of the reasons that the platform is seen to ignite aggression and hostility). Most lifestyle gurus traverse a range of social media platforms. They use these technologies to bring a desired self into being. In all cases, information is carefully selected and edited by users to appeal to their audience and to present themselves in a favourable light. The persona presented is a curated self that can be constructed, shaped and edited. How people choose to present themselves on these platforms – including what information they provide or omit – reveals how they want to be portrayed and perceived by others. Self-promotion triumphs achievement.

Social media both enables and encourages people to become the curators of their own lives by writing themselves into being. The difference for lifestyle gurus is that engineering their image through self-branding is usually driven by commercial interests. There is a basic template to achieve lifestyle guru status online that has shown to be a recipe for success. While content may vary depending on the lifestyle topics they cover and the audience to whom they perform, the template includes the following components:

- A *carefully constructed persona* that is not only aspirational, but relatable, emulatable and accessible to fans and followers.
- A *compelling narrative* revealing their transformation from a state of pain and misery to one of success and well-being. They may present their journey as an ongoing struggle, but in order to validate their programme and products they must demonstrate a degree of self-improvement. Descriptions of this kind will usually be found on their social media profiles and in the 'about me' section of their blogs.
- *Attractive images* are used to curate their social media profiles. Photographs and videos are the central means of communication

as they verify the claims of lifestyle gurus, highlighting who you too could be if you were to purchase their products and services. There is a common conception that women are the primary target of advertising imagery. While self-presentation techniques are highly gendered (e.g. men using muscle shots to signify virile strength; women communicating health and beauty through slim, toned physiques), both men and women use 'selfies' (self-portrait photographs) and imagery on social media to communicate an idealised self to their audience (Twitter and Reddit to a lesser extent – see Baker and Walsh 2018).

• *Metrics* often accompany images and blog posts to support lifestyle advice. The emphasis on metrics corresponds to the quantified self movement where weight and performance can be tracked, measured and analysed in greater detail as a result of the proliferation of digital devices, health apps and wearable technologies. The emphasis on quantification is particularly common among male lifestyle gurus, who promote themselves as strategists (Tony Robbins), bio hackers (Dave Asprey) and practitioners of lifestyle design (Tim Ferriss). This process of managing the body is often referred to as 'biohacking', a term that refers to tricks or shortcuts (i.e. 'hacks'), which enable people to take control of their genetic material. Life hacking refers to any hack that increases productivity and efficiency in life. Social media driven metrics in the form of 'likes', shares, comments and follower counts provide credibility by signifying status and influence online.

The formula is replicable, but in order to stand out from the crowd, lifestyle gurus must portray themselves as unique.

One of the primary concerns of aspiring lifestyle gurus is how to present themselves to appeal to fans and followers. In *The Presentation of Self in Everyday Life* (1959), Erving Goffman conceptualised identity as a performance. He suggested that, analogous to actors performing on stage, individuals present themselves strategically in everyday social interactions to adapt to different audiences and social situations. These performances are often rehearsed 'back stage', where 'the performer can relax'; 'drop his front, forgo speaking in his lines, and step out of character' (Goffman 1959: 488). While Goffman explored face-to-face interactions prior to the digital age, his dramaturgical approach lends itself to understanding self-presentation in digital contexts. Whereas physical and verbal cues, such as gestures and facial expressions, indicate how the individual is perceived by others during co-present interaction, social media primarily uses metrics to evaluate the user's performance. Popularity, status and influence are quantified online in the form of likes, comments, retweets and view counts. Rather than relying on another's physical or verbal cues to ascertain how their actions are perceived, these metrics operate as a form of social validation. The tendency to rank and rate status online, and to reduce one's value to metrics on social media, reveals the ways in which technology informs knowledge and human behaviour.

One of the difficulties that individuals experience online is how to present themselves to different audiences. In everyday social life, Goffman describes how individuals tailor their performances to suit different audiences and settings. Individuals perform different roles in different settings: for example, as a wife, a daughter, a mother and a friend. While some roles may overlap (e.g. simultaneously performing the role of a wife and mother in a domestic environment), there are situations where these roles must be segregated to ensure that the behaviour performed is compatible with the audience and situation. Goffman employed the term 'audience segregation' to describe the process by which individuals segregate the roles they perform to suit different audiences. Audience segregation is important because there are certain cultural norms and expectations that govern social interaction. If one failed to adapt the way they behave around others (e.g. swearing at a child the way they swear around friends), their behaviour would seem inappropriate – possibly offensive or embarrassing – and discredit their character. As Goffman (1959) explains, the performer would lose face and credibility, and risk appearing like a 'phony'. Audience segregation is important because it enables people to present a consistent character, compatible with the situation, which means individuals are more likely to appear authentic and believable to others. The American psychologist and philosopher, William James, made a similar observation a century earlier:

> Properly speaking, *a man has as many social selves as there are individuals who recognise him* and … about whose opinion he cares. He generally shows a different side of himself to each of these different groups. Many a youth who is demure enough before his parents and teachers, swears and swaggers like a pirate among his 'tough' young friends. We do not show ourselves to our children as to our club-companions, to our customers as to the laborers we employ, to our own masters and employers as to our intimate friends. From this there results what practically is a division of the man into several selves; and this may be a discordant splitting, as where one is afraid to let one set of his acquaintances know him as

> he is elsewhere; or it may be a perfectly harmonious division of labor, as where one tender to his children is stern to the soldiers or prisoners under his command. (James 1890 [italics original])

Audience segregation is more difficult to achieve online. Goffman's work described interaction rituals during standard face-to-face interactions. Offline, segregation is relatively easy to achieve due to the boundaries of time (e.g. human memory rather than digital footprints) and space (the different ways you interact with people in different contexts, e.g. home, work, social settings). Online, conversely, multiple audiences that were previously kept distinct are often 'collapsed' into a single context (Marwick and boyd 2011). In the case of social media, user profiles may be visible to multiple audiences comprised of colleagues, friends, family and strangers, which means that the individual's profile must be managed to a higher degree to maintain consistency and to avoid discrediting their persona. While audience segregation can be achieved on some social media sites by applying privacy settings (e.g. creating friend lists on Facebook), it requires a degree of knowledge and technical proficiency; particularly because most social media sites are public by default. The dilemmas of audience segregation are highly relevant to the self-presentation strategies of lifestyle gurus in the digital age given that their fame relies mostly on social media. Lifestyle gurus treat their audience as an undifferentiated collective. Social media marketing manuals repeatedly advise aspiring bloggers about the importance of brand consistency by maintaining a consistent identity across a broad range of platforms (Zarrella 2009; Martin 2017). One of the problems that lifestyle gurus encounter is how to navigate conflicting concerns around the drive for publicity and privacy.

Confession and Self-disclosure

Traditionally, the relationship between fans and celebrities was established and maintained at a distance by the media. The mass media were the primary channel by which to access celebrities, with that access limited to print, screen, stage and radio. The mediation of celebrity presupposes a certain level of distance from their fans and followers. There is physical distance in that most contact with celebrity is experienced by way of media representations, but also distance in the sense that these representations are stage-managed by media corporations, agents and managers. This distance was often accentuated by the super-star qualities projected onto celebrities in terms of their achievements: a charismatic movie star, a talented athlete or a musician with an incredible voice. The fascination with celebrity led to an interest in their personal lives. Entire industries were established around probing and exposing the personal lives of celebrities, most notably the tabloid press and paparazzi. Graeme Turner (2013: 8) suggests that once the public takes an interest in the private life of a public figure, as opposed to merely reporting on their talents and achievements, they pass into celebrity status. While fans have an insatiable appetite for celebrity, maintaining a certain level of distance from their followers adds to a celebrity's mystique and enables them to 'disappear' into a role.

As a result, many celebrities have sought to protect their privacy. A celebrity may be required to perform public duties by attending promotional events and press releases, yet their private lives tend to be either guarded or selectively displayed by way of interviews and photo-shoots with the media that benefit them in some way (e.g. self-promotion, altering public perception and so on). While the paparazzi and tabloid press have traditionally been perceived as threats to a celebrity's privacy, personal information is regularly leaked by celebrities to compete in an oversaturated market. Common examples include sex tapes, staged controversies and scandals. We often associate such acts of self-promotion with D-list celebrities, using savvy means to gain visibility and attention; the sex-tapes used to boost the fame of the reality-television stars, Paris Hilton and Kim Kardashian, is a case in point. However, celebrities have long used the media to shape their public profile with public relations agencies, managers and agents working with the media to influence public perception. Examples include televised public confessions as an appeal for forgiveness and redemption or acts of self-disclosure in print media (Thompson 2000; King 2008). A significant example of this shift towards the blurring of public and private life was the public staging of the private breakdown of Charles and Diana's marriage in the tabloid press. In 1985, the couple took part in a televised interview, 'The Prince and Princess of Wales Talking Personally', in an attempt to quash rumours regarding the state of their marriage. While the public relations exercise initially appeared to be successful in shaping public opinion, the couple's decision to 'talk personally' with the press represented a significant departure from the British Royal Family's stoic reserve and played a direct role in the public's appetite for gossip and scandal (Baker 2014). It is now commonplace for celebrities of all kinds to self-promote on social media and leak news and photographs to the tabloid press. This is because who the celebrity is seen to be (e.g. straight, gay, an alcoholic, a family man) influences their public face and commercial appeal (Rojek 2001). Publicity is not risk proof. There is the hazard of misinterpretation or appearing staged. The degree of criticism that those who feature in the tabloid press are subjected to is a warning against the dangers of over-exposure. So too is the online criticism that social media and internet users experience from 'haters' and trolls.

Part of the difficulty for micro-celebrities is discerning what information to keep private in a culture that encourages self-disclosure. Lifestyle gurus are encouraged to have regular interaction with their followers to keep them informed and interested, with news about their daily lives. Examples include social media posts, such as, 'outfit of the day', 'what I ate in a week', and weekly pregnancy vlogs documenting a baby's development and the mother's experiences throughout her pregnancy. The content shared may appear trivial, but each revelation and image shared with their followers combines to form a greater understanding of, and connection to, the lifestyle guru. Lifestyle gurus often choose to disclose personal information online because confessional content and controversy sparks interest and attention. Algorithmic steering has encouraged a preoccupation with sensational and controversial content. Algorithms do not distinguish between loyal followers, haters or trolls, all constitute engagement and potential advertising revenue. Because views can be monetised, social media encourage dramatic content that stands out from the noise. Posts of this kind are commonly rewarded with a higher follower count and increased engagement with followers (e.g. likes, comments, shares), which results in a more lucrative brand. A case in point is 'mummy blogging'. Some of the most popular mummy blogs involve revelations of miscarriage, post-natal depression, divorce and loss. While sharing their personal experiences can provide consolation and assist those who have endured similar hardships, much self-disclosure is manufactured online in the quest to attract followers and increase viewer engagement.

The cultural trend towards self-disclosure pre-dates the internet. Psychoanalysis established and expanded its authority in the twentieth century. It was institutionalised as a profession at universities and medical organisations and percolated into everyday vocabularies (Illouz 2008). Part of the appeal of these models is that they addressed a public for whom gender norms around marriage and sexuality were in flux, offering 'new narrative models', metaphors and language to make sense of life (Illouz 2008: 36). The late-twentieth century saw a surge in confessional television programmes and the genre of talk shows, in which participants discussed various topics with a talk-show host. The topics discussed were typically of an intimate nature (e.g. divorce, cheating, deceit, incest), often echoed by the talk-show host's own revelations of trauma and abuse. Oprah Winfrey, Phil Donahue, Geraldo Rivera, Ricki Lake, and Montel Williams exemplify the cultural trend of talk-show hosts revealing personal troubles publicly. The talk-show genre led to a sub-genre of lifestyle and self-help programmes, that featured a host (often a medical practitioner, therapist, or counsellor, such as Dr Phil or Doctor Oz), and guests who sought intervention, described psychological problems or offered advice. Programmes of this kind represent a shift from emotion norms of self-restraint (e.g. the stiff upper lip) towards self-disclosure. Frank Furedi (2003) has termed this shift towards the confessional, 'therapy culture', to describe a cultural phenomenon characterised by the blurring of public and private life.

One of the implications of living in a therapy culture is that private life is rendered a legitimate area of public concern. This shift is evident in the topics discussed by lifestyle gurus. In the case of mummy bloggers, the most popular videos on YouTube are concerned with private issues. One popular mummy blogger (known as 'Scary Mummy') announced her divorce on Facebook by revealing that her husband is gay. Constance Hall (2016), another popular mummy blogger, accumulated a huge public following after she released a Facebook post on what she termed 'parent sex'. The post was liked over 173,000 times and shared 39,931 times on Facebook. Since releasing the post, Hall has shared intimate photographs of herself in her underwear following the birth of her child, sitting on the toilet texting in front of her children, and of her toddlers having tantrums. To many viewers, these posts appear vulgar and inappropriate, too private to release in the public domain. Yet, the prevalence of this type of confessional content, and the tendency to share these images publicly, is revealing. It is suggestive of a cultural shift around norms of self-disclosure with the popularity of bloggers derived precisely from the personal content they share with their followers. Micro-celebrities are often encouraged to overshare details about their personal lives in an attempt to stay relevant in an oversaturated market. Confessional content (including revelations and staged bloopers) appeals to viewers because it presents lifestyle gurus as vulnerable, authentic and relatable compared to the polished, airbrushed documentation of celebrities in the mainstream media. It was a practice popularised by lifestyle gurus, such as Oprah, and is now mainstream.

The confessional content and style of lifestyle gurus can provide consolation to those who are suffering. For example, forums provide a space for people to seek knowledge, advice and support to help them cope with challenging circumstances and to share their everyday experiences with those in similar situations. Some posts are written by experts, but the majority of advice is produced by a large, opinionated crowd with content crowdsourced from users. The internet has allowed people to express their opinions and share their experiences anonymously online. Historically, identity was guaranteed through embodied, face-to-face interaction. If you had a problem, you could seek advice from someone you knew personally or trusted as a result of their credentials or professional expertise. Technology enables users to communicate anonymously at a distance. While there are growing concerns that anonymous communication can lead to mistrust, misidentification and misinformation, the anonymity enabled by the internet is part of the reason that digital platforms have become such popular spaces to share personal experiences and seek advice. Instead of seeking advice from a health professional or family member, users can discuss sensitive topics with others, anonymously, from the comfort of their own homes.

Part of the appeal of forums, chat rooms and social media is their ability to facilitate a sense of identity and belonging. Online, one can find spaces dedicated to niche interests on a range of lifestyle topics from parenting, to yoga, fashion and veganism. The internet helps users to connect with people whom they perceive to be like themselves, whether they share a common interest, medical condition or life problem. A quick Google search enables users to track those they would not necessarily be able to locate in physical proximity from a desktop computer or on a mobile device. In seeking advice online, one can connect with communities structured around similar lifestyle concerns and interests. In addition to acquiring advice and knowledge from others online, the internet can facilitate membership into a specific lifestyle community (Baker and Walsh 2018). While social network sites are structured around friendship, other social media sites provide new opportunities for group membership outside the user's established social network. For example, the social news site, Reddit, structures content around shared topics of interest rather than personalities while hashtags on sites like Instagram and Tumblr afford users the capacity to connect with others around shared issues and topics. A case in point is the Tumblr account, *The Last Message Received*. Founded by teenager, Emily Trunko, from Ohio, the site was designed as a shared platform on which people could post the final message they received from a loved one or friend. Some of the messages document breakups, others unexpected deaths; most chronicle sadness and loss. By contributing to the collection of letters and text messages sent by those like themselves, the result is that people feel they are not alone in their suffering. When people share advice online with those perceived to be similar to them, they foster a sense of community and connection. This process facilitates 'mimetic vertigo', the recognition that the object represented also represents you (Taussig 1992). In many ways the experience of identifying with, and relating to, another online resembles the experience of identifying with a character in a novel or a film. The result of this process of identification, is a feeling of connection and intimacy with online group identities. It is conceived as a form of intimacy and an antidote to the social fragmentation characteristic of modern life.

While social media thrives off making people's private lives public, the relationship between lifestyle gurus and their fans remains typically one-sided. Since both users and celebrities on social media occupy the same sites, there is a sense of presumed intimacy with celebrities (even though there is no technical requirement of reciprocity on social media and ordinary users tend not to be followed by celebrities in return). For example, in 2018 the singer, Taylor Swift, had 114 million followers, but chose not to follow a single Instagram account. Similarly, the musician, Beyonce, had 123.1 million followers, but also followed none in return. Despite being the seventh and eighth most popular accounts on Instagram in 2018, the relationship followers have with these celebrities is not reciprocated. The same is true of micro-celebrities, who mostly follow those in the public eye. Micro-celebrities can share information online with their followers without requiring further participation on behalf of the micro-celebrity, resembling the previous forms of one-to-many broadcast models they are commonly defined in relation to. Micro-celebrities may occasionally respond to questions and comments online; however, in most cases this interaction is more about conveying the *impression of accessibility* – the perception that they are approachable – rather than fostering genuine, intimate exchange. As such, the relations between followers and those who achieve fame online tend to be 'para-social' in nature with the internet multiplying para-social access to celebrities. This is due, in part, to the frequency with which one may engage with micro-celebrities online, as well as the direct forms of communication afforded by these technologies. Blogs and social media provide relatively frequent exchange, while the affordances of these technologies (e.g. the comments section on Instagram or the @reply feature on Twitter) provides the *potential* for direct, dialogic exchange. Social media is especially potent in establishing para-social relationships of trust and intimacy because sites are structured and communicated as an exchange between equals. They dispense with the paraphernalia of hierarchy that separates the attention capital of the star from the fan. Instead, they emphasise authenticity and social inclusion, despite the fact that many of these relations are performed for fame and profit.

Manufacturing Authenticity

One of the most popular bromides in social media marketing is 'be authentic'. Aspiring micro-celebrities are frequently reminded by marketing experts about the importance of authenticity. In self-help literature, self-improvement is often framed in terms of self-discovery wherein the imperative is to discover one's supposedly unique and authentic self (McGee 2005: 16). The phrases that characterise self-help literature – 'Discover your passion', 'Follow your dreams' and 'Realise your calling' (Sinetar 1989) – thrive off the idea of achieving authenticity by way of self-discovery; ignoring the fact that the self develops *in relation* to others. This notion of authenticity as self-discovery was propagated by Oprah, who taught principles for 'cultivating your authentic power' and 'developing an authentic self'. Her intention for the show became 'to inspire women to be the best version of their most authentic selves' (Winfrey 2019). 'To be authentic', for Oprah, 'is the highest form of praise. You're fulfilling your mission and purpose on earth when you honour the real you' (Winfrey 2018a).

In social media marketing, authenticity is generally used as a synonym for being genuine and 'real'. Aspiring bloggers are advised, 'Be genuine and be yourself' (YouTube 2017). This advice is employed in a self-descriptive manner by lifestyle bloggers with mummy blogger, Anna Saccone Joly, telling her followers, 'No filter and no fakery here … you all know I like to keep it real!' (Saccone Joly 2018). In this context, authenticity has a relational meaning; it is defined in relation to being fake. To be fake is to be perceived as contrived, disingenuous and insincere. The point of demarcation here is with the mass media. Whereas the media is criticised for manufacturing the news, spinning stories and airbrushing images for ratings and profit, lifestyle gurus perform authenticity through managed self-disclosure. They commonly stage private moments for public display; sharing content featuring outbursts, confessions and revelations with their followers in heightened emotional displays – what Laura Grindstaff (2008) terms 'the money shot'. Posts of this kind aim to foster the *impression of authenticity* by taking the viewer 'backstage' to get a glimpse of their personal lives.

The idea of authenticity presents a tension between popular associations of authenticity with interiority and the increasing need to brand oneself for market demands (McGee 2005: 167). Engineered around the quest for 'likes' and followers, social media rewards visibility and attention, emphasising performance and how we appear to others. In a world preoccupied with looking out, there is nostalgia for an authentic world 'found' from within. Hence, as social media sites become increasingly commercialised, the importance of authenticity has increased. Popular understandings of authenticity as denoting that which is genuine and 'real' resonate with Web 2.0 ideals of trust, openness and transparency. What these common-sense understandings of authenticity miss is the performative nature of authenticity (Alexander 2017: 13). Authenticity is not to be found in the behaviour of the actor alone, it signifies the fusion of the actor and audience in an authentic performance.

The emphasis that lifestyle gurus place on authenticity is about establishing meaningful connections with fans and followers. Authenticity is strategically enacted by lifestyle gurus to increase their engagement rate and online following. In the article *How to Connect with Website Visitors in an Authentic Way* (2016), A. J. Agrawal suggests that authenticity is the new currency when it comes to marketing. He emphasises the importance of connecting with followers authentically to create customers who are loyal to your brand:

> Wondering why I keep talking about authenticity? It's because being recognised by your audience as inauthentic doesn't just weaken your brand, it can destroy it completely – along with the relationships you've built with your customers. When people get the feeling that they're being strung along with nonsense in the hopes that they'll fall into the 'trap' of buying, they leave and they don't come back.

The demand for authenticity can be understood in this context as symptomatic of the eroding reputation of corporate institutions and distrust of corporations (Gilmore and Pine 2007). Authenticity operates here as a form of social capital. It is a means of building trust with followers. To appear trustworthy, aspiring lifestyle gurus must appear authentic. In her study of *Camgirls* (2008), Theresa Senft highlights that authenticity is integral to maintaining micro-celebrity status. Whereas the idea of celebrity conventionally implied distance and separation from fans, online popularity depends upon connection to one's followers (Senft 2008: 25–6). This connection is predicated on the idea of micro-celebrities as 'real' people with 'real issues' rather than staged celebrity personas (although, as we have argued, the value of authenticity was already present in the late-twentieth century with the likes of Oprah). It is precisely because followers enabled these individuals to achieve micro-celebrity status that micro-celebrities have certain ethical obligations to those who made them 'what' they are; their fame is dependent on their followers rather than manufactured by the entertainment industry, as is typically the case with celebrities.

Micro-celebrities use various techniques in order to display authenticity. Authenticity is performed by sharing 'backstage' moments and personal online exchange through photos and videos that provide insight into their private lives (e.g. #nofilter or 'make-up free' selfies, 'what I ate in a day' videos, exercise tutorials, emotional outbursts and personal revelations). Social media gives celebrities and micro-celebrities the opportunity to present snapshots of themselves rehearsing for a show, preparing for an event, making breakfast or interacting with their family, thereby, feeding the public's desire to know intimate details about their personal lives. The format of Instagram, as a platform to document life visually, means that posts of this kind tend to be frequent and expected. While insight into celebrities' private lives is far from new, previously these were reserved for documentaries and magazine interviews that were less frequent, indirect and more overtly edited. By contrast, the documentation of the self on social media via selfies, 'make-up free' or 'no filter' photographs, bloopers and self-depreciating pictures 'gives-off' the impression of authentic, spontaneous exchange (even though these images are often highly edited and monitored by agents and managers). What these images communicate is not who a lifestyle guru is, but how they want to be seen by others.

One of the reasons for the cultural drive towards disclosing one's inner life on social media is because vulnerability and self-disclosure establishes immediate intimacy with followers. Confessional posts attract high levels of engagement as indicated by the likes, view counts and comments on YouTube videos documenting personal concerns. The confessional is used as a way to connect with followers and encourage them to invest in one's brand (King 2008). Here authenticity is commonly conflated with transparency. Going behind the scenes and revealing intimate images and personal information, is a way of appearing trustworthy and authentic by displaying human vulnerability unlike a 'faceless corporation' (Agrawal 2016). Despite their common concern with revealing information, there are important differences between the terms. While authenticity is concerned with being genuine, transparency is primarily about visibility. Analogous to looking through a window, transparency is concerned with how much of your life viewers can see. The view can be restricted or completely transparent. People display different levels of transparency in terms of what information they are willing to share and with whom they are willing to share it. In this regard, there is a strong connection between transparency and privacy. Privacy varies according to the user. It also varies according to the platform. Most users limit what information they share online. For example, children may feature in a lifestyle guru's narrative, especially if they define themselves as a mother, but they can limit how much they reveal about their children online to maintain their privacy. Lifestyle gurus also conceal those parts of themselves that do not align with their online persona. Users categorise and compartmentalise their beliefs and opinions to adapt to their audience and protect their brand. The drive for authenticity on social media is about building relationships. To build relationships online people share different levels of information (degrees of transparency) with their audience. The cultural norms around transparency also change over time. Increasingly, the idea of authenticity combines the need to share personal information and to maintain a consistent persona across all social media platforms.

Some of the most successful lifestyle gurus are guarded about their private lives. This is a strategic move. Rather than boost their online following through revealing personal and intimate information about themselves, they focus on presenting a consistent persona online. Consistency is an important aspect of self-branding. It facilitates trust with fans and followers, and enables brands and companies to know what to expect when hiring lifestyle gurus to promote their products and services. Chelsie Kenyon, a social media coach and entrepreneur, expressed this understanding of authenticity as consistency in a YouTube video entitled, *Being Authentic and Consistent in Your Branding on Social Media*. Authenticity, she explains, is 'about being consistent with yourself, your branding and the image that you want to portray'. She highlights the importance of 'always presenting your best possible self … no matter what's going on with your day' (Kenyon 2016). Kenyon then proceeds to provide techniques that aspiring lifestyle bloggers can use to alter their mood and manage their emotions. Emotional management is regarded as an important skill for helping to maintain a brand's image and customer satisfaction. Paradoxically, despite the emphasis on self-disclosure as a means of displaying authenticity, these displays must be closely managed to ensure that a consistent and appropriate persona is presented online. Authenticity is conceived of here as a marketing strategy that encourages 'emotional labour', the management of personal feelings (also known as 'emotion work') in exchange for pay.

Emotional Labour

While social media marketers emphasise the benefits of emotional management for brands and celebrities, there are costs associated with emotional labour. Emotion work – 'the act of trying to change in degree or quality an emotion or feeling' (Hochschild 1979: 122) – is an ordinary part of everyday social life. A wife, for example, may feel obliged to express gratitude to her husband for assisting with domestic duties when the same praise is not shown in return. Or, an irritable parent may suppress their feelings of frustration during a toddler's tantrum in the quest to remain calm. In these instances, the individual's feelings are managed to produce a certain outcome in the context of family life. Whereas emotion work refers to acts performed in a private context where they have 'use value' (Hochschild 1983: 7), these activities become 'emotional labour' when they are performed in an employment setting for a wage, 'sold as labour' with an 'exchange value' (Hochschild 1983: 7, 19).

There are hidden costs associated with emotional labour. In *The Managed Heart* (1983), Arlie Hochschild discussed the consequences of emotional estrangement. Her study of flight attendants demonstrated that presenting 'artificial elation' has a personal cost, especially when the feelings presented are dissonant with how the performer feels. In these situations, employees can feel emotionally estranged from their feelings and selves, which can lead to a sense of alienation. Whereas Marx argued that alienation emerges when workers are unable to control the means of production, Hochschild contends that alienation emerges in contemporary society when workers are unable to control the relationship between what they must do and how they feel – what she terms, 'the managed heart' (Hochschild 1983). In these instances, corporations control workers at a deeper level because they manage their private lives and inner experiences. The company dictates not only the physical motions involved in their role, but their emotional thoughts and actions.

Emotional labour has cultural pertinence with regard to lifestyle gurus. The self-presentation techniques employed by lifestyle gurus resembles Hochschild's work on emotional labour. When emotion work is put into the public marketplace as emotional labour it operates like a commodity: 'the demand for it waxes and wanes depending upon the competition within the industry' (Hochschild 1983: 14). Despite the appeal of fame and celebrity, and the commercial success lifestyle gurus may receive as a result of their work, there are downsides to engaging in emotional labour. As the market becomes more saturated, lifestyle gurus are under pressure to create more interesting content to remain relevant and popular. Many speak of the pressures of creating the perfect content and persona. These pressures have an emotional cost, motivating numerous lifestyle gurus to quit blogging and social media. For example, Josi Denise quit her popular blog, *The American Mama*, when she realised that the pressure of chasing lucrative sponsors turned her family life into a charade. She explained that she would post photos of her children that appeared happy, even if they were miserable, because she needed content for advertisers. Recollecting an example of a fake Father's Day post that she produced for a tea company, she explained: 'We had to do it a month out so that I had the photos edited in time for Father's Day. So it wasn't authentic, it wasn't on Father's Day, it did feel very stage directed' (Denise 2016). While lifestyle gurus trade on appearing trustworthy and authentic, it was these feelings of dishonesty (constantly curating advertising content – that did not look like an ad) and insincerity that prompted Josi to quit blogging:

> I made thousands of dollars during months I was focusing and working hard to dig through box after box of shitty as-seen-on-tv like products and share 'my 100% honest opinion' about them, that weren't at all influenced by the page after page of 'key messages' the brand requested that I include in my review. You won't find most of those posts on this blog today. They aren't gone forever, and I do plan to revive some of them. But for the most part, they are dead and I want them to stay buried forever. Because, like 90% of the fake nonsense I used to share on the internet as a mommy blogger writing about my fake life and oh-so-happy marriage, they are pure bullshit. (Denise 2016)

Other lifestyle gurus have expressed the emotional strain associated with maintaining fame online. The criticism and abuse they are subjected to by 'haters' and trolls is coupled with the pressures of pursuing status and attention. Essena O'Neill, a micro-celebrity from Australia, was a teenage girl who amassed half a million followers on Instagram by posting selfies and content related to beauty, fitness and fashion. At the height of her fame, she quit Instagram describing the site as 'contrived perfection made to get attention'. After deleting over 2,000 photos on Instagram, she renamed her account: 'Social Media Is Not Real Life'. She also changed the captions on the photos remaining with frank anecdotes to reveal the companies that sponsored posts, the careful editing required to produce the images she posted and the pressure she felt to look perfect in the quest for validation. One photograph featuring her wearing a bikini on the beach was replaced with the caption,

> NOT REAL LIFE – took over 100 in similar photos trying to make my stomach look good. Would have hardly eaten that day. Would have yelled at my little sister to keep taking them until I was somewhat proud of this. Yep so totally #goals. (O'Neill in Sherriff 2015)

Other captions revealed the degree of preparation, editing and effort involved in the apparently 'spontaneous' selfies that she shared with her followers. The revised captions repeated the similar message that 'THERE IS NOTHING REAL ABOUT THIS [social media]' (O'Neill in Sherriff 2015 [emphasis in original]).

While O'Neill's separation between the offline world as 'real' and the online world as fake is problematic given that all forms of self-presentation are curated, what her comments speak to is the greater capacity to control and manipulate how we cast ourselves online. Photoshopped images and airbrushed editing techniques once reserved for magazines and professionals are now readily accessible due to the availability of easy to use social media filters and photo editing apps. The usability and availability of this software has led to concerns about people's quest to present their online lives as perfect and to present an appearance that is a distortion of how they appear offline. Criticisms of this kind rely on a traditional, albeit basic, understanding of representation as denoting a reflection of reality. For example, a lifestyle blogger may use filters on Instagram to enhance the colour of their skin and various apps to make their body appear more toned, thereby distorting their physique in ways not readily available in standard face-to-face encounters. Offline, a lifestyle blogger can strategically modify their self-presentation through exercise, cosmetics, surgery or fashion. However, the ease with which self-presentation can be modified online, especially as these spaces become increasingly commercialised, is what has come under scrutiny. In essence, these critiques are about truth and fakery with online self-presentation seen as facilitating less 'real' and 'authentic' forms of interaction than the offline world. Our concern with self-presentation precedes the internet, as evidenced by Goffman's famous work on *The Presentation of Self in Everyday Life* (1959). However, social media affords us with greater capacity to control involuntary behaviours (e.g. fumbling, blushing, stammering), our digital personas and the information that we share about ourselves online; even though there are limits to our ability to control the information others share about us online (e.g. photographs shared by friends on social media). What is more, if we share content that we decide at a later point in time is incongruous with the image that we wish to project, this may be concealed, edited or deleted. An online response can also be delayed, considered and canvassed with others before replying, making online exchange qualitatively different from face-to-face encounters.

Social media has intensified the negative consequences of emotion management. Emotions are not only managed for commercial purposes; they are managed in the quest for acceptance, approval and validation. Social media sites are built around the desire for status and attention with the user's value reduced to metrics: the validation derived from a video view, an Instagram like or a new follower. O'Neill (2015) described the pressures associated with quantifying herself online, 'I let myself be defined by numbers.' Consumed by social media and obsessively checking the metrics of the photos she uploaded online, her appetite for views, likes and followers was insatiable: 'It was never enough' (O'Neill 2015). O'Neill was later criticised for using the controversy to publicise her new website, *Let's Be Game Changers* (discontinued in 2015), which encouraged people to reconsider the way they used social media. Nevertheless, her decision to quit social media due to the pressures involved in seeking approval and validation online, points to something larger.

As lifestyle gurus compete for attention in a saturated market, some employ unethical techniques, such as rigging and 'like farms', to compete for status. In 2018, it was revealed that more than a hundred celebrities had purchased Twitter followers from the company, Devumi. This included business leaders, sports stars and television personalities, who sought to increase the value of their brand through increasing their follower count on social media. Devumi sold counterfeit Twitter followers and retweets to people and brands who sought to appear more popular or exert influence online. With an estimated stock of 3.5 million fake accounts (bots), sold to users many times, the company sold more than 200 million Twitter followers (Confessore et al. 2018). Those who purchased artificial followers said they did so because their careers had come to depend, in part, on the appearance of having influence on social media. 'No one will take you seriously if you don't have a noteworthy presence', said Jason Schenker, an economist who purchased 260,000 followers. The pressure for celebrities and micro-celebrities to increase their follower count reflects the fact that, in many cases, their market value is proportionate to the number of followers they have on social media. The emotional costs of lifestyle blogging are not particular to O'Neill, they are symptomatic of the ways these technologies are designed: configured around the drive for status and attention under the guise of sharing and connection. Although celebrities also engage in these strategies to enhance their online status, the defensive structures available to celebrities are not always available to micro-celebrities (Marwick 2013) and micro-celebrities experience additional pressure to appear popular as their fame is dependent on their online following (Senft 2008).

The Trouble with Authenticity

The twenty-first century has witnessed the rise of a new form of lifestyle guru, the micro-celebrity. Micro-celebrities are assigned high status on social media by a niche community of followers; in the case of lifestyle gurus, those interested in various lifestyle pursuits. Micro-celebrity is strategically performed online using a series of self-presentation techniques designed to achieve status and attention. These include carefully constructing an online persona, sharing personal information about themselves with their followers to establish the perception of intimacy and 'friendship', and presenting themselves as authentic in an attempt to distance themselves from traditional media by appearing trustworthy, genuine and 'real'. The internet affords new ways of experiencing the self and relating to others. Social media enables lifestyle gurus to inhabit the same online spaces as celebrities and to occupy a celebrity subject position by addressing followers as fans. However, the fact that micro-celebrities achieve fame as a result of their followers alters the dynamic of fandom with fans demanding authenticity from those they promote and follow.

Despite their claims to authenticity, for the most part, the personas of lifestyle gurus are highly manufactured, edited and controlled, conforming to commercial ideals that dictate socially acceptable modes of self-presentation. On social media authenticity is a form of social capital designed to establish affective relations of trust and intimacy with followers. It is not about revealing one's true self, but about appearing believable to others by presenting a compelling persona, narrative and performance. Authenticity is performed online by disclosing intimate details about their private lives. There is a tension here between revealing information to connect with followers and limiting what one shares to ensure privacy and brand consistency. These issues are further complicated on social media given that sites collapse multiple audiences into a single context. In contrast to standard face-to-face encounters, users must decide what information to reveal and conceal from their entire audience to achieve audience segregation online. To the degree to which they are able to present a believable persona and narrative to their audience, they have achieved authenticity.

Micro-celebrity is a form of labour designed to achieve fame. While lifestyle blogging may promote self-actualisation, it can also produce alienation. Just as the industrial worker described by Marx was alienated from the product they produced, the emphasis on emotional management can alienate lifestyle bloggers from themselves and others. Although social media is premised on Web 2.0 ideals of content creation and sharing, these platforms are highly competitive. The introduction of the 'like' function as a way to express regard for a photo or video, has intensified users' quest for validation, as approval can be measured and quantified. Metrics in the form of likes, view counts and followers are used to quantify status. They signify influence and reputation by quantifying and publicising visibility and attention. The fact that there are entire industries built around increasing people's follower count and engagement rate with their followers, reveals the power of metrics to demonstrate public esteem and social standing. The drive for status and visibility is built into the design of these platforms. As Sean Parker, the founding President of Facebook, explains:

> The thought process that went into building these applications, Facebook being the first of them … was all about: 'How do we consume as much of your time and conscious attention as possible?' And that means that we need to sort of give you a little dopamine hit every once in a while, because someone liked or commented on a photo or a post or whatever. And that's going to get you to contribute more content, and that's going to get you … more likes and comments. It's a social-validation feedback loop … exactly the kind of thing that a hacker like myself would come up with, because you're exploiting a vulnerability in human psychology. The inventors, creators – it's me, it's Mark [Zuckerberg], it's Kevin Systrom on Instagram, it's all of these people – understood this consciously. And we did it anyway. (Solon 2017)

Beyond the gratification of being 'liked', metrics have a tangible impact on lifestyle gurus' status and commercial success. As a result, the self must be strategically presented online to increase status and attention. Not all micro-celebrities are commercial, but the pressures of seeking approval, and the need for many to adhere to commercial ideals, has a cost. When people use social media to self-brand, they are encouraged to regulate, edit and 'filter' themselves. Self-curation is not new, but the saturated market of lifestyle blogging accentuates these pressures as users compete to become visible and heard among the noise of lifestyle advice. The perception of authenticity is key to achieving a loyal online following. The irony is that the ideal of authenticity promoted by lifestyle gurus is driven by commerce, competition and status-seeking over genuine, spontaneous interaction.

4

'Your Person as a Product': Commodifying Influence

In 1997, Tom Peters wrote an article, *The Brand Called You* (1997). The article generated the self-branding movement. He wrote:

> It's time for me – and you – to take a lesson from the big brands, a lesson that's true for anyone who's interested in what it takes to stand out and prosper in the new world of work. Regardless of age, regardless of position, regardless of the business we happen to be in, all of us need to understand the importance of branding. We are CEOs of our own companies: Me Inc. To be in business today, our most important job is to be head marketer for the brand called You … The good news – and it is largely good news – is that everyone has a chance to stand out. Everyone has a chance to learn, improve, and build up their skills. Everyone has a chance to be a brand worthy of remark. (Peters 1997)

Self-branding is the idea of turning yourself into a brand. It is the practice of marketing oneself as a commodity to be sold to others (Page 2012; Marwick 2013: 166). Self-branding involves using a series of advertising and marketing strategies to brand the individual. Individuals apply the branding strategies of major corporations to themselves, becoming what Peters (1997) terms, the 'CEO of Me Inc.' The idea of self-branding was popularised in a series of bestselling marketing books including: *Be Your Own Brand* (McNally and Speak 2002); *The Brand Called You* (Montoya and Vandehey 2002); *Authentic Personal Branding* (Rampersad 2008); *Me 2.0* (Schawbel 2009); *Crush It!* (Vaynerchuk 2009) and *The 10Ks of Personal Branding* (Mobray 2009). What these texts share in common is that they act as manuals for self-branding, providing readers with a set of techniques for strategic self-promotion that is outwardly demotic in being available *in principle* to everyone. Self-branding has been facilitated by the internet with people using social media to promote themselves as a product to be consumed by others. These platforms enable people to create, collaborate and share information online (Schawbel 2009), giving them visibility and an audience of potential consumers with whom they can interact for social and economic gain (Page 2012). The accessibility of these tools make self-branding more achievable online compared to traditional media channels (e.g. television, radio, print advertisements), which are beyond the reach of most starting a company.

While the rapid growth and popularity of online social networks have made self-branding widely possible, the 'promotional culture' of self-branding is not an innovation of social media (Page 2012). Rather it draws on the marketing strategies of corporations and is evident in reality television (Hearn 2008), whereby fame is conferred on ordinary people – those 'formerly known as the audience' (Rosen 2006) – by virtue of the 'demotic turn' (Couldry 2002; Turner 2010). As discussed in previous chapters, this logic was manifest in the late-twentieth century with the celebration of ordinary people on talk-shows and reality television. Self-branding has had a direct bearing on the rise of ordinary people branded as lifestyle gurus with Peters reminding his readers, 'you've got to be an exceptional expert at something' (Peters 1997). In *Me 2.0*, Schawbel (2009) echoes this advice, encouraging aspiring bloggers to contribute to publications to reinforce their image as an expert. The idea is that expertise is accessible to anyone with native experience in an area rather than a talent or skill that needs to be achieved by way of formal training or credentials. What is novel about lifestyle gurus today is how they use social media for self-branding. Social media enables micro-celebrities to use self-branding to monetise their following. When a micro-celebrity uses self-branding for profit, they are referred to as a social media influencer.

Social Media Influencers

Social media influencers (from here on in referred to as influencers) pursue fame professionally as a vocation. They have been able to self-brand a public persona successfully transforming their online fame into a business. Like micro-celebrities, influence is achieved using social media. Most lifestyle gurus today are influencers. They have achieved influence in various lifestyle domains with people seeking their opinions, advice and guidance as a result of the popular content they share online. Their content curates the mundane, ordinary aspects of everyday life; their knowledge and advice supported through lived experience rather than professional training. Whereas a micro-celebrity may not receive commercial rewards for their fame (e.g. acquiring fame accidentally in a viral video), to be an influencer is regarded as an occupation given that many monetise their following by integrating sponsored content and ads into their blog and social media posts. Those with large followings can command tens of thousands of dollars for posts that publicise products or services. Attesting to their commercial appeal, elite modelling and celebrity management agencies now represent influencers. There are also digital strategy training courses, such as YouTube's *NextUp* programme, and media agencies specifically designed to train influencers to produce commercially lucrative content, boost engagement and grow their online following. Despite emerging online, an influencer's fame can transfer offline resulting in modelling contracts with major brands and other forms of mainstream advertising. However, unlike traditional advertising, which is typically overt and recognisable, influencers mostly engage in personalised forms of marketing.

The degree to which an influencer can monetise their status depends on their capacity to convert their fame into persuasive, commercially driven content. This mostly involves creating content that revolves around their persona and product placement. The approach mimics the relationship that brands have with their media partners, the fundamental difference being that influencers exist outside of the traditional power structure as the content producer and editor of their site. Traditionally, a celebrity's commercial value might be measured in terms of their net earnings, modelling contracts, record sales or box office hits. Conversely, an influencer's commercial potential is measured by quantifiable metrics: a high follower count and engagement rate with their followers in the form of comments, shares and likes. By assessing influence through quantifiable metrics, online influence can be 'objectively' evaluated.

The commercial appeal of an influencer also depends on the quality of their followers. Brands have begun to advertise on social media using 'nano influencers', people who have as few as 1,000 followers (Tort 2018). They might not be as famous as an influencer, but their commercial value is that they have high engagement rates with their followers, facilitating peer-to-peer marketing. The audiences of lifestyle gurus are invested in their personal stories. It is an 'economy of affect', not just attention (Roberts 2005; Abidin 2018: 95). A range of software now exists that enables marketing firms to find influencers whose followers align with the corporate, sanctioned values of specific brands. These programmes typically operate by locating a brand's desired consumers based on key demographics, such as age and location, as well as who they follow on social media and how they shop online. These criteria are then matched with an influencer's followers. Influencers appeal to brands when they are liked and trusted by their followers. Whereas traditional celebrities appear remote in their skills and achievements (e.g. possessing rare beauty or acting talent), influencers trade off their apparent affable ordinariness, using a series of techniques to reduce the aesthetic distance between them and their followers. Part of the commercial appeal of influencers is the means by which they establish intimacy and trust with their followers through sharing 'exclusive', inside tips and producing content that gives the appearance of authentic, 'unfiltered' exchange. It is their lives as documented that is central to their fame and commercial success.

Commodifying Influence: Social Media as Advertising

A series of technological changes has contributed to the rise of lifestyle gurus as a commercial industry. In the twentieth century, radio, television and print were the primary channels of communication and advertising. In the mid-2000s, marketers and advertisers were surrounded by a range of new media. Internet-based communication tools, such as blogs and social media, captivated the attention of millions of users, with social media rapidly becoming an ubiquitous mode of communication. In the late 1990s and early 2000s a range of blogging platforms emerged, together with video sharing and social media sites such as Facebook (2004), YouTube (2005), Reddit (2005) and Twitter (2006). These technologies not only transformed how users published and consumed content; by giving people the ability to self-broadcast, they enabled users to interact with brands through creating, commenting on, and sharing content. As social media ascended in popularity, so did the commercial relationship between marketers and influencers. While the mainstream media continued to play a pivotal role in the dissemination of information, these traditional channels (e.g. radio, television and print) were influenced by online conversations on blogs and social media. Influencing these conversations were popular social media users with relatively large public followings. Although most did not have the volume of fans of a celebrity, they were characterised by a niche community of loyal followers and tended to have high engagement rates with those who followed them. Influencers provided brands with new ways to access consumers and intervene in online conversations. Their niche following enabled brands to reach their target market of certain demographics, while their engagement rate with their followers could make them more influential than celebrities paid to endorse a product. Advertisers cottoned on that online influence could be commercialised by paying influencers to post photos, write reviews and curate videos endorsing a brand on blogs and social media.

The role of influencers would be to persuade their followers to desire a specific brand or product. The traditional two-way model of selling to potential buyers via advertising was succeeded by a new three-way relationship between buyers, sellers and reviewers. Social media is central to the consumer experience, with consumers seeking advice and assurance about the quality of brands in the form of customer recommendations, commentary and reviews from those who occupy positions of influence online. Influencer marketing is a billion dollar industry. Valued at 1.07 billion USD in 2017, the global influencer market is predicted to reach 2.38 billion USD in 2019 (Statista 2017). Influencer marketing has not replaced celebrity endorsements. Instead, it forms part of a broader cohesive digital strategy designed to create brand awareness and loyalty through 'conversation' and 'community' (Gillin 2008).

Social media has changed the way we think about life with others and how to measure influence online. What made these tools so useful for marketers was not only their ubiquity, but the fact that influence could be more precisely measured and analysed via quantitative criteria, such as search engine rankings, website traffic, unique visitors, page views, hits, positive or negative comments and subscribers (Gillin 2008). These metrics proved more reliable than previous measures of audience awareness or customer satisfaction, particularly among younger demographics, who were readily adopting social media. While the methods for determining influence are dynamic and changing, the plethora of tools and services for evaluating influence reflect the importance of digital advertising and social media. Part of the appeal of digital marketing is that the internet provides brands with new methods to track and report campaign results. Online marketing campaigns are instantly measurable due to the click-through rate of the various products and services. 'Click-through rate' (CTR) is a metric that measures the ratio of clicks an advertisement receives per impression (the number of times it is seen). Clicks are valuable to brands because clicking on an ad transfers users, all of whom can be converted into potential consumers, to the merchant's website. These metrics can be collected and analysed using a series of web services to boost a site's search traffic and performance. Click-through rates for online ad campaigns vary. While banner ads once boasted high click-through rates, their effectiveness has decreased following the rise of ad-blocking technology to prevent commercial interruptions online. Perceived to be obstructive to the quality of user experience, people have learned to ignore these interruptions (what is referred to as 'banner blindness'). Banner ads have been replaced by 'native advertising', a subtle and highly personalised form of advertising where the ad experience follows the natural form and function of the user experience in the context in which it is placed. Because the ad blends with the content, it is less likely to interrupt the user experience and therefore perceived to be more effective. As a result, the mainstream media increasingly employ native advertising to advertise products and services. In many cases, influencer marketing proves more persuasive as influencers are trusted by their followers and can drive brand awareness through leveraging off their niche community of loyal followers.

Influencer marketing has altered the fabric of marketing as it existed for the last century (Gillin 2008). Influencers have always been an important part of marketing, yet the means of achieving influence have changed in the digital age. Credibility was traditionally assigned by the media via magazine covers and features signifying influence. Advertising was largely a one-way mode of communication designed to persuade consumers. Editors would select what advertising content would be featured in radio, print and television. To complement these methods, public relations agencies would hire models and celebrities to attend events to publicise brands. Images would then circulate of these high-profile individuals attending staged events in the social pages of popular newspapers and magazines. This mode of top-down, one-to-many model of communication has been challenged by social media. Now brands use influencers to help tell their story by creating branded content that influencers can share with their followers online. Influencers have a two-way mode of communication with their followers. Followers can engage with their content through commenting, sharing and liking their posts. Comments might take the form of questions about how to use a certain product or where to buy it. In the case of lifestyle blogging, a follower might comment on a post featuring a green juice and ask the influencer for the recipe or where they sourced specific ingredients. Influencers can also share the posts of those that they follow. The key difference with influencer marketing is that social media enables influencers to engage in instant dialogue with their followers. This capacity for dialogue, whether realised or not, facilitates the impression of direct relationships between influencers and their followers. Rather than explicitly trying to sell a product, their influence rests on the fact that, in addition to being inspirational, they are perceived to be accessible and trustworthy. Influencers are not held to the same standards of objectivity expected of the institutional media. Their 'straight talking', direct form of address is an important part of their appeal. Consumers follow influencers because they are interested in their opinions and relate to their brand. This means that when influencers endorse a particular product, their followers are likely to view it positively and be influenced by their opinions.

As influencers became a primary feature of digital marketing, the industry began to settle on some broadly agreed-upon standards to measure influence. One of the primary ways to measure online influence was using *Klout*, a social media analytics tool that rated users' audience reach and engagement on social media by awarding them with a *'Klout Score'*. *Klout* assigned users with a numerical value between one and one hundred, quantifying their influence according to its scoring algorithm. The more followers and interaction a user had with their followers (e.g. via comments, retweets, shares and mentions), the higher their score and perceived influence. *Klout* was the major tool for measuring influence until 2018 when the company was acquired by Lithium Technologies. One of the problems with these tools is that they are subject to platform algorithms. When engineers change the scoring methodology and weightings given to different forms of online interaction, they result in new scores and metrics. Metrics are significant because they translate into profit. The commercial appeal of being perceived to have high influence has resulted in a series of counterfeit methods to boost one's engagement rate and online following. Users can purchase fake followers (referred to as 'bots') and 'likes' through companies and 'like farms' to boost their status (see Chapter 3). Savvy users can also game the system by helping each other to increase a post's engagement rate through algorithmic manipulations, including rapid-fire commenting and liking (Baker and Walsh 2018). As a result, a series of social media marketing services have emerged to detect how trustworthy accounts are by looking for certain periods where users have gained a huge spike of followers in a day (through purchasing followers) and checking their engagement rate. With social media platforms and digital marketing firms cracking down on counterfeit practices, users have established new, legal methods to appear influential online. These include collaborations between influencers designed to increase audience reach by sharing their viewership. Collaborations expose each influencer to the other's followers. An example could be a blogger posting a video of a fitness tutorial featuring another wellness guru. Or, a fashion blogger collaborating with another fashion blogger in a featured blog post.

Influencer Marketing

Social media is intrinsic to the commercial success of influencers. Influencers use the internet to monetise their brand through advertising and marketing. The primary way in which this is achieved is through sponsored posts (also referred to as 'advertorials' or 'brand features'), where an influencer receives monetary compensation or gifts for featuring or reviewing a product on their blog or social media. Other common ways influencers earn money online is through selling products on e-commerce stores and affiliate marketing. Affiliate marketing is a form of advertising where an affiliate, such as a blogger or influencer on Instagram, is remunerated by a business for each new customer they attract through their marketing efforts. Affiliates usually place links or discount codes on their blogs or social media posts that direct viewers to the website of the business they are partnering with. As an affiliate partner, they receive a commission for every 'click through' (or sale) that can be tracked back to their content. An example would be a fashion blogger, who sells a brand's clothing on their website, or a lifestyle guru, who places a link for a specific cooking utensil at the end of a recipe on their blog. What is important here is that advertising is understated, personalised and integrated into the content by promoting products consistent with their brand and of interest to their audience (the bloggers audience is who appeals to the company employing them as an affiliate). Whereas an ad for clothing in a magazine is generally overt, influencers typically blend advertising into their social media content; in the case of fashion, posting pictures of themselves online with affiliate links to the products worn embedded in the post.

There is an important connection between content and products, with influencers using subtle techniques to monetise advice through e-commerce stores and affiliate links. Most of these transactions occur on Instagram, given the visual nature of the platform, that lends itself readily to advertising. Many brands and companies are represented on the site, meaning they can be tagged in posts. In this regard, Instagram can be viewed as a collection of ads. Affiliate marketing programmes, together with these social network sites, allow influencers to earn a commission by endorsing a particular brand or product and monetising their following. This would not be possible if mobile digital devices and online social networks were not established in popular culture. The rapid increase of 18 to 24-year-olds with a smartphone and social media accounts means that ads are likely to be viewed more frequently by a larger proportion of the population. The online social networks instantly accessible to today's social media influencers are remarkably different from the methods of transmission available to Smiles, Beecher and Beeton in the nineteenth century; they also provide influencers with a 'networked audience' of vastly greater magnitude than print, radio and television afforded Oprah and Stewart in the twentieth century. Social media has not only enabled lifestyle gurus to communicate directly with their followers, but to commodify their online influence. While the commodification of advice can be traced back to the emergence of lifestyle media in the twentieth century, these technologies have enabled influencers to enter into commercial relationships with advertisers and flourish as an industry in the twenty-first century.

Most influencers attempt to minimise the commercial motivations behind their posts and interactions. Followers may be aware that they are promoting a product, but their commercial motivations cannot be seen to compromise their brand otherwise they jeopardise their relationship with their followers. As discussed in Chapter 3, the appeal of influencers rests largely on the impression of trust and intimacy they foster with their followers. One of the reasons that it is more powerful when a product is endorsed by a third party, such as a friend or family member, rather than the brand itself, is because their advice appears to be genuinely 'coming from the heart' rather than driven by commercial interests. The same is true of celebrities. Celebrities may be inspiring, but given that their endorsements are often commercially driven, celebrity endorsements tend to be less trusted than friends and family. Influencers occupy a position between these groups. Unlike actors or celebrities in a commercial playing a role, they provide their followers with the appearance of genuine connection and intimate transaction. In occupying the same platforms as their followers, they convey the impression that they are not managed by intermediaries (whether this be the case or not given that most successful influencers are managed by agents). It is their apparent ordinariness, autonomy and accessibility that makes influencers appear trustworthy. Influencers promote this perception by addressing their followers as 'friends' (rather than fans, which implies distance) and claiming to 'be authentic' (see Chapter 3). The problem influencers face is how to commercialise their content without risking the relations of trust they have established with their followers. Most make it clear that they only promote products they 'believe in' and repeatedly reject offers from companies that do not align with their brand. In this regard, trust depends upon authenticity. It is about influencers telling a compelling story and sharing their experiences with their followers. For influencer marketing to be successful, followers need to believe that influencers genuinely like the products they endorse. Trust and authenticity is what distinguishes them from appearing like another celebrity paid to endorse a product. Hence, the overwhelming number of claims influencers make about being 'authentic', 'true to oneself' and one's brand. Influencers are a brand.

Relations of managed trust and the perception of authenticity are the basis of their credibility.

When an influencer's brand appears to be compromised by commercial interests, it threatens their claims to authenticity. As a result, the most effective influencers limit the visibility of their commercial relationships. This has led to a blurring of the lines between advertising and editorial content, which, in turn, has generated confusion and frustration among consumers about when content is advertising. In response to these methods, in the UK the Advertising Standards Authority (ASA) established new rules in 2011 requiring users to disclose to their followers when they are being paid to promote a product. Influencers must reveal when they have a financial partnership with a brand. They must also declare when they have been rewarded with gifts or loaned a product to endorse goods or services. Current practices for labelling online ads include adding the hashtags #ad, #advert, #advertising or #advertisement. Instagram encourages users to add the hashtag #paidpartnership to paid posts. Other labels used by influencers to indicate when a commercial relationship exists are less clear, such as #spon or #sp (abbreviations for #sponsored content), #collab, 'thanks to … ', 'in association with …' or @ mentions. Influencers have become savvy about how they include these labels, so as to minimise the appearance of ads. For example, by burying them in a collection of hashtags. In principle, marketing messages on websites and social media are subject to the same regulations as the mainstream media. The decisive difference is that, whereas television and newspaper ads are generally overt (native advertising an exception), online advertising can be highly personalised and unclear.

Most influencer marketing is situated alongside editorial content of a similar style, so it is not always obvious when a post is informative or an ad. It is often difficult to discern when a blog, vlog, tweet or Instagram post is an ad because advertising is cleverly camouflaged as lifestyle advice. This is part of the commercial appeal of influencers to brands in so far as their message appears free from much of the 'market logic' associated with traditional advertising. The fact that influencers achieve popularity among niche communities means the advice they convey tends to be of interest to their followers. For example, when a follower sees a post of an attractive influencer wearing a dress on social media, they will often ask in the comments section where the influencer purchased it. In this regard, the ad is seen to benefit the consumer rather than intruding on their leisure time, as is typically the case with advertising. Another key difference between traditional advertising and influencer marketing is that if an influencer no longer appeals to a follower, they can opt out of viewing their content. As such, ads can be tailored to a niche market of interested consumers and leverage off consumers invested in an influencer's lifestyle.

The Democratisation of Advice: Blogging as a Community of Equals?

Part of the popular appeal of lifestyle gurus is the way they position themselves as alternatives, often in opposition to big business and elites. Despite their commercial leanings, those lifestyle gurus who achieve influence online are presented as ordinary individuals who have achieved success through passion and effort. Web 2.0 discourses enhance this ideology by emphasising that, unlike the hierarchical structure of the mass media system, these platforms can be used by anyone with access to the internet. This quality of being an 'ordinary' participant of an egalitarian system is an important part of self-branding. For it bridges the distance between influencers and their followers, facilitating trust and intimacy. It also enables influencers to advertise products and services as being relevant to a mass market. For example, images documenting an influencer's physical transformation after consuming certain supplements, testify to a product's effectiveness and relevance to the masses. This idea of blogging as a community of equals is built on a series of inter-connecting discourses.

1. *Egalitarianism.* This depicts the blogosphere and social media as a democratic, inclusive public space. The idea is that the internet in general, and social media in particular, gives everyone an equal voice, thereby destabilising the hierarchical, corporate structures that formerly governed the media. Blogs are seen to provide a user-friendly, communal space for guidance, nurturing, growth and friendship. In contrast to the one-to-many broadcast model of the mass media, lifestyle gurus emphasise the many-to-many model of blogging and social media is based on participation, dialogue and interaction.

2. *Authenticity.* Lifestyle gurus trade off their perceived authenticity. They present themselves as ordinary individuals, with a passion for lifestyle issues and self-discovery, just like their followers, which defines them in contrast to the received order of experts and elites. It is common for lifestyle gurus to exaggerate

their 'everyman' status through stories of vulnerability, hardship and personal confessions. Authenticity here is *performed*. It is more about fostering relations of trust and intimacy with their followers than a set of inherent characteristics. Being perceived as authentic is important because it distinguishes influencers from Big Media and corporations. In claiming to 'be authentic', lifestyle gurus are reminding their followers that they should be trusted as folk heroes because they are outwardly 'genuine' and scrupulously only promote products and services they believe in. This is said to differentiate them from mainstream advertising, which are ruled by commercial interests (despite the fact that they often are heavily intertwined with advertising and marketing industries).

3. *Access.* This conveys the patina of proximity and friendship. The ideal of access is fundamental to lifestyle gurus and one of the factors that differentiates them from traditional celebrities. Interaction with their followers in the form of @replies, comments, retweets, reposts and direct messages creates the feeling of connection. It gives lifestyle gurus direct access to their followers in contrast to traditional celebrities, who typically are mediated by cultural intermediaries.

4. *Autonomy.* This is the idea that blogging is a creative enterprise that exists outside of the system. In contrast to the mainstream media, which garners legitimacy as a result of reputation and a shared code of ethics, lifestyle gurus exercise charismatic authority through establishing para-social relations with their followers (Weber 1968). As such, it is common for lifestyle gurus to speak about the importance of 'following your passion' in order to achieve success, thereby, implying that their success is meritocratic.

These discourses are ideals rather than a reality. Despite Web 2.0 discourses about democracy, participation and equality, Web 2.0 is not a meritocracy. Meritocracy is built upon presuppositions that success is deserved. As an idea, it presupposes that status and success result from talent, effort and achievement. The corollary is that failure is also deserved. What ideas about meritocracy ignore are that the skills, privileges and resources required to achieve influence online and, crucially, how others are involved in the co-creation of our success. At the most basic level, lifestyle blogging requires internet access and a camera (for many, social inequalities prevent access to these technologies). The ubiquity and access to digital technologies lower the barriers for entry, enabling more people to participate online, but it does not guarantee influence, visibility or attention.

To achieve influence demands more than participation; you must perform convincingly in order to bring others into confidence. Exercising persuasion online involves acquiring and deploying certain skills and resources – knowledge about how to establish and maintain a blog, how to take high quality photographs and edit a video, for example. Lifestyle bloggers also require time to write blog posts, edit photographs and videos. To distinguish oneself from the noise online, lifestyle gurus must be trained and skilled in the methods of production. This usually includes purchasing a digital single-lens reflex (DSLR) camera (rather than a smartphone), photography equipment and photo editing software to produce high resolution photographs, and acquiring knowledge on how to use these devices. Most successful bloggers have friends or partners with specialist skills and knowledge about photography, video editing and marketing. Producing quality content also requires time, a resource unequally distributed among the population.

Authenticity and access are important attributes of influencer marketing. To appear authentic depends upon more than a personality type. As discussed in the previous chapter, it requires strategic self-presentation and knowledge about what information to share online (as well as what to exclude). Performative skill rather than self-discovery is crucial. The same applies to access, which in most cases remains para-social: unequal and one-sided. Finally, the idea of autonomy overlooks the degree to which influencers are motored by commercial objectives. That is, part of the system they outwardly define themselves against. Commercial forces influence how we interact online. Discourses of bloggers as autonomous conceals the ways that blogs resemble traditional sites of production. Once bloggers start to mobilise sponsors, their distinction from traditional media outlets becomes blurred. Their brand depends on their capacity to build a following to attract advertisers. As such, influencers succumb to the same institutional and commercial structures as the magazine and television industry.

The Wellness Industry

One of the most striking examples of the commodification of lifestyle advice is the creation of the wellness industry. The preoccupation with living well tends to occur in contexts where longevity and survival are more commonplace and secure. By virtue of the fact that we live longer, there is an increasing interest in how to maximise the quality of our lives. For most of history, humans have had an interest in living well. For the Ancient Greeks, the concept of *eudaimonia* referred to a state of well-being. This contented state was not confined to mere pleasure; it was the result of performing right action through cultivating virtues that align with reason, more akin to human flourishing than contemporary understandings of happiness. The Greek's philosophical enquiry into the 'good life' was shared by various Eastern philosophies and the Judeo-Christian tradition. The ideal of rational self-mastery to which these traditions aspired informs much of what we identify today as the self-help movement (McGee 2005: 18). The principle of self-improvement presumes that the consumer is lacking in some way. A sense of absence, often vague and indefinable, is the happy hunting ground of the lifestyle guru. They comport themselves online as the antidote to the problems of others; 'friends' who can guide us from a state of inadequacy to perfection through various step by step programmes and regimes. A key difference is that whereas well-being was traditionally achieved through introspection and moral training, well-being is now commonly infused with medical discourses around vulnerability, health and illness.

During the twentieth century there were shifting understandings of health, which saw health emerge as a synonym for well-being. An early example of this can be found in the definition adopted by the World Health Organisation (WHO) in 1946 where health was defined as 'a state of complete physical, mental and social well-being and not merely the absence of disease or infirmity' (World Health Organisation 2018a). This definition of health is noteworthy for several reasons. It provides a more holistic understanding of health as comprised of interconnected modalities: physical, mental and social well-being. Wellness was not only perceived to be located within the individual, as it had been previously, but contingent on their social positioning in the world and environment (including their material resources and social relationships). The use of the term 'well-being' as a synonym for health also conveys health as a positive concept – a state of 'wellness' – rather than the mere 'absence' of illness and disease. Despite attempts to broaden the scope of what is meant by health so that it includes physical, mental and social well-being, ironically this more holistic approach to health has resulted in a preoccupation with the individual. In striving to achieve 'complete health', well-being has been recast from a state free from illness to an unattainable goal. This understanding of well-being is more in line with individualised conceptions of health as a matter of personal choice and responsibility (Baker and Walsh 2018).

Although lifestyle gurus promote the quest for health and wellness positively in terms of choice and freedom, critics conceive of the intrusion of politics over ostensibly individual concerns of diet and lifestyle as a governmental mechanism designed to control the citizen consumer (Mayes 2015). In prescribing new techniques and rules for living, lifestyle gurus promote and validate certain models of 'good' citizenship (Lewis 2008). The techniques for self-improvement, which dominate lifestyle guru sites, offer instructive templates on how to live. Drawing on Foucault's (1977) conception of governance as the 'freely' chosen 'techniques' for directing human behaviour exercised by the self in liberal societies, critics contend that the rise of neo-liberalism in the 1980s has shaped modern understandings of the self-governing citizen (Rose 1989, 2010). Self-governance is enabled here by what Nikolas Rose (2010) terms the 'diagnostic gaze', wherein psychological models of selfhood govern subjectivity. While Rose's analysis focuses on 'experts of psy' – psychology, psychiatry, psychotherapy and other 'psy' disciplines that have played a key role in understandings of the self – the charismatic authority of today's lifestyle gurus adheres to a similar logic. Everyday existence is recast as a series of life problems to be managed by the autonomous individual seeking self-improvement, self-fulfilment and happiness. Life solutions embrace the practice of self-discovery, positive thinking, being kind to oneself, building self-esteem, stress reduction, eating well and engaging in physical activity. The result is that health and happiness are conceived of as a voluntary pursuit (Rose 2010: 77).

Lifestyle management is presented as involving pleasure and responsibility (Lewis 2008). Enticing health related posts on Instagram are regularly accompanied by discourses of responsibility as exemplified by the hashtags: 'determination', 'motivation' and 'healthy choices' (Baker and Walsh 2019). Robert Crawford coined the term 'healthism' to refer to this 'new form of health consciousness' (1980: 365). The term is used to describe the political ideology, which emerged in the US during the 1970s, that positioned 'the problem of health and disease at the level of the individual' (Crawford 1980: 378). Inherently person-centred, healthism locates health solutions within the domain of the individual, assuming they have the capacity to resist advertising, culture, institutional and environmental constraints and disease. Those who view this shift positively tend to discuss well-being in terms of freedom and empowerment. Critics, on the other hand, perceive this shift to be a result largely of the privatisation of the health care system in late modern societies; a move away from a traditional welfarist model of health, in which responsibility resides with society to provide the conditions that promote well-being (Raisborough 2011), towards the promotion of the individual, fee-paying, neo-liberal citizen.

Whether viewed from a positive or negative angle, the emphasis on well-being reframes health as a matter of self-management and personal responsibility (Benford and Gough 2006). In this context, 'being healthy' becomes not just an individual undertaking, but a moral responsibility (Raisborough 2011: 78). Wellness and self-improvement are framed here in relation to narratives of risk; well-being is about optimisation and striving to avoid the threat of contamination and disease. Nikolas Rose refers to this concern with self-management as the 'will to health', a cultivated set of individual obligations that 'encode an optimisation of one's corpo-reality to embrace an overall "well-being" – beauty, success, happiness, sexuality and much more' (Rose 2001: 17). From this standpoint, health and well-being are glorious ideals; they are not merely defined in terms of the absence of illness and disease, but are articulated in relation to self-improvement and moral virtue. Hence, the rise of lifestyle media and reality television makeover shows dedicated to the topic of well-being: *The Biggest Loser*, *The Big Fat Truth* and *Queer Eye for the Straight Guy*, to name a few. These shows both reflect and reinforce assumptions about what it means to be healthy, successful and desired.

Wellness has become synonymous with medicalisation and is now used to treat a range of health problems. Whereas wellness was formerly associated with psychological growth and development, it is increasingly presented as a substitute for conventional medicine (Donelly and Toscano 2017). In a saturated market, wellness has become a buzzword. It is promoted as an antidote to today's most pressing medical threats: mental illness and cancer. Part of the appeal of the wellness movement can be understood by the 'placebo effect'. The placebo effect is a beneficial effect produced by a placebo drug or treatment. The benefit cannot be attributed to the properties of the placebo itself (the drug or treatment in question), but rather to the patient's belief in, and expectations about, the treatment. One of the striking discoveries of the twentieth century was that the placebo effect can result in tangible effects. It was suggested that around 35 per cent of patients with a variety of conditions could be improved or cured by placebos (Beecher 1955). In passing, we might note that these hypotheses were proposed in the nineteenth century by William James. Having used his belief in God to overcome depression,

James emphasised the power of the mind in his essay, *The Will to Believe* (1896).

> ... often enough our faith beforehand in an uncertified result is the only thing that makes the result come true. Suppose, for instance, that you are climbing a mountain, and have worked yourself into a position from which the only escape is by a terrible leap. Have faith that you can successfully make it, and your feet are nerved to its accomplishment. But mistrust yourself, and think of all the sweet things you have heard the scientists say of maybes, and you will hesitate so long that, at last, all unstrung and trembling, and launching yourself in a moment of despair, you roll in the abyss. In such a case (and it belongs to an enormous class), the part of wisdom as well as of courage is to believe what is in the line of your needs, for only by such belief is the need fulfilled. Refuse to believe, and you shall indeed be right, for you shall irretrievably perish. But believe, and again you shall be right, for you shall save yourself. You make one or the other of two possible universes true by your trust or mistrust, both universes having been only maybes, in this particular, before you contributed your act.

What these enumerated studies reveal is the inexorable relationship between mind and body. The placebo effect is both individually and culturally defined. For example, consumers are likely to be influenced by advertising if they live in a culture surrounded by advertising (Goldacre 2009: 81–2). On an individual level, the placebo effect reveals the power of the mind. There are strong parallels here with the self-help movement in so far as discourse about wellness takes the basic truth about the power of our mind to shape our reality and exaggerates it by promoting alternative, 'non-hierarchical' therapies as cures for cancer and disease.

There are obvious benefits of adhering to a positive outlook and a healthy lifestyle. The problem with much of the discourse around wellness and self-help is that they exaggerate these claims for profit and commercial success; profiting from the fact that consumers feel empowered by such advice, believing that they can achieve health and happiness in life. Positive thinking feeds into our cognitive biases, which make us susceptible to the belief that we can control our future. While our thoughts shape our reality, we tend to imagine that we can control forces beyond our control, expecting a higher probability of success than probability would warrant. This phenomenon is referred to as the 'illusion of control' (Langer 1975). It operates in a range of contexts from gambling and investing, to the way we assess risk and our perceptions about our health and prosperity (Caulfield 2015: 170–1). There is a large body of psychological literature that shows how these tendencies are tied to cognitive biases: confirmation bias, the tendency for people to focus on corroborative evidence and to ignore evidence that contradicts their preconceived notions, and optimistic bias, the tendency to think that negative events are less likely to happen to oneself than to one's peers, feed these illusions (Kahneman and Tversky 2004; Kahneman et al. 2011; Sharot 2011). Our proclivity for positive thinking, together with the modern Western ethos of personal responsibility, inform contemporary understandings of vulnerability and well-being as an ongoing individual project susceptible to commodification.

Cleansing and Detoxing: The GOOP Phenomenon

While humans have had a preoccupation with living well for thousands of years, it was in the late-twentieth century that the wellness industry was formed. During this period, wellness was commercialised in a range of products and services with practices that were formerly considered esoteric becoming mainstream. Wellness programmes, retreats, detoxes, cleanses, yoga and meditation now infuse popular vocabularies. Much of the discourse around health and wellness is informed by celebrity culture. Given that health and wellness is largely about beauty and desirability, it is not surprising that celebrities are enlisted to market and popularise health goods and services. A case in point is our cultural preoccupation with detoxing and cleansing. Cleansing and detoxing is driven largely by celebrity endorsements. Celebrities have contributed to the popularity of cleansing, detoxing and juicing by using their brand and testimonials to verify products and services. Gwyneth Paltrow advocates Dr Alejandro Junger's *Clean Program*, the reality-television star, Khloe Kardashian, promotes *Flat Tummy* detox shakes and the rapper, Cardi B, promotes *Teami* detox tea. These products are marketed as a remedy for common health ailments: stress, anxiety, depression, insomnia and fatigue. In a world where people feel overwhelmed and overworked, discourse around fatigue, burnout and stress is compelling. The concepts of cleansing or detoxifying are based on ideas of purgation and purification. These practices rest upon the belief that the modern world – our environment and the food we eat – is inherently toxic. As a result, we must 'cleanse' or 'detoxify' our body of these impurities. The metaphor is one of removal, namely removing toxins from your somatic house (Junger 2009).

The image of cleaning up your house as a precursor to well-being is persuasive. It invokes ideas about cleanliness and order that most of us intuitively believe to be true. However, once these metaphors are examined more closely, it becomes evident that the language of cleansing and detoxing is deliberately vague. There are references to toxins, pollutants, and dirty environments, but rarely are these terms consistent or well defined. Instead, they appeal to common-sense thinking about purity and cleanliness. Scientists have highlighted that our bodies do not require detoxification given that we have organs, such as the kidneys, liver, skin and colon that perform these functions (see Goldacre 2009). There is no evidence to support the claims that cleanses, comprised of specific supplements and vitamins, evacuate toxins from the body. Instead, what is taking place in most cases is caloric restriction achieved through intermittent fasting: a practice shown to increase weight loss and mood (Martin et al. 2006). The benefits attributed to intermittent fasting result from consuming less calories in a specific timeframe; they do not require the support of branded products and services. In this regard, the modern preoccupation with detoxification is a marketing myth.

> The detox phenomenon is interesting because it represents one of the most grandiose innovations of marketers, lifestyle gurus and alternative therapists: the invention of a whole new physiological process. In terms of basic human biochemistry, detox is a meaningless concept. It doesn't cleave nature at the joints. There is nothing on the 'detox system' in a medical textbook. That burgers and beer can have negative effects on your body is certainly true, for a number of reasons; but the notion that they leave a specific residue, which can be extruded by a specific process, a physiological system called detox, is a marketing invention. (Goldacre 2009: 10)

Detoxing is a cultural product. It aligns common-sense thinking with scientific terminology to persuade consumers of the need to engage in the ritual of detoxification. But the appeal of detoxing and cleansing is also largely the result of celebrity endorsements and an issue with language. The term has emerged as a synonym for 'abstaining' from something perceived to be harmful. Hence, the phrase 'digital detox' to imply a break from our addictive behaviours pertaining to internet use. As Goldacre notes, after periods of unhealthy eating, excessive drinking and poor sleep, most people make a conscious effort to rest and eat well; celebrities 'detox'. This has led to an entire industry of detoxing products (e.g. supplements, vitamins, juices) aimed at assisting a natural process. Despite having no scientific evidence to support these claims, detoxes, cleanses and juicing programmes are now estimated to be a $5-billion-dollar market with the wellness industry growing at an accelerated rate (Caulfield 2015: 8; Sense about Science 2009).

Arguably, one of the most notable celebrity lifestyle gurus in the twenty-first century is the Hollywood actress, Gwyneth Paltrow. In 2008 Paltrow launched her lifestyle site, *goop*. Created several years before Instagram was founded, the site was comprised of a weekly newsletter designed to share helpful lifestyle tips and recommendations with her readers. As a well-travelled Hollywood actress, afforded the privilege of a luxurious lifestyle, Paltrow's aim was to share the life knowledge she had accumulated over time. In an in-depth feature about the company with *The New York Times*, Paltrow explained how when she started the business, she only wanted to recommend things: where to buy the best gelato in Italy, or where to find the best coffee in London. The first iteration of *goop* was only these lists – 'where to go and what to buy once you get there' – published via a newsletter she emailed out of her kitchen (Brodesser-Akner 2018). It was intended to be unbiased (at least, commercially) and based on authentic experience. After meeting with a venture capitalist one evening, Paltrow was encouraged to monetise her blog. Instead of simply sharing advice online, Paltrow learned how to profit from her advice through advertising and manufacturing her own products. Martha Stewart – who Naomi Klein (1999: 2) referred to as 'one of the new breed of branded humans' – had commodified domestic lifestyle advice in print, television and radio decades earlier. However, Paltrow was one of the first celebrities to capitalise on digital media (the success of Stewart's lifestyle site hindered by her public fallout following her felony charges and the dot.com crash). With *goop* emerging as one of the pioneer lifestyle brands in the digital age, Paltrow was joined by a list of other celebrities building and investing their attention capital to create lifestyle brands online. In 2011, the Hollywood actress, Jessica Alba, founded the wellness brand, *The Honest Company*, to help parents find 'safe, effective products that perform' (Honest Company 2018). In 2014, Meghan Markle, the former actress turned Duchess of Sussex, launched the lifestyle brand, *The Tig* (2018). The site featured posts on food, travel, living, fashion and beauty as well as a column that showcased influential women. In 2019, the reality-television star, Kourtney Kardashian launched the lifestyle site, *Poosh*, as 'a place of discovery'. Echoing Oprah's mission statement, *Poosh* describes itself as a modern guide to 'LIVING YOUR BEST LIFE'. The brand's mission is to 'EDUCATE, MOTIVATE, CREATE, and CURATE a modern lifestyle, achievable by all' (Poosh 2019 [emphasis original]).

What makes *goop* stand out as a lifestyle brand was that it approaches 'wellness' comprehensively and from a position of privilege. In contrast to

Martha Stewart, whose aspirational lifestyle brand was attainable to the masses at the department store chains, Kmart and Macy's, Paltrow appeals to a niche market of privileged customers. Past products sold on goop include a £1,614.00 cashmere-blend sweater, a £2,364.00 Trunk Accordion Bag, a £1,212.00 casserole dish and a private Island in Belize priced at £4,545,558. The products sold by *goop* are the same items that Paltrow is believed to use. By purchasing them, consumers are able to experience a glimpse of her lifestyle and vicariously enter her life-world. As Paltrow explained when questioned about her lifestyle brand, 'It's crucial to me that we remain aspirational. Not in price point, because content is always free. Our stuff is beautiful. The ingredients are beautiful. You can't get that at a lower price point. You can't make these things mass-market' (Brodesser-Akner 2018). The success of *goop* as a lifestyle and wellness brand is a testament to the value we attach to celebrity lifestyles and their influence over our aspirations and conceptions of well-being.

Goop's commercial success has transformed the site into a powerful platform for wellness advice. Having departed from its original iteration as a homespun weekly newsletter where Paltrow shared 'her unbiased travel recommendations, health-centric recipes, and shopping discoveries for friends', *goop* is now a major lifestyle brand producing content across six key pillars: wellness, travel, food, beauty, style, and work. Within these pillars, the company curates and sells products as well as its own goods. *Goop* is primarily a lifestyle site targeted at women (although in 2019 the lifestyle brand launched 'Goop Men', dedicating part of the site to products and content marketed around men's lifestyle and wellness). The site appeals to the common strategies designed to achieve intimacy online discussed in the previous chapter, presenting itself as 'a place where readers can find suggestions about where to shop, eat, and stay from a *trusted friend* – not from an anonymous, crowd-sourced recommendation engine' (Goop 2017). It is this combination of appearing trustworthy and aspirational that appeals to consumers. 'I want to help you solve problems', explains Paltrow. 'I want to be an additive to your life' (Brodesser-Akner 2018). Though the site features interviews with 'experts', *goop* positions itself as an alternative source of wellness information to established mainstream Western medicine. At the *In Goop Health Wellness Summit* held in New York in March 2019, where tickets sold for $1,000USD per person, Paltrow greeted the 600-person audience with Caroline Myss, a self-proclaimed 'medical intuitive' gifted with 'bio-spiritual consciousness'. This condition, Myss explained, allows her to sense illness and disease in people before they have been diagnosed by a physician. 'I have friends with chronic issues that Western medicine isn't healing', nodded Paltrow. At the summit, the pair praised attendees for their open-mindedness to alternative medicine. 'You're here because you're a part of a new wave of thinking', Myss explained (Griffin 2019). *Goop* is part of an alternative wellness movement open to psychedelic medicine, antipills, psychic mediums, 'clean' makeup, superfoods and Reiki energy healing.

Over time content on *goop* has expanded the generic wellness topics discussed in Paltrow's original newsletters (e.g. detoxes, cleanses and meditation) to include posts about mindfulness, sexual health and spirituality. As the wellness industry becomes increasingly saturated, the health advice on *goop* has become bolder. Beyond advice about cleansing, detoxing and vitamins, past posts include recommendations about steaming your vagina to balance female hormone levels, inserting 'jade eggs' into one's genitals to enhance sexual energy, drinking 'Inner Judge Flower Essence Blend' to prevent depression and spraying 'Psychic Vampire Repellent' around your aura 'to protect from psychic attack and emotional harm' (Shop.goop.com 2018). Paltrow has received criticism from scientists and medical experts for promoting pseudoscience that is not only false, but dangerous (Caulfield 2015; Gunter 2018). In 2018, the company was also forced to pay $145,000USD to settle allegations it made unverified health claims (Griffin 2019).

Far from defaming Paltrow's image, the controversy caused by such advice appears to be part of *goop*'s business strategy. During a talk at Harvard Business School, where Paltrow was invited to speak about how to create a 'sustainable competitive advantage' in relation to her lifestyle brand, she explained how she could profit from controversy. Negative publicity derived from the content on *goop* drives traffic to her site. Once there, people might decide to purchase a product. 'I can monetise those eyeballs', she said. Paltrow insists that the controversial content produced by *goop* is not clickbait – content whose main purpose is to attract attention and encourage visitors to click on a link to direct them to a particular web page. Instead, she describes content as a 'cultural firestorm' when it generates controversy (Brodesser-Akner 2018). Nevertheless, the parallel is unmistakable. Each controversy caused by content on *goop*, results in people clicking on the site. As such, Paltrow can capitalise on the attention (and 'monetise those eyeballs', as she puts it). The strategy has proven to be effective. As of June, there were 2.4 million unique visitors to *goop* per month. *Goop*'s podcast receives 100,000 to 650,000 downloads each week and the company is now estimated to be worth $250 million USD (Brodesser-Akner 2018), with most of its revenue generated through product sales and its own product lines (e.g. clothing and dietary supplements).

What is taking place here is the commodification of controversy. In 2017, it was announced that *goop* planned to collaborate with the magazine publisher, *Condé Nast*, to create a multi-platform content experience, including launching *goop* in print (Condé Nast 2018). One of the reasons that *goop's* magazine venture with *Condé Nast* collapsed was because Paltrow objected to a third party fact-checking the articles. The collaboration would also prevent *goop* from using the magazine as part of their contextual commerce strategy by selling *goop* products on their site. In response to a series of popular articles, *goop* had begun to manufacture its own line of products; *goop-Skincare* (a collection of creams, cleansers, beauty oils and 'superpowders') was launched in response to a much-read article about natural beauty products and *goop-Wellness*, a series of vitamin 'protocols' for women with different concerns, such as THE MOTHER LOAD for pre- and postnatal women, was launched following a popular story about 'postnatal depletion' (Goop 2018a). More recently, Paltrow has documented her own story of menopause. In a video shared on *goop's* Instagram account, Paltrow revealed that she's currently experiencing symptoms of perimenopause, a precursor to menopause characterised by the ovaries producing less oestrogen. 'I think when you get into perimenopause, you notice a lot of changes. I can feel the hormonal shifts happening, the sweating, the moods – you know you're just like all of a sudden furious for no reason', Paltrow explained. 'I think menopause gets a really bad rap and needs a bit of a rebranding' [sic] (Instagram 2018). With Paltrow's statement coinciding with the release of *goop's* perimenopause and menopause support supplements, *Madame Ovary* (Goop 2018d), her revelations appear to be part of *goop's* marketing strategy. Paltrow's video post on Instagram forms one of many articles on the topic of perimenopause produced by *goop* in 2018 (Goop 2018a, 2018b, 2018c). Not only are there unresolved issues around some of the ingredients in the product (e.g. high levels of vitamin A have been associated with increased cancer risk – see Gunter 2018), these products are much more expensive than purchasing vitamins from a pharmacist with *Madame Ovary* selling for $90USD for thirty packets (approximately one month's supply). The success of *goop* as a lifestyle brand demonstrates the power of compelling narratives and personalised celebrity content to sell products and services. She is drawing on the same marketing techniques popularised by Oprah and Martha Stewart on television, decades earlier, to commodify lifestyle advice.

The Commodification of Advice

There is an ironic turn of events at play here. In mainstream culture there is widespread disdain for advertising and marketing. Conversely, people appear more tolerant towards influencer marketing. Whether it is because their personalised advice appears to be helpful or tailored towards their specific concerns, consumers are more accepting of the commodification of advice online. While lifestyle advice is of potential benefit to consumers, what is often understated, or hidden, are the commercial interests driving lifestyle advice. Take, for example, the slim pills promoted by influencers and celebrities on Instagram. Cardi B, Khloe Kardashian and Iggy Azalea have all been paid to endorse 'detox teas' as weight-loss solutions on social media. Companies of this kind are renowned for contacting slim influencers and celebrities to promote their products on Instagram. As a result, confounding the cause and effect of the product by representing the product (i.e. 'detox tea') as the origin of the influencer's slim physique when, in fact, it has no conclusive bearing upon their physical appearance. In this regard, the logic of influencer marketing and commercialised lifestyle advice has parallels with mainstream advertising. Instead of a corporation hiring a model or actor to promote a brand, the lifestyle guru uses their influence to persuade their followers to covet and buy certain products and services. What is more pronounced is how the perceived authenticity of influencers informs the ways in which these messages are communicated. Although there is a history of product placement in reality television, integrating media content and advertising in entertaining ways (Hudson and Hudson 2006), influencer marketing is often obscured within a personalised, 'authentic' narrative of vulnerability and lifestyle advice. Consumers may be aware that lifestyle bloggers are sponsored by commercial entities, but part of the branding of a successful influencer is the assumption that they only endorse products that they genuinely believe in. In a saturated market, the drive to appear authentic must negotiate the need to 'stand out' from the crowd by producing content that captures attention.

The commercialisation of lifestyle blogging means there is an incentive to embellish health advice with sensational headlines and clickbait rewarded through profit and attention. Controversial health products and lifestyle advice function as clickbait and lead magnets reducing complex topics to digestible stories (e.g. four tips to improve health; three types of toxic relationships and how to avoid them). While much of this advice is innocuous, the medicalisation of wellness renders the commercial underpinnings of lifestyle blogging more harmful. Controversial advice about 'wellness' and alternative therapies are joined by evocative headlines promising knowledge about the causes and cures for Alzheimer's disease, cancer and mental illness. Paltrow's response to her critics is that she is demotic, making room for alternative views. She also claims to interrogate promising topics and share information rather than advice. What statements of this sort overlook is the capacity for celebrity endorsements to *influence* consumers to purchase certain products and services. By virtue of the fact that celebrities and influencers appear aspirational, they stand as 'proof' of a product's effectiveness. Social media has contributed to the rise of the wellness industry by affording ordinary users, most of whom have no scientific credentials, with the ability to disseminate advice on the same platforms as celebrities and powerful elites. Arguably, influencers are more effective at health and wellness marketing due to their perceived accessibility and the feelings of trust and intimacy that they establish with their followers. One of the issues that we face in the digital age is how to regulate health information online. It is not altogether clear how to distinguish between posts advising and misinforming people about health and those sharing information of a personal nature; something Paltrow exploits by promoting her lifestyle site as a platform to discuss interesting holistic alternatives for women rather than being 'prescriptive' (Griffin 2019). This conundrum is explored in the subsequent chapter.

5

'Don't Eat That!': Lifestyle Gurus as Unregulated Advisers

The lifestyle guru phenomenon involves the mobilisation and articulation of interests, invariably for commercial ends. However, the interests concerned both reflect and reinforce unprecedented demographic and technological conditions. To begin starkly, there are more people in the world than ever before. The *Population Reference Bureau* (2018) estimates that the current world population is 7.5 billion; it is projected to rise to 9.8 billion in 2050, of whom 1.4 billion will be young people, under the age of eighteen. In addition, the social structures that condition choice and entry into the attention economy are far more permeable than in traditional society. In the latter, ascribed, authoritarian social hierarchies, usually cemented by religious belief and a salaried clergy, set a mainline to public debates about self, possibility and society. Very simply, today there are more narratives, with more stories to tell, and more counter narratives to oppose them, than ever before. A corollary of this is that we experience more difficulty in deciding who to believe. There is a surfeit of opinions, many of which are conflicting, to be found online. The deluge of conflicting advice creates the soil for lifestyle gurus to compete and clamour for influence and attention. Simultaneously, digital technology has created more opportunities to access others than at any point in history. Currently, it is estimated that there are 3.9 billion active internet users worldwide (Statista 2019a). Chat rooms, forums, help lines, drop-in-platforms and dedicated online advice sites are flourishing. Together, this extraordinary combination of forces change the rules of lifestyle management.

Today's lifestyle gurus are located at a crossroads between unparalleled volume and unprecedented velocity. Two aspects need to be separated. Firstly, the web does not merely inform and educate, it also builds what might be called an *envy playground* in which the lives of others may be automatically interpreted as more colourful, attractive and desirable than the viewer's lot. Paltrow's lifestyle site, *goop*, embodies this. Social media gives the general impression of compressing the distance between celebrities and the public. It entices ordinary people to make comparisons with celebrities who are presented and very often, initially at least, perceived to be 'just like us'. The participation of micro-celebrities in lifestyle issues simply raises the envy stakes. For they appear more accessible, and their aspirational lives more emulatable, than conventional celebrities, who, in the institutionalised system of the mass media, appear remote in their exceptional glamour, skills and achievements. Envying the lives of others is as old as history. However, with the internet it reaches a new pitch, encouraging what we call *lifestyle combing*: sweeping around websites for strands of useful knowledge and good practice to weave together to enhance acceptance, approval, validation and attention capital. Lifestyle combing is compatible with hybrid identities and heterodox outlooks. As with so much else about web relations, these are massive unintended consequences of the web supply chain. They also correspond to the idea of meritocracy. That is, the notion that with courage, effort and imagination anybody can be somebody. We submit that a consequence of the envy playground is the cult of what we propose to call *affirmative perfectionism* (see pp. 132–4).

The global reach of the web heightens social consciousness of cultural relativism and sharpens populism. The web shows that everyone matters, everyone is special, everyone has a voice, everyone deserves to be heard and amplified, it is the life duty of all who are lucky enough to be alive in this age of boundless opportunity to affirm. The desire for the affirmation of self-feeling places relentless, many-sided pressures for self-improvement and maximising attention capital to keep pace with fluctuating standards of perfection. What is primarily affirmed by subscribers on lifestyle guru sites is seldom talent, skill or accomplishment. Rather the acknowledgement of mere co-presence in the world is enough. Hence, the banal representations of selfhood exchanged on sites like Instagram such as dishes on the table, scenes from car and train windows, and of course, perfectly ordinary selfies. These examples of 'lifestreaming' – the continual sharing of personal information of the unfolding self to others – presuppose an audience. These images are not documented merely for the self, they are designed to be publicly broadcast and shared with others. A picture of a meal or a holiday can be categorised, via hashtags, with similar content, categorising the self in relation to a wider international social network. Being ordinary is thus transformed by a sort of sorcery from being unexceptional to becoming the necessary passport to communication. For if nothing else, it serves public notice that one is different from those who have not registered online co-presence.

This brings us to our second point. We no longer necessarily look, first and foremost, to primary networks (consisting of kith and kin relationships) or secondary relationships (consisting of friendship, peer group, school or work circles) as the privileged transactional field in which life-help data are exchanged, and processes of self-validation are confirmed. Para-social tertiary relationships, forged in the institutionalised mediasphere (television, film, radio, print culture) and online, now rival primary and secondary relationships as salient sources of purposive self-conduct and validation. Needless to say, the rules of face-to-face encounters that previous generations of sociologists elucidated continue to have relevance. 'Real' people have not, as it were, vanished to be replaced by some sort of alchemy of online presence that makes them everywhere and nowhere at the same time. Conversely, tertiary relationships introduce new para-social markers of acceptance, approval, self-validation and attention capital. In the course of this, multi-layered, complex sign economies of self-help and validation have arisen to take on the privileges of primary and secondary relationships. As with the online staple of communication on social media, the methods that online lifestyle gurus conventionally use are designed to rapidly and unequivocally elicit affirming relations of presumed intimacy given that they inhabit the same online spaces. In pursuit of this goal, nothing is more effective than the face.

Facemethods

Facebook is called Facebook for a reason. It affords schematised transactions. By the term 'schematised' we wish to draw attention to the calculated nature of communication. Of course, schematised transactions are an ordinary feature of everyday encounters. For example, when we go on a first date with someone, or attend a job interview, we attire and comport ourselves in order to make a favourable impression. In ordinary life, judgements made about the integrity of the exchange are counterbalanced by observing mannerisms, grooming, motivations, tics and body posture when the individual is not verbally interacting that bear upon how the worth of the relationship is perceived and judged. Ambience and physical presence mesh in face-to-face relationships. The information taken via ambience is very often just as important as the issues verbally and visually communicated through direct physical interaction. This is much curtailed in online transactions. Lifestyle gurus work through the face to elicit *preferred readings* of their composure and interlinked narratives.

At this point an insight from the sociology of portrait photography made by John Tagg (1988) is germane. Tagg contends that in the nineteenth century portrait photography concentrates repetitively on the head and shoulders, 'as if those parts of our bodies were our truth' (Tagg 1988: 32). He goes on to remark, that the focus on the head and shoulders draws upon theories of physiognomy that rest upon 'sedimented notions' of respectability, honesty, worth and decency (Tagg 1988: 32). In a society with very different values on punishment and welfare from our own, the pictorial poses that criminals or inmates of the workhouse or lunatic asylum were asked to adopt by portrait photographers, exploit and confirm wider perceptions of 'the dangerous elements' and those 'in want' and 'misery'. At the other end of the social scale, the same is true of the poses that the rich, the celebrated and the influential were required to adopt. The decisive point that Tagg intends to convey is that, by the technical means of the use of lighting, arranged bodily posture and compositional contrast, nineteenth-century portrait photographs bear inscriptions of the history and place of their subjects in the wider social schema. Subjects are not simply photographed, they are also *positioned*. In these photographs there is always another narrative belt besides the focal point in the frame. The subject in question is the constellation of power in which the focal point is addressed, and which the photographer aims, by technological means of composition, to make immediately (but tacitly) 'true' and 'incontrovertible'.

In privileging the face (and, in the case of lifestyle gurus, the body), online, lifestyle gurus downplay the other details we require to determine the veracity of exchange and the prudence of following the advice imparted. It might be objected that the interactive nature of online exchange makes the comparison with nineteenth-century portrait photography and its relation to theories of physiognomy weak. What this ignores is all of the things that are subtracted from conventional online interaction. We have in mind, the mannerisms and behaviour of lifestyle gurus when they are off-camera; their use of aids for impactful interaction that are not made visible or transacted online; the research they have conducted through qualitative and quantitative methods on the needs, desires and anxieties of their audience; the considerations they make in representing online 'fronts' of dress, bearing, grooming, entitlement and how this has been concocted in relation to what might be called 'the general physiognomy of achievement'. The online encounters of lifestyle gurus possess a choreography that is designed to bring the audience into confidence. In fine, the online face is *abstracted from history*. While lifestyle gurus often adorn their websites with personal narratives of the circumstances that led them to self-revelation, the construction of the methods they use to achieve fulfilment and endorsements from others who have benefited from following their programmes are difficult and time consuming to corroborate. Typically, these take the form of statements of self-disclosure that are not buttressed by independent objective evidence. Despite the richness of online data sourcing, it is often very challenging to produce independent verification that self-disclosure statements are truthful. As with so much about online exchange with lifestyle gurus, the weighting in the encounter is upon taking, and accepting, things at face value.

In abstracting the online face from history, digital exchange also separates it from culture. Of course, the producer and consumer are embodied subjects, interpreting content from a particular cultural position in time and space (Haraway 1994). However, the apparatus of online lifestyle exchange does not make much allowance for cultural, ethnic, racial, religious or economic variation. For example, when Kourtney Kardashian addresses her followers on her lifestyle site, *Poosh*, the assumption is that her success as a single, working mum is a template of meritocratic achievement accessible to the masses:

> PEOPLE ARE CONSTANTLY ASKING ME HOW I DO IT ALL, FROM BEING A SINGLE MOM TO WORKING FULL-TIME TO STILL MAINTAINING A SOCIAL LIFE … SO I DECIDED TO CREATE POOSH, A CURATED EXPERIENCE AND A DESTINATION FOR MODERN LIVING. (Poosh 2019)

What discourse of this kind overlooks is the position of privilege from which Kardashian's success is derived – the nannies, personal trainers, chefs, housekeepers, assistants and helpers crucial to her achievements, yet unavailable to the majority of single, working mothers. Instead, an abstract, universal subject, with standard needs, desires, hopes, fears and anxieties is invoked as the principal currency of exchange. Hence, incidentally, the general lack of interest in lifestyle sites with orthodox questions of organised politics. For what has class, gender, race and religion got to do with anything when the name of the game is centred around self-discovery and self-improvement? The online portraiture of lifestyle gurus varies in many particulars. Those who present themselves as advisers on matters of relationships, differ from those who put themselves forward as agreeable guides to finance, fashion, health, vulnerability and well-being. However, categorically speaking, all are so many face iterations of the general physiognomy of achievement. This is usually imbricated with the patina of positive thinking. The universal subject that they address is invited to join 'the journey'. The journey is ever upwards and the reward is more acceptance, more approval, more attention capital and ultimately, self-validation.

There is a palpable difficulty with this. Subjects are not universal. To some extent, the disciplines of anthropology, political science, sociology, economics and psychology, may all be understood to be inventories of particularity. The more one enters into them, the less persuasive a one-size-fits-all model of human behaviour becomes. In foregrounding the face while, at the same time curtailing data-bearing social, cultural and historical aspects, online communication disables the social mechanisms that we ordinarily rely upon in habitual, physically co-present, transactions to judge truth from lies, fact from fiction and worth from waste. There is no purchase in contending that it *prevents* one from making judgements about integrity and veracity. However, when all is said and done, in omitting so much information from the picture, the online face offers generous opportunities to draw us *into confidence* without providing supportive evidential proof regarding the methods or content of advice and guidance on offer.

One consequence of this is the emergence and development of a new gestural economy of online mannerisms that build presumed intimacy (Rojek 2016). The vocabulary of shared vulnerability, narratives of self-reconstruction and advance, traits of behaviour that convey implied complicity against 'the system', all contribute to building an ethos of shared ground and common purpose. All are based in the feeling state of the self, rather than the fibre of collective subjects. As such, the limit horizon of their advice stretches no further than presenting the self in an affirming light so as to achieve acceptance, approval, social impact and self-validation. Generally speaking, there is no interest in collectively transforming the existing social and economic systems in which the self is situated. You don't discover yourself by making an inventory of the poor or cataloguing the apparatus of inequality. On the contrary, conditions of poverty and inequality are mostly left unaddressed. When lifestyle gurus voice humanitarian issues and environmental concerns, these problems are usually framed as an individual undertaking (e.g. switch plastic for glass, stop using straws) that become persuasive reasons to endorse fairtrade merchandise, eco brands and organic, 'non-toxic beauty' products (Poosh 2019). The impetus for change is located firmly with the individual and not within the civic or political sphere. Society may change for the better, but only if individuals change their behaviour (and products) rather than because of regulatory or political intervention. To have any chance of changing them, one must obviously and urgently, first change what it is at least realistic and manageable to change: yourself. The acceptance of what is being communicated at face value by lifestyle gurus, and the stated consequences of exchange and dedicated practice, are presented as all the knowledge and truth one needs to go forward. As a corollary, it is assumed that social impact is inconceivable unless one first makes a success of yourself. By working on yourself all of the systemic factors that get in the way of achievement – class bias, sexism, racism – can be vanquished.

Diet and Nutrition

A case in point is the rise of lifestyle gurus as leading figures in the field of nutrition. One of the problems in the present age is that there is so much conflicting scientific advice available about health and nutrition. This is propelled, though not caused, by the internet. The proliferation of blogs and social media accounts in which people, most of whom have no certified credentials, document their diets and lifestyles provides an array of suggestions about how to achieve optimal health and well-being. The result is that consumers tend to select information that supports their pre-existing views (what is referred to as 'confirmation bias' – see Chapter 2). Rarely will people welcome new information that challenges their beliefs or change their opinions. Instead, the field of nutrition assumes a quasi-religious character in which devotees of a particular diet fervently defend their preconceived beliefs and practices. In this context the lifestyle advice we choose to believe is largely predicated on who we believe, and who we believe is influenced by our cultural context and political values (Haidt 2012), which inform what advice *feels* right and *appears* compelling.

Food is a strong carrier of meaning. Theological language has long pervaded discourse around food. Food is described as sinful, leading 'devotees' into temptation when they indulge in guilty pleasure. Emily Contois (2015) demonstrates how religiosity of this kind operates within dieting approaches that are generally considered to be secular. Diet manuals propagate the belief that weight loss requires conversion, sacrifice and commitment, health elevated as a form of salvation achieved through rituals, such as, counting calories, tracking minutes and weighing oneself (Contois 2015: 114). Dieting theology assigns a moral value to food by constructing a dichotomy between 'good' and 'bad' foods and right and wrong ways of living (Baker and Walsh 2018, 2019). Lifestyle gurus draw on the moral dimensions of food by using food imagery and photographs of aesthetically pleasing subjects to stand in for moral virtue and character.

Social media sites, such as Instagram, prioritise the visual by documenting social life in photo and video form. The image has an overriding influence in shaping belief over textual advice. Lifestyle gurus capitalise on this using a series of carefully constructed and highly edited photographs to document their health journey and support their claims (Baker and Walsh 2018). The accessibility of social media, combined with the lack of regulation online, means that in principle anyone can claim expertise in lifestyle matters. Diplomas can be purchased on the internet, as can likes, comments and followers on social media (see Chapter 3). The way social media sites are engineered means that credibility is based more on metric-driven status (e.g. likes, followers) and attractiveness rather than qualitative data. After all, who is more persuasive, a slim attractive influencer explaining that she achieved dramatic weight loss by avoiding gluten or a dietician who proposes a diet based on consistency and moderation? Lifestyle gurus promise simple solutions to complex problems, using the image to provide instant evidence. The emphasis on the image has been accentuated by social media; it did not carry the same weight in the text-based lifestyle manuals of Smiles, Beecher and Beeton. In this regard, social media and digital devices shape our understanding of social life and ourselves in it. It is not that the power of the image is new – people have been influenced by imagery for centuries and many of those who appear healthy in person could be secretly living unhealthy lives; rather these technologies prioritise status and the visual as the central means of communication and are highly susceptible to manipulation through choreography, editing and filters. Moreover, because these technologies give users access to broad social networks, the advice put forward by lifestyle gurus has unprecedented audience reach and impact.

Take, for example, the popular food blogger, Ella Mills (nee Woodward), author of the blog and bestselling cookbook, *Deliciously Ella*. Mills employs the common heroic trope to narrate her journey from illness to self-recovery. In her book, she notes how she 'overhauled her diet and lifestyle', using food to heal herself from a debilitating illness, Postural Tachycardia Syndrome. This involved adopting a plant-based diet and eliminating common food villains; 'saying goodbye to gluten, dairy, refined sugar, processed food, additives and meat' (Woodward 2016: 7). Her advice is instructive; informing readers that 'healthy living has totally transformed my life and I think it will transform yours too' (Woodward 2016: 7). While Mills was formerly known as one of the leading proponents of clean eating – a popular dietary trend based on restricting certain food groups perceived to be unclean and impure – she now distances herself from the movement, stating that foods should not be classified as 'good' or 'bad'. She explains how 'the blog was originally intended to be a personal project, a way to encourage myself to fall in love with plant-based eating and eat as healthy a diet as I could' (Mills 2018), thereby exempting herself from claims that she has encouraged disordered eating. Despite their similarities to diaries and journals, there are key differences in the types of communication that blogs afford. Whereas the former conceives of documentation as the end goal of self-reflection, blogs use documentation as the primary mode of communication with a public audience. The information is designed to be shared with others with sharing inscribed into blogs and social media. When they reach a critical mass, blogs have tremendous influence. In this regard, the information shared online is not inconsequential; it can have significant public reach – Mills herself noting that her blog has had 'over 130 million hits!' (Mills 2018).

Important questions arise here with regard to how authority and influence are constructed online. Much of the research on diet and nutrition is fuzzy, not least because the methods for measuring the effects of diets are confounded by issues of reliability (see Goldacre 2009: 76–80). Evidence-based science requires randomised controlled trials. Nutritional research, conversely, is exceptionally difficult to study due to the inability to produce controlled, long-term research on people's diet and lifestyle. Instead, most studies provide correlations based on animal studies and anecdotal evidence. Lifestyle gurus base their advice on anecdotal evidence, drawing upon personal experience and feelings to support their claims. The triumph of feelings over facts is symptomatic of a 'therapy culture' (Furedi 2003) where feeling good is pursued as an end in itself. This phenomenon is exemplified by the rise of lifestyle gurus as advisers of health and wellness in the place of established expertise, where to have a popular Instagram account comprised of attractive images and likes makes one more trustworthy and credible than a registered doctor or dietician.

Lifestyle gurus occupy a peculiar position where they appeal to scientific knowledge to support their views while at the same time positioning themselves as being an alternative resource located outside of the system and against professional expertise, diagnosis and treatment. This is particularly the case in the field of nutrition where lifestyle gurus promote a range of conflicting diets from veganism and pescatarianism, to the paleo, ketogenic and carnivore diet. The Australian celebrity chef, Pete Evans, recently self-published a paleo cookbook for children, *Bubba Yum Yum, The Paleo Way for New Mums, Babies and Toddlers* (2015), co-authored by blogger

Charlotte Carr and naturopath Helen Padarin. These self-described 'health crusaders' describe their recipes as incorporating 'modern science' together with the 'wisdom of ancient traditions' (invoking the ancient Greek physician, Hippocrates', famous quote, 'Let food be thy medicine'). Books of this kind are positioned against 'conventional' food production practices. While diverse diets label themselves as 'clean' (e.g. vegan, ketogenic or paleo), the clean eating movement is fuelled by a common narrative which constructs modern farming and technology as artificial and impure in relation to an idealised past when food production and consumption was simpler and less refined (Baker and Rojek 2019).

There is good reason for public distrust of the food system. Changing expert opinions regarding dietary guidelines, conflicting dietary advice and the conflict of interest involved in scientific research funding (e.g. studies funded by Kelloggs and Coca-Cola) further erodes public trust in professionals, governments, experts and elites. Distrust of the food industry is particularly high in the US, which has an established history of food industry lobbyists informing dietary guidelines (Baker and Rojek 2019). These feelings of distrust have inspired many consumers to turn towards the internet to search for answers and to take their health into their own hands. It is not surprising that the ethos of individual responsibility thrives in low trust societies. What is surprising is the degree to which deference to the professional expert has been replaced by deference to the lifestyle guru, many of whom advocate lifestyle solutions configured around political and commercial interests.

A prominent example of a contemporary lifestyle guru in the field of nutrition is Vani Hari. The self-proclaimed 'Food Babe', has built a huge social media following around criticising the food industry. Her homepage features a glamorous picture of herself holding a book and a looking glass next to the statement, 'hot on the trail to investigate what's really in your food!' (Hari 2018). Like most successful lifestyle gurus, Hari uses her own personal story of self-transformation through diet and lifestyle change to establish her authority as a lifestyle guru. Her story is supported by visual accounts of weight loss and physical transformation into an ostensibly happier, more glamorous woman. Before and after photos, together with videos documenting 'what I used to look like before the Food Babe Way'; testify as evidence of reasons to 'Join Me!' (Hari 2018) by subscribing to Hari's newsletter and lifestyle philosophy. Hari's mission follows the common theme of empowerment, 'to empower individuals to take back control of their health and become their own food investigator' (Hari 2018). Self-taught – 'I didn't go to nutrition school to learn this. I had to teach myself everything' (Hari 2018) – she describes herself as an 'activist', calling on her followers to join 'the Food Babe Army', alluding to a revolution. Hari's message has reach and influence. Her website boasts that she is a *New York Times* bestseller, who has featured on various global media outlets and was listed by *Time Magazine* as one of the '30 most influential people on the internet' (Hari 2018). She is defined against the system – as 'Public Enemy No 1. of big food companies', 'a crusader for truth', 'a modern-day David', 'a protector of our health and well-being' and, importantly, as one of 'the people' (Hari 2018). But beneath the language of mateship, 'truth' and support, is a strong commercial incentive. Hari's statement, 'LET ME HELP YOU RIGHT NOW' followed by links to her various products and services: meals plans, sugar detox and juice cleanse programmes, 'how-to guides', affiliate links to supplements and protein powders, and her books, *The Food Babe Way* (Hari 2015), a 21-day plan in diet and lifestyle change, and *Feeding You Lies: How to Unravel to Food Industry's Playbook and Reclaim your Health* (Hari 2019). The food industry has rightly come under criticism. However, alternative approaches have their own political and economic incentives.

There is a commercial incentive behind denigrating expertise. Survey data show that disappointment with mainstream medicine correlates with people seeking alternative therapies (Goldacre 2009: 84). In response to public concerns about mainstream science and medicine, lifestyle gurus present themselves as an alternative source of knowledge. The term 'nutritionist' is an unregistered title (McCartney 2016). Unlike a dietician, a title which requires certified training, anyone can claim to be one. Nutritionists are alternative therapists who brand themselves as scientists (Goldacre 2009). Most appeal to food myths (i.e. pseudoscientific ideas about evolution) and employ common-sense thinking that people intuitively believe to be true: eat more fruit and vegetables, exercise more, reduce alcohol and sugar consumption, and so on. In many cases, however, the advice put forward by lifestyle gurus is misguided and contradictory. For example, 'sugar-free' recipes that include high-sugar substitutes, such as honey, maple syrup, dates and coconut sugar. Advice is itself susceptible to commercial forces with lifestyle gurus promoting 'superfoods' as a panacea and expensive substitutes for sugar, such as agave nectar and coconut sugar, which are metabolised by the body in similar ways to regular sugar yet are much more expensive than other varieties. A case in point are Ella Mills' 'Deliciously Ella Hazelnut and Raisin Balls', which are marketed as a 'vegan friendly', healthy snack despite being comprised mostly of highly concentrated dried fruit (dates and raisins) and containing

43g of sugar per 100g. Advice can also be extreme as exemplified by the celebrity chef, Pete Evans', paleo cookbook for babies.

One example, which has gained recent traction, is the carnivore diet. The carnivore diet requires its adherents to consume only beef, salt and water. It has been promoted for improving autoimmune disorders by a series of bloggers, such as, Shawn Baker and Mikhaila Peterson. While Baker is a doctor, Peterson has no medical or scientific qualifications. Her advice is based primarily on anecdotal evidence. At the age of seven, Peterson was diagnosed with Juvenile Rheumatoid Arthritis. She also experienced autoimmune issues and depression. After years of taking high doses of medication, and undergoing a hip and an ankle replacement caused by joint deterioration from her arthritis, she began an elimination diet to see if she could control her arthritic symptoms. On her blog she explains how 'after a successful elimination diet for one month (and much less scepticism), my arthritis went away. Three months later my depression disappeared. Five months later my fatigue disappeared. I lost thirty pounds. The story is a lot more complicated but that's the gist of it.' In short, Peterson highlights that all of her medical problems were 'diet related' and 'fixable'. This experience is said to give her the credentials not only to document her health journey on a blog, but to offer 30-minute and 60-minute consultations charged at $75.00CAD and $120CAD respectively (Peterson 2018). Peterson neither has medical qualifications nor a bachelor degree, yet the implication is that her native experience and independent research on the topic provides her with the knowledge necessary to inform others about how best to live.

It is likely that Peterson's elimination diet has genuinely assisted her health issues as a consequence of caloric restriction, mimicking the benefits of fasting and preventing food sensitivities by eliminating high allergen foods. She presents her blog more as a mode of documentation than a forum for advice, noting that her 'blog chronicles how my family and my parents eat and what it's done for us'. The problem, however, is that her personal story, whether intended or not, provides a general one-size-fits-all approach to health that others will follow. By virtue of the fact that this information is shared publicly, it is designed to influence. The provocative title of her blog, 'Don't Eat That', and the caption on her Instagram page – 'For info on treating weight loss, depression and autoimmune disorders with diet, check out my blog or fb page!' – reaffirm this message. This advice is not innocuous. People influenced by Peterson are likely to mimic her diet and only consume meat. They may feel better in the short term (mostly due to caloric restriction), but the long-term effects remain unknown. While eliminating gluten or dairy is unlikely to be harmful, extreme dietary changes, such as consuming only meat, can have serious health repercussions. Peterson's approach is not unique, it is part of a genre of lifestyle advice emerging in the blogosphere and social media on nutrition. In essence what these food bloggers share in common is a simplistic understanding of nutrition. Their claims exemplify the ideology or paradigm of 'nutritionism', which is characterised by a 'reductive focus on the nutrient composition of food' as key indicators of health (Scrinis 2008). They provide simple solutions to complex issues, such as nutrition, which often require a nuanced understanding about the interplay between diet, genetics, the microbiome and other variables. In the past, of course, dietary advice could be solicited by friends or family with no expertise, but the key difference is that the internet makes this information available at an unprecedented speed and scale. Some perceive this shift in terms of the democratisation of knowledge where blogs and scientific articles are increasingly made accessible to the broader public. What is often overlooked is that scientific journals are written by experts for experts and experienced practitioners with a deep understanding about the subject. Moreover, these experts are held accountable by the institutions that employ them and the standards of the administering health-related bodies of which they are a part. By contrast, lifestyle gurus occupy a media landscape with little or no regulation.

Regulation and Lifestyle Combing

The protocols for online social exchange are fuzzy (David 2017). In the USA the Telecommunications Act (1996), published during the presidency of Bill Clinton, guaranteed that the internet would not be chained by regulation. Section 230 absolved tech platforms from any responsibility for any material that appeared on them. In the UK, a variety of legislative measures exist to regulate web transactions (e.g. *The Data Protection Act 1998*, *The Disability Discrimination Act 1995*, *E-Commerce Regulations 2002* and the *Companies Act 2008*). Leaving the question of legislative provisions aside, it is in the nature of the worldwide web to prosper and grow beyond the resources of optimal policing. The multiplier effect of online transactions generates statements, passions and opinions at a greater rate than the capacity of independent verification and legitimation to catch up with them. In all of this there is an important 'just in time' quality that needs to be differentiated. The sheer multiplicity and velocity of data exchange on the web contributes to a general sense of living in hiatus, where ordinary rules of certainty and truth are either suspended or do not apply. The words of assured wisdom offered by Smiles, Beecher and Beeton seem obsolete. They belong to a lost era. This is because they enjoin readers to think of their advice and guidance as a sort of secular bible, based in examples and role models from history, unfailingly fit for every type of occasion and challenge. What lifestyle gurus pointedly grasp and convey, is that our world is one of perpetual change and that it is our responsibility to embrace change positively. The fate of the times is to live in a 'liquid world' in which history has, so to speak, dissolved (Bauman 2007). Those who insist in hanging on to the verities of the past risk being left behind.

The data deluge partly reflects real transformations in everyday social life. For example, fifty years ago domestic space required a good deal of physical space for the household hi-fi system and record collection. Now you can carry your entire record collection on a mobile phone in your pocket, However, it is all too easy to get carried away by the metaphor of liquidity and work on the presumption that everything is changing and as a result, all relations are uncertain and ambivalent (Rattansi 2017). To be sure, most lifestyle guru websites make a fetish of living optimistically in the face of change. For example, the Joe Wicks *Body Coach* site describes Joe as 'a man with a mission to rescue people from the awful dieting industry ... I created this plan to educate people and give them the knowledge they need to get a lean, healthy strong body without going hungry' (Wicks 2018). Wicks has become a lifestyle celebrity among his demographic. His bio details list him as having '1 degree in Sports Science', '5 years as a personal trainer', '3 years as an Online Nutrition coach' and achieving '100,000 Client Transformations'. *The Body Coach* site claims that it will take only '90 days to transform your body' (Wicks 2018). The speed and decisiveness with which positive results are guaranteed is not untypical in today's lifestyle guru sites.

Competing for visibility in a saturated attention economy, the programmes for self-transformation offered on most lifestyle guru sites, are calculated to capture public attention by offering accelerated, simple solutions to life's complex problems. Corey Wayne's site in the USA is more exhaustive than *The Body Coach* (Wayne 2018). Wayne describes himself as a coach in 'self reliance and peak performance'. Itemised coaching skills on his website relate to relationships, self-help in the areas of pick-up, dating, seduction, business, health, leadership, goal setting, success, liberty, life, happiness, overcoming challenges, corporate / team turnaround, fulfilment and wealth building (Wayne 2018). It is as if these sites undertake to restore subscribers to factory settings and to reboot them in order to achieve acceptance, approval, social impact and self-validation. Born of the media, they often cultivate an incestuous relationship with the media to enhance their profile and market appeal. For example, Wicks' *The Body Coach* site highlights that it has featured in *The Daily Mail*, *Women's Health*, *Men's Fitness*, *The Times*, *Cosmopolitan*, *Grazia*, *ES Magazine* and *Forever Sports*. The questions of how it has been featured, and what has been written about it, are left blank. What matters in a site dedicated to achieving social impact for subscribers is the gold standard of demonstrable, serious social impact (i.e. to be recognised by the official, institutional media). Recognition slides into approval, acceptance and self-validation without any independent confirmation that this is, what Joe's '100,000 client transformations' have actually achieved. In the online world of the face, face-value is all. In addressing the market for immediate lifestyle challenges, lifestyle websites generally take care to create legacy markets. To rely upon methods of acceptance, approval, social impact and self-validation today that worked perfectly well yesterday, may be to unintentionally cultivate competitive disadvantage. The cult of perfection is a full-time job because the representations and standards of what passes for perfection are comprehended to move ahead at a galloping pace. He who stands still with his secular bible of lifestyle management, is he who will be left behind. Today's consumption of a programme of peak performance carries with it the likely necessity of top-up regimes in the future.

Modernity Again

It goes without saying that much of this was anticipated, and indeed covered, in the nineteenth and twentieth-century debates about the nature of modernity (Frisby 1985). These debates were largely conducted in freedom from the Christian eternal verities that inspired the likes of Smiles, Beecher and Beeton and emboldened them to construct total, assured semi-religious life plans of lifestyle management. In the debate on modernity perpetual movement in technology, medicine and social change was understood to force the necessity to perpetually revise questions of how to *be* among others and *what* to expect from them. Old expectations about roles and lifestyle could no longer be taken on trust. The seizure in social consciousness by what Baudelaire, in *The Painter of Modern Life* (1848, tr. 1986), called 'the transitory', 'the fugitive' and 'the contingent', changed the rhythm and cadence of life with others (Frisby 1985: 2). The observation, and general acceptance, of the transitory, fugitive and contingent nature of our deepest inner convictions stimulates the senses, disturbs stultifying, encrusted features of normative order. One aspect of this highlighted in the debate around modernity is that life was interpreted as growing more 'abstract and advanced' (Simmel [1918] 2010: 3). Thus, for many years, the man in the street assumed that only professionals really knew and understood what is going on in the world. The ideology of professionalism exploited and developed this popular perception. It decreed that the monopoly over authoritative, scientific knowledge and application demanded certifiable competence. In turn, this required regimented training in specialised, certified reserves of objective knowledge, open testing and the development of a language that constantly reminded others of the complexity involved in the life issues that professionals dealt with, and the precision and objectivity required to express things accurately and correctly (Hawkins and Shohet 2012; Elliott 2014).

Today, two factors coalesce to erode professional authority. In the first place, on many fronts, from the economy to the environment, from schooling to legislation, from diplomacy to well-being, professionals are deemed to have got many things wrong. For example, recently globalisation and cosmopolitanism, in particular, have explicitly emerged as examples of so-called professional myopia and error (Nichols 2017). Hundreds and thousands of people in the North American rust belt and the industrial Northern cities of the UK, lost their jobs as home-grown businesses exploited cheaper labour markets in the developing world. Enhanced investment in North American and Western European economies in the knowledge, information and service sectors resulted in an influx of skilled migrant labour. Added to this was an incoming stream of unskilled and semi-skilled labour, that had either been displaced from internal conflicts in external countries, or were striking out on their own journeys of self-discovery and self-improvement. In the European Union, the volume of refugees from strife-ridden Syria threatened to overwhelm the welfare system. In member states the pressure on local and national labour markets and welfare services was intensified by the migration of significant numbers of workers from Eastern Europe following the *Treaty of Accession* (2005). An increase of supply of labour, often unskilled or semi-skilled, drove down wage rates. Domestic workers, who for decades had just got by, now found themselves being out-priced by foreign workers willing to accept lower wages for the same work. In these circles, professionals were now defined as part of the problem rather than the solution (Nichols 2017). Likewise, professional advice on health, environment, child rearing, financial investment and many other matters, central to the quality of life, have been judged by the court of popular experience, to be frequently threadbare. Moreover, scandals in the fields of science and technology, whether due to negligence or corruption, contributed to people's growing distrust of experts and elites (Beck 1992). All of this is anticipated in the classic debate on modernity.

In answer to Hegel's philosophy, which portrayed the world as the unfolding of spirit towards a state of serene maturity, Adorno characterised the world as imprisoned in the contradictions of what he called, 'negative dialectics' (Adorno 1990, 2008). Whereas Hegel envisaged the world as moving towards wholeness and stability, Adorno pictures it as spinning in perpetual fragmentation and endless division. The advice put forward by today's lifestyle gurus confirms Adorno as the victor of these competing views of world history. In Hegels' famous view of the necessity of rule by reason, thesis produced antithesis and evaluation of the two culminated in synthesis – the resolution of conflict. Against this, Adorno's negative dialectics portray a world in which thesis and antithesis proliferate without end. The modern condition is to live without synthesis. This is of course, a major reason why lifestyle gurus currently thrive. They purport to offer solutions to problems that are psychologically experienced as intractable and overwhelming. This is reinforced by the popular sentiment that fragmentation and division in the world is now moving into a higher stage of unprecedented complexity and acceleration. It is as though professionals have been stranded by the sheer speed of change and the unexpected, practical lifestyle problems of vulnerability, isolation and confusion that have accrued like tumbleweed in the backdraft. Moreover, what renders them most fallible is their insistent, unapologetic adhesion to science as the jewel of knowledge and practice. The antinomies and failures of science have opened the lid on non-scientific resources. Folkways, religion and faith in self-reliance have, in particular, emerged as ways of bringing light to bear upon personal problems. As such, it is no wonder that lifestyle gurus seize and exploit a wide popular demand for support and guidance, which utilises what is instrumental in science but shows a willingness to enter into the realm of non-scientific resources to find their way forward.

This brings us to the second point, on which we have already briefly touched. The monopoly power of professionals has been compromised (although not caused) by social media and the *digital data deluge*. By this term we mean an over supply of conflicting data that exceeds the capacity of human consciousness both to absorb and resolve (Nichols 2017). The result is a widespread sentiment that life today is burdened by constant back-peddling against a torrent of information that creates discontinuity between the land-ho of professional certainty and the perfect storm of random, discordant, unstable, inhospitable, churning data. The data deluge made available on the internet conspires against the power and mystique of professionals in various ways. It has subjected professional authority to a pincer movement. On one side, the quasi-monopoly power of professional knowledge and modes of application are checked by lay alternatives; on the other, the velocity of social change means that no sooner than articulated, the wisdom of professionals in response to the new, altered circumstances becomes outmoded. Surplus data increase the supply of information and make professional expertise look like navel-gazing. Professional authority has not been unseated. It is not the case that lay alternatives have universally risen to replace them. Rather, the data deluge has imbricated all aspects of life with, as it were, a permanent second opinion.

Deference and obedience were previously heralded as the appropriate responses among people who had little or no knowledge about a particular subject, against professionals and experts who proceeded on the basis of having superior, objective, certified scientific standing. The data deluge stands this conventional, accustomed way of thinking upon its head. People may know nothing, or next to nothing, about a particular subject. But the sheer volume and torrent of data on the internet provides them with the right to have an opinion on virtually everything. All of this has made the adventure of self-discovery more urgent and essential. For the effect of modern life has been to turn the self into *a city of fragments*. In a world where the volume and velocity of data would have astounded our ancestors in the days of Smiles, Beecher and Beeton, there is more chance of staying afloat and being carried forward, if the self is viewed and experienced positively as changing fragments rather than a solid body of weight and *gravitas*. Against Smiles, Beeton and Beecher, self-discovery is not about building a permanent, solid self fit for all purposes. Rather, in line with the discourse of Oprah and Stewart, it is about creating an outlook on personal life, that is always open and provisional. Data from *The Body Coach*, Corey Wayne's 'self-reliance and peak performance' platform, and similar sites, are presented and perceived as helping one stay afloat and swim against the tide. In contrast, the lapidary advice provided by Samuel Smiles, Catharine Beecher and their ilk, is now regarded as all that one needs to sink like a stone.

The Scuttling of Democracy?

All of these factors combine to threaten expert knowledge and modes of application with latent mistrust and perpetual scrutiny (Nichols 2017). Social media has enabled citizens to monitor and challenge elite power. As a result, some commentators claim that representative democracy is undergoing an epochal transformation (Runciman 2018). The traditional, cyclical order of representative democracy has been scuttled. Voters are no longer comfortable for representatives to speak for them. Social media equips them with the apparatus to have their own say. Digital society multiplies power-monitoring and power-contesting mechanisms that supplement and, in some cases, surpass the official electoral process. That is, a form of democracy in which power is being massively decentred, away from majority rule / representative assemblies in favour of mobile, liquid networks of popular opinion able to disperse and regroup rapidly. Technology is central to this process, but the uses to which it is being put reflect important historical changes in the composition of Western democracy. John Keane uses the term 'monitory democracy' to pinpoint the issue (2009: 585–839). Monitory democracy is the system of plebiscitary government in the age of trans-national human rights watch, progress and development organisations, founded in the ideals of good governance, social inclusion and justice. Keane uses the adjective 'monitory' to describe this stage of democracy because he wishes to highlight its watchful, judgemental, borderless nature. Samantha Power (2013), who responds fully to the logic of civilisation and watchfulness, argues that it is not just transnational organisations that need to scan the world and be prepared to intervene in cases of human rights abuse, it is also a responsibility of mature liberal democratic states and civilised citizens to do so. The United Nations 'World Summit' (2005) seized upon this line of thought and codified it in the famous 'Responsibility to Protect' (R2P) Statement. This document decreed that all signatories to UN membership had the responsibility to ensure that their citizens are protected from four threats of *genocide, war crimes, ethnic cleansing* and *crimes against humanity.* The Statement calls upon 'the international community' to take responsibility to pre-empt or eliminate the same four threats by means of direct action (Haas 2018: 115–16). Leaving aside the enhanced foreign-policy duties to intervene in the affairs of 'faulty' states, R2P unambiguously makes every civilised citizen of the mature democracies a world citizen, conscious and willing to 'make a change' in the lives of the oppressed and physically threatened. Logically, this is based upon having at least a minimal opinion about human rights abuses and the uses and misuses of power. The data deluge is fit for this purpose.

The new stage of democracy to which we are alluding, might be called *post-monitory democracy*. It is attached to many of the same goals of monitory democracy, but technological innovation has overturned the codes and authority of the institutions that marked this anterior stage. What is involved is a decentring of power from Parliament, the state and associated trans-national bodies to anyone who can afford and use a digital communication device. Lifestyle citizenship does not need a voting booth. Rather it is a life issue which is increasingly politically honed to best effect in online data gathering and exchange. Human rights issues and civil injustice is brought out of the court room, the Senate and the television studio and turned over to the smartphone and tablet. It does not require a leap of imagination to see how these changes reflect and reinforce the growth of lifestyle gurus who view it as their responsibility to intervene positively in general life issues. We have noted that most lifestyle guru sites are not explicitly political in the sense of following party politics. However, the positive lifestyle citizenship issues that form their staple fare have obvious political dimensions. Lifestyle citizenship is fundamentally DIY Citizenship (Ratto and Boler 2014). That is to say, it bypasses the system of representative, electoral politics and demands that citizens become carpenters of their own lives. This does not take the form of organising and mobilising to replace one political system with another. Rather, emblematic of the general drive towards 'privatising' and 'personalising' civic and political concerns (Chouliaraki 2013), the unity between the personal and political today is more concerned with keeping constantly and openly informed, being watchful and cultivating an optimistic 'can do' attitude in respect of literally, anything that might come up. For some, this constitutes a qualitative extension of the public sphere (Castells 2012). As is perhaps well-known, in the sociology of Jürgen Habermas (1962), the public sphere refers to a public space wherein individuals exchange information and by means of rational debate eventually achieve consensus. Of course, Habermas recognised that within the public sphere power differences between groups potentially obstruct undiluted democracy. For cyber-optimists, the qualitative leap made available by the technology of digital society is the deliverance of meaningfully networked public sphere. Under it, potentially, the entire globe is embraced and empowered. The fragments of humanity that were notionally championed under monitory democracy are now able to speak directly for themselves. In the course of this, popular understanding of awareness and agency has been reconfigured. Local and national issues no longer set the boundaries of what citizens may meaningfully address.

The logic of populism means that individuals can play an energetic part in this without actually being conversant with the complexities of the social problems and remedies that they absorb and exchange. The general ethos calls upon everyone to become an active, conscious and meaningful citizen. The 'can do' ethos of 'making a difference' and accepting the responsibility of 'acting for positive change' at the level of international relations finds its parallel in everyday self-management transactions. For, where better to start making a difference than a positive life change that combines DIY research with the lifestyle guru guidance? In the struggle to cope with the common problems thrown up by an ever-changing world there is a certain native wisdom in choosing to fall back on your own common sense and the lifestyle advice of people who appear to be just like you. The lifestyle networks that have emerged in the last ten to fifteen years are redolent of this way of thinking about the self, and about personal responsibility. Despite the progressive capacities of the internet enjoined by cyber-optimists, on the whole we agree with those commentators who hold that talk of the dawning age of 'cyber utopia' is massively premature (Fuchs 2014: 201). While in some respects, the internet contributes to positive aspects of post-monitory democracy, it also brings about the blurring between reputable news (based, in principle, on professional accuracy and verification – even though there are cases where this ideal falls short) and amateur outlets with no responsibility for attempting objective truth statements. The current media landscape, coupled with distrust of the news media, has further encouraged the ethos of personal responsibility characteristic of the modern West.

Today, a socially credible subjective orientation to personal well-being and life with others places critical responsibility upon keeping up with the inexorable data deluge and expanding and refining lifestyle citizenship. It is in the nature of the web for information to be de-territorialised and invulnerable to effective jurisdiction. Facts, quasi-facts and off-the-cuff advice are tossed into the data deluge without a sense of amalgamated purpose and direction. In contrast to their nineteenth-century predecessors, such as Smiles, Beecher and Beeton, lifestyle gurus today exploit and develop a just-in-time philosophy on advice and guidance. Today's lifestyle gurus propagate the importance of delivering advice and programmes of social impact and self-validation that are explicitly *au courant*. This befits the widespread sense of living fully and positively at a moment of profound, uncertain change along many fronts. The form and content of their knowledge and practice is categorically different from their nineteenth and twentieth-century predecessors. Were Samuel Smiles, Catharine Beecher and Isabella Beeton alive today, they would doubtless regard websites like Corey Wayne's *Self Reliance and Peak Performance* site to be irresponsible and vacuous. Nineteenth and early twentieth-century writers on lifestyle advice prided themselves on being part of an undertaking of epochal social progress. It is the absence of social progress as a problematic that is deeply revealing about the true character of today's lifestyle guru sites. Categorically speaking, it is one differential characteristic among many. These differences point to a notable shift in the ideological counterparts of twenty-first-century lifestyle guru advice and guidance from the ideology of their historical predecessors.

6

The Two Cults of Lifestyle Perfectionism

Putting aside for the moment the question of the details that significantly differentiate them, what unites nineteenth and early twentieth-century sites of lifestyle advice and guidance with today's counterparts, is *the cult of perfectionism*. By this term, we mean the system of beliefs and practices designed to elicit the best possible version of the self in social interaction. Smiles, Beecher and Beeton were bourgeois missionaries of an exhaustive system of time management, self-regulation and domestic economy that was presented and intended to be consumed as a total, failsafe life-plan of perfectionism. Ultimately, it was based in an ideology of class superiority. The bourgeois class regarded their adhesion to science, and their application of rational principles of life management, to be qualitatively superior to aristocratic precedents and folk alternatives. Their outlook identified the perfection of the self as the key to the wider, and more important goal, of social progress.

Today's lifestyle gurus are more populist. They possess no obvious class ideology. Yet, class remains a fundamental concept to apply in order to understand how they influence and inspire. Lifestyle gurus construct and operate in a lifestyle citizenship ethos in which an imagined, global middle class is encouraged to take on and overcome barriers and threats to personal success, planetary well-being, creating opportunities for young people to succeed. They generate, distribute and monetise advice that users can absorb and apply as cultural capital to fulfil their own ambitions. Lifestyle/DIY citizenship is a response to the alarm widely felt in middle-class circles that normal politics is no longer providing peace, prosperity and progress (Ehrenreich 1989). This approach to lifestyle issues focuses on personal life problems. Tackling challenges is not framed as forbidding or unpleasurable. On the contrary, ludic metaphors of life as a game or a contest for sport predominate. Lifestyle gurus reflect and reinforce the founding principle of lifestyle citizenship, which is that life should be lived gamefully (McGonigal 2016). The challenges and problems they address are presumed to apply to every Western-based intelligent citizen, irrespective of class background or affiliation. Smiles, Beecher and Beeton believed that they were carrying the standard of social progress forward. Generally speaking, today's lifestyle gurus have no interest in bearing such a standard. Instead they assume that the present state of Western society is all that there is, or can be. Since there is no valid alternative in prospect, the action is all about making the most of oneself in the material and historical conditions in which one finds oneself. Hence, the almost complete absence of party political issues in online lifestyle management websites and further, the strength of the invocation to change yourself rather than change society. We have used the term 'ideology' thrice in the foregoing paragraphs of the chapter. As we regard the types of perfectionism we are dealing with here to be twin, contrasting ideologies of self-help, it is perhaps worth stating what is meant by the term. An ideology is an idealised set of ideas and practices referring to freedom, association and optimal behaviour, which operates as the lode star for agency and self-definition. It may be that ideology stops people from doing what they want to do. More commonly it provides the energy for them to do anything at all and, consequently, operates as the back stop to enable them to judge and believe whether what they do is useful or useless, right or wrong. The two systems of perfectionism examined here are understood to be the reflecting pools in which the *Looking-Glass Self* gains substance and freedom to grow from generalised and significant others. So much for preliminaries. We propose to categorise these systems as *assured perfectionism* and *affirmative perfectionism*. Their key characteristics are as follows.

Assured Perfectionism

Assured perfectionism is an approach to the organisation and presentation of the self that is based in principles of psychological rigour, rational organisation and determined, inflexible application. Crucially, it presents itself as a finite, authoritative method of lifestyle planning and intervention that is affixed to the wider goal of social progress. At one and the same time the principles of rigour, rationality and application that are advocated as the means to transform the self are also seen as the same means to transform society. Self-discovery, self-improvement and social progress are understood to go hand-in-hand. In a word, this is lifestyle governance by *rote*. The high-water mark of this regime was in Victorian society. Court Society undoubtedly took a lively interest in the conduct of the population. Encouraging training in military skills as a means of being prepared for war was practised since at least, the days of William the Conqueror (Morris 2016). However, it was not until the eighteenth century, with the emergence and substance of the public sphere, signalled by the elimination of so-called 'rotten boroughs' and the increasing assertiveness of a Parliament consisting of elected, accountable representatives, that emotional life-stuff became an acceptable, regular feature of public discourse and class-based planning (Habermas 1962). The bourgeois public sphere championed the aspirations of freedom and equality. Initially, the separation between state and society presupposed a property qualification. Perhaps mindful of the examples of the American (1776) and French (1789) Revolutions, the aristocracy was only prepared to extend the franchise to men of property. In Britain, the 1832 Reform Act enshrined this principle. Undoubtedly, a new public, with genuine political power was delineated. However, its foundation lay not in education, skill or patriotism, but in property ownership (class membership). In so doing, political reform unintentionally accentuated a sense of grievance among artisan strata and unskilled labourers, who were already, in effect, debarred from formal political culture. In the long run, working-class agitation, organisation and mobilisation extended the franchise to propertyless men and women. The initial extension of the public sphere inalienably presupposed organised, class demarcated closure. The key to being formally acknowledged as having a stake in society did not primarily rest upon demonstrating strong patriotic sentiments, acquiring schooling and recognised qualifications, or anything of that sort. The key was having money that translated into legal property ownership (Calhoun 2012: 128–35). The vote belonged to a minority of property owners, leaving the majority of propertyless, wage labourers without an officially sanctioned say in the conduct of society.

These broad historical brush strokes are necessary because it is our contention that the roots of assured perfectionism overwhelmingly reside in class relations. The rising power of the bourgeois class in the late-eighteenth and early nineteenth centuries created an audience for lifestyle issues regarding marriage, household management, sanitariness, child-rearing, dress, grooming, behaviour in public places, recreation, vice and related intimate and self-image questions. The bourgeoisie saw it as their Christian duty to offer muscular lifestyle advice and guidance to the spendthrift aristocracy and the eligible lower orders. This was of course, not the age of the internet, nor of fully developed professional society. Nonetheless, it was a vibrant, invigorating period of expanding mass communications, debate and, by no means fortuitously, seismic structural change. The perfectionism that was popularised largely through print culture at this time was *assured* because it operated on the assumption that it was exhaustively superior to aristocratic and folk alternatives. For the most part, the agents of awareness that catered to this new audience hailed from similar privileged backgrounds. Writers like Jeremy Bentham, Thomas Malthus, Samuel Smiles and Isabella Beeton wrote from the seat of well-to-do families about respectable, rational, best-life practice. Their property qualifications were an indispensable element in accounting for their audience appeal. Property automatically equipped the new agents of awareness with *gravitas*.

The other side of this coin was that the property franchise was like a lock set to exclude the participation of artisanal strata and unskilled labourers from meaningful participation in the official political process. The historical consequences of this cannot be underestimated. Above all, an alienated, parallel audience, formally disenfranchised from official political culture, and intent upon recognition and empowerment, was created. Contemporary notions of feeling 'left out', 'underestimated' and 'ignored' by civil society have their origins in this political history. Autodidactism and the organised movement for universal, free education, were historically decisive responses to this state of affairs. In the fullness of time, working-class organisation, agitation and mobilisation turned the key that unlocked the bolts of the property franchise. Needless to say, this did not achieve the ideals of individual freedom and inequality integral to the concept of the bourgeois public sphere. The inequalities in wealth, access to networks of social influence and the cognitive division of labour, that made Gramsci's concept of hegemony so compelling in the analysis of social relations in the twentieth century, already obstructed freedom and equality (Gramsci 1971). Even so, working-class action was, eventually, successful in extending the franchise by making it a right of maturity rather than of property. In as much as this is the case, it is legitimate to speak of the 'opening of the public sphere', albeit with the consecutive acceptance that many areas of darkness, most notably with respect to questions of gender, race and religion, were still, so to speak, obscured by the light.

Assured perfectionism was a perspective that the rising bourgeois class developed to assert their new status in public life. This was only tangentially expressed in the advocacy of bodily modesty, cleanliness, exercise and frugality (Springhall 1977; Allen 2005). The *cause célèbre* of assured perfectionism in the sphere of intimate, respectable relations was the control of sexuality. In this regard, an influential text, written by the essayist, William Godwin, was *Political Justice* (1842) – published in the buoyant aftermath of the French Revolution. It elaborated some of the central arguments set out in his *Enquiry Concerning Political Justice* (1793): Godwin, who was a child of the Enlightenment, contends that mankind is infinitely perfectible. As befits the public mood of the time, his analysis identifies class inequality as a core issue in overcoming the imperfection of society. A major precondition of perfectibility, declares Godwin, is the equitable distribution of private property. This is because true individual freedom and common justice depend upon redistributive justice. To some, for whom money remained closest to self-interest, this revisionist suggestion was deemed to touch quite closely enough upon matters of intimacy! Nonetheless, Godwin's ideas about human perfectibility did not stop with questions of money and property; they encompassed the topic of the moral regulation of sexual behaviour. He holds that perfectibility requires the restraint of carnal appetite. To his way of thinking, the achievement of equality and justice is within the grasp of mankind. The one large and immutable caveat is that the population of the world must not be permitted to out-run the fecundity of the Earth's productive resources. According to Godwin, should this condition come to pass, equality, justice and the cause of perfectibility must be fatally compromised. For it would mean that an insufficiency of the world's surplus is available in relation to the demands of a rising population. Godwin's conclusion is that lifestyle must be made subject to class-based, dutiful, morally informed, benevolence in order to pursue the perfection of mankind. It is impossible to ignore the prototypical of lifestyle guru-ship in these sentiments.

Godwin's ideas were famously seized upon and countered by a cleric and gentleman scholar, Thomas Malthus (1798). Again, as with Godwin, the unlicensed, 'native' character of the lifestyle advice that Malthus imparts is striking. His contribution became so widely celebrated that it eventually entered the language as a collective noun: Malthusianism. Malthus' argument combines elements of science with folklore and moral sanctimony. It holds that two unalterable laws define the human condition. Firstly, food and drink are necessities for survival. Secondly, sexual passion is an unavoidable fact of human existence. To Malthus' way of thinking, in the course of human history, especially in the industrial era, the two are unequivocally at odds with one another. In the long run, agriculture must struggle to keep pace with population explosion. Famously, he formulates the tension in mathematical terms. Population growth, if unchecked, increases by *geometric* ratio, while agricultural subsistence is bound by *arithmetic* ratio. Partly, Malthus' target was Godwin's utopianism. Specifically, he was concerned to demonstrate that redistributive justice is folly. However well-intentioned it might be, the result will merely be to augment numbers in the lower orders, doomed to live in conditions of want and misery which will, in turn, be a threat to the order of society. Worse, Malthus submits that privation must be expected to lead to moral decline, since the remedy to want and misery among the non-eligible lower orders is inevitably, vice.

Both Godwin and Malthus are writing about the requirement to develop a prudent, rational sexual lifestyle as a precondition of effective moral rectitude. Long before the phrase was coined, they fully appreciated that 'the personal is political' (Halmos 1978). Applying very different, inimical rationales, they favoured delayed marriage as the means to optimise the relationship between the population and scarce resources. Their ideas attracted a vast readership. Godwin counted among his readers, Wordsworth, De Quincey and Coleridge (Thompson 1993: 14). The works of Godwin and Malthus influenced how their readers thought about planning for life, motivation, rational and irrational customs and conduct. What more basic life plan could there be than one that offered advice and guidance on when to get married, how many children to have and how to invest surplus resources? Such were understood to be the fundamental matters of self-discovery and self-improvement. But in both cases their central arguments depended less upon sophisticated knowledge and accurate comprehension than upon common or garden prejudice. There was no verifiable or tested basis to Godwin's proposition that mankind is infinitely perfectible. Equally, Malthus' grand proposition that population proceeds by 'geometric ratio' while agriculture obeys 'arithmetic ratio' blithely ignored the experiments in crop rotation, seeding and irrigation that were improving agricultural productivity in his own day. Yet upon these grounds, elaborate moral philosophies of virtue signalling, that conditioned and regulated social behaviour were nurtured and allowed to flourish. Godwin and Malthus differed in their advice on lifestyle planning and practice. But the authoritarian nature of their philosophies derived in large part from the conviction to which each held fast, namely that to deviate from the lifestyle path that they outlined would to lead to perdition and ruin. They were offering fixed, total, finite principles of rational lifestyle planning and practice that were intended to be applied rigorously and inflexibly respected. There is hardly any provision for collaboration or dialogue with their audience in their respective narratives. In summary, notational form then, the main features of the doctrine of assured perfectionism may be represented thus:

1. A class-based ideology of self-improvement and social progress based in the resources of scientific knowledge and rational principles of planning.
2. A system of total life governance dedicated to moving towards the perfection of the species that beheld itself to be superior to aristocratic precedents and proletarian alternatives.
3. An exhaustive approach to life's secular questions that appealed to Christian doctrine for its ultimate authority.
4. An ideology of progress that regarded folk ways and folk knowledge as backward-looking and defective when set against the example of science.
5. A philosophy of knowledge that operated with a division between professional and lay strata and insisted that the summit of knowledge and practice lay in the hands of certified scientific experts and professionals.
6. An attitude to lifestyle management which advocated a rote-practice alignment to dealing with life's issues, with the proviso that revolutions in the paradigms of scientific knowledge and professional methods would always require rote-alignment to be adapted to ever improving benchmarks.

Affirmative Perfectionism

Remnants of the ideology of assured perfectionism are to be found in the advice and guidance schedules of today's lifestyle gurus. For example, the notion that personal life can be totally turned around by pedagogy and practice; the idea that lifestyle management connects up with acceptance, approval, social impact and self-validation; the conviction that it is the duty of all in life to get the most out of oneself, are common ground; and the implication that to ignore neighbourly advice is to flirt with perdition and die unnoticed. All the same, the differences are obvious and full of meaning.

Most obviously, the ideology of affirmative perfectionism is not overtly class based. Elitism is spurned in the attack on professional power. The cultivation of an ideology, which places wellness celebrities and micro-celebrities on the same playing field as their followers, is the antithesis of class. Gwyneth Paltrow's lifestyle site, *goop*, does not situate her as morally, economically or politically *better* than her followers. Though perceived to be aspirational, it contrives to assemble the impression that she is just like you: interested in what works, suspicious of received professional opinion and, above all, vulnerable. This may be deluded. We have already noted that lifestyle / DIY citizenship can be best understood as filtered though middle-class values and beliefs (see pp. 29, 123, 148). Be that as it may, the face that affirmative perfectionism shows to the world is beyond class and status. Moreover, the tone of affirmative perfectionism is strategically dialogic. It acknowledges that the activism of self-transformation draws on a plethora of resources rather than a single, authoritative voice representing a fixed, concrete, unimpeachable system of rote-alignment. So far from this being the case, it is striking that lifestyle guru sites that espouse affirmative perfectionism are based in the doctrine that true believers must be prepared to forsake all that they hold to be firm and sacred and replace it with a willingness to respond in alert ways to the ever changing circumstances of the world in which we are situated. Self-knowledge and self-development are presented as a process of contingent, experimentation and trial and error, rather than submitting to an unvarying catechism of lifestyle management and rote learning. In addition, a more wary attitude is cultivated with respect to the value of scientific knowledge, the rule of reason and the formations of professionals and experts encamped around them. The conflation of self-improvement with organised social progress that characterised nineteenth and early twentieth-century perspectives, is almost entirely absent. Smiles, Beecher, Beeton and their ilk, presented knowledge of lifestyle management as an evolutionary benefit rooted in the best practice of role models from the past and scientific know-how. In contrast, today's lifestyle gurus have virtually no historical perspective, and utilise an eclectic, selective, instrumental, pragmatic approach to science. The idea of Lifestyle Citizenship to which they are attached sees social change much more in terms of a 'demonstration effect' rather than mobilisation, organisation and protest. That is, developing an optimistic, positive, informed outlook on life which makes a virtue of eclecticism and barrierless knowledge, will, by reason of its glamour and apparent optimal input into goal achievement, encourage others to join the adventure. Interestingly, the volume and velocity of information in the data deluge encourages today's lifestyle gurus to emphasise the provisionality of knowledge over supposed everlasting systems of lifestyle management. Whereas the science of life that Smiles, Beecher and Beaton thought they had discovered enabled them to claim to be building a new Jerusalem, today's lifestyle gurus see change as omnipresent and contingent. Affirmative perfectionism calls upon followers to be alert and self-critical. Resting upon your laurels is fatal. The future is to accept your role in life as a small, mobile, alert, intelligent unit who can make a difference. Revealingly, a common motivation for turning to lifestyle advice and guidance is designated in the notion of a crisis in the life course. Nineteenth and early twentieth century advisers portrayed lifestyle guidance as part of the cycle of maturation in an intelligent individual and a civilised society i.e. it is a normative part of growing up. Today's lifestyle gurus are more likely to encourage their audience and subscribers to turn to their pedagogy and methods to solve an immediate crisis – a dislocation in the life course or an urgent anxiety about arrested development in the business of achieving acceptance, approval, social impact and self-validation.

One concept that helps to bring all of this together in the outlook and approach of contemporary lifestyle gurus is the *Reset*. Directly or implicitly this is very common in lifestyle guru websites that espouse affirmative perfectionism. It refers to the conscious, planned, dedicated reversal of personal convictions and traits of behaviour that obstruct and hinder affirming oneself to the utmost in order to achieve acceptance, approval, social impact and self-validation. The Reset wipes the slate of negative thanking and bad practice clean. History is neutralised and replaced with the invitation to start again with a new slate, but, of course, with the added bonus to hand of the lifestyle programme that leads the way to peak performance. The Reset presents itself as the means to allow people who have broken wings to join the race, take wings and fly.

Additionally, breaking the cycle requires 'the Decisive Act'. That is an act that commits to change one's lot by deliberately discarding the obstacles and clutter in one's life-history that are blocking self-affirmation and unlocking the real you. By implication, sites insinuate that those who lack the courage to take the decisive act are doomed to teach people only to repeat the same mistakes. They will never be able to soar into the light. A corollary of the lifestyle guru's decisive act which turned things around in their own lives is the expectation that followers and subscribers will be persuaded to walk in line and eventually find their own ways forward. The online promulgation of the Decisive Act is meant to elicit imitation on the part of subscribers which, needless to add, is generally sealed by a cash transaction to access start up programmes and up-dates. For example, Sue Stone's bio on her website describes her as hitting a low point in which she once only had '£10 left in her purse' and felt 'depressed', 'desperate' and 'full of fear' (Stone 2018). From this nadir, through an inspirational combination of will power, positive thinking and hard-headed self-analysis she achieved 'an incredible life transformation' and is now 'totally at peace, happy, financially free and a TV secret millionaire' (Stone 2018).

By subscribing to Sue's lifestyle programme, subscribers are invited to take the same adventure. Stone's website is one of the few to explicitly offer help to the unemployed. Yet, the probability is that online sites are particularly attractive for low income groups who are keen to catch the adventure of becoming happy, positive and achieving well-being, but lack the money to make a programme of expensive appointments with private professionals. Stone's site reinforces the message that is universal in online life coaching sites: anyone can be happy and fulfilled if only one has the guts to take the *Decisive Act* and *Reset* one's life.

In similar vein, Johnny Wimbrey's website includes access to podcasts with titles like, 'Born To Win', 'Jump into the Wealth Development Club', 'I Mastered a Failure But Look at Me Now' (Wimbrey 2018). His online bio describes him as an 'incredible rags-to-riches story' who 'transformed his life from poverty and abandonment into wealth and opportunity'. Moving on, Stella Frances' site describes her as once being desperately trapped in the rat race, 'juggling family responsibilities and an unwanted divorce' and suffering from 'fibromyalgia, chronic fatigue and heavy depression' (Frances 2018). 'Eventually', she continues, 'stress and exhaustion caught up with me. One day at work I just collapsed. When I was driven home that day, I had no inkling that I would ever return.' From this low point, the healing process started with some difficult questions: 'How could I have failed so miserably? How did I get myself here and, more importantly, how could I get myself out?' (Frances 2018). The Reset and Decisive Act that turned a 'breakdown into a breakthrough' was achieved by positive thinking, 'programming' and developing 'a system based on the laws of life and the principles of success'. All of these sites utilise the archetypal myth of the hero's journey from adversity to triumph and serenity. They seek to replace complexity and ambiguity (Stella Frances refers to 'the mind's negative chatter box'), with boldness and simplicity of manner and purpose. Tacitly, the courage to make the leap into managed self-discovery is presented as sorting out the successful from the sheep. It as if the registration of on-site interest automatically makes one different and special. For it proves the questing spirit which is, in the end, the engine of self-validation, self-improvement and the attainment of social impact.

Not all motivational sites employ the technique of self-narrated crises and the archetypal myth of the hero's journey. Others draw on a collection of self-narrated *vitae* listing enviable backgrounds of success that magnanimously, they want to share with subscribers. For example, Penelope Trunk's site lists her as playing professional volleyball, before studying English at Grad School, then working for software companies, founding her own start ups, writing columns for Business 2.0 magazine, before moving on to create a platform offering advice on how to create 'happy enduring relationships', 'make money selling your ideas' and 'open doors and change the world' (Trunk 2018). Similarly, John Assaraf's (2018) site comes with the strapline, 'Train Your Brain to Change Your Life'. In his online bio he describes himself as 'a self-made multi-millionaire, international bestselling author … (who has) built five multi-million-dollar companies in real estate, internet software, business coaching and brain research'. What worked for Assaraf is presented as achievable by any subscriber, if only they have the courage (and money) to subscribe. Gary Vaynerchuk's site describes him as 'a serial entrepreneur' and CEO of *VaynerMedia* (Vaynerchuk 2018). He 'rose to prominence after establishing "one of the first commerce wine sites *Wine Library*"'; he founded a new publishing company 'started after acquiring leading women's lifestyle property PowWow', and is a partner in the athletes representation agency *VaynerSports* (Vaynerchuk 2018). Vaynerchuk's site reproduces a common motif in lifestyle sites dedicated to supplying programmes to achieve success in life. Namely, it conflates physical, bodily fitness with fitness to scale in the business world and win.

The differences between assured perfectionism and affirmative perfectionism are now emerging in sharper relief. Assured perfectionism addressed able people who wanted to improve themselves by means of science and rational lifestyle management. In contrast, the foundational principle of the ideology of affirmative perfectionism is that most people are victims. Subscribers fall into two markets, two camps. Either they are designated as damaged people who need a full body–mind Reset, or they are under-achievers who need the example of success leaders to move to the next level. Instead of succumbing to futile, self-indulgence of willed failure, the ideology of affirmative perfectionism offers various strategies of positive thinking and programmes of self-development to climb out of the pit. The aim is to create the most exciting version of you. Sites and platforms dedicated to affirmative perfectionism either dilute or eliminate the hierarchical component found in assured perfectionism. They make hay from advertising themselves as informal, collaborative and empathetic. Symptomatically, 'I'm Your New Best Friend', is the strapline of Veronica Varlow's platform (Varlow 2018). It offers a programme of awakening and change that purports to guide communicants and subscribers back to semi-forgotten 'raw instinctual power' by 'primal and ancient' forms of 'magic', 'sacred ceremony', 'tantra' and 'fourth-generation initiatives' (Varlow 2018). Throughout, the process is presented as participatory, egalitarian, enabling, interactive, ludic and dialogic: 'We're not about preaching or judging, we're about exploring and conversing. This isn't a monologue, it's a dialogue', explains Kardashian's lifestyle site, *Poosh* (2019). By this means the communicator stands to learn as much from the digital transaction as the communicant.

In addition to making a virtue of dialogic exchange, affirmative platforms generally self-present as being located, and working, outside the system. Rather than looking up to professionals or falling back upon resources of kith and kin, they typically assume, either directly or indirectly, that to use Stella Frances' pitch, the hand of life has dealt them superior knowledge of 'the laws of life' (Frances 2018). One case that usefully illustrates the quality of knowledge exchange and the play on emotions above reason involved here, are the Twitter and YouTube accounts of the Canadian transgender vlogger, Julie van Vu (Princess Jules). The site content addresses medical/ surgical transition and beauty/ make up issues from the standpoint of activism and advocacy. It also combines this material with commercial objectives. Who can disagree that Vu's site is exemplary in focusing on personal transformation as a goal? However, while self-realisation and self-transformation are taken as givens, self-reliance is treated as intrinsically provisional and constantly subject to additional qualification. The site works with the 'just in time' principle that is so characteristic of the ideology of affirmative perfectionism. The surgical, transitional and beauty applications that the site promotes are portrayed as a renewable, lifelong processes. Because of this, the site has been criticised for promoting 'explicit self-commodification' (Raun 2018). Transgender, online networker's have hitherto, generally prioritised advocacy and activist elements over commercial considerations (Raun 2018). By and large, they have been at pains to snub corporate advertising or endorsement fees in advice relating to surgical, transition and beauty/ makeup issues, on the grounds that monetisation compromises the authenticity and sincerity of intimate exchange.

The majority of transgender platforms are no different to the majority of lifestyle guru sites. They operate on the principle of presumed intimacy (Rojek 2016). As with any type of deliberate human action, presumed intimacy involves goal-setting and the mobilisation of energy. Recently, the concept of *affective labour* has gained currency to describe the combination of energy and goals involved in monetised intimate relations. The main characteristics of the concept are accessibility, availability, confidence, co-presence, affinity, informality and trust (Hardt 1999; Gregg 2009). In transgender lifestyle networks, Vu's site is controversial because it breaks with convention by monetising advice and intimacy. The affective labour that she offers on her site begins with the acknowledgement of vulnerability and complicity. Communicants are presented with accounts of what has worked for Vu in the surgical and transitional challenges that she has faced. However, the communication process does not advance very far, before communicants are implored to become subscribers. The credit/debit card is the gateway to getting the complete Reset on what works to the uppermost, in transgender surgery, transition and cosmetics. On Vu's site this is apparent in two respects. Firstly, she tries to generate financial capital by submitting to sell product reviews and accepting sponsored videos. Secondly, she utilises some of the familiar means of persuasion adopted in Celebrity Society to generate *attention capital* for herself. In nakedly combining considerations of financial and cultural capital, Vu's site confirms the premonitory remarks made by Senft about the general tendency of directional drift in social media platforms (Senft 2008, 2013).

If we might take the liberty of expressing this drift in the shape of a general law it would amount to this: Wheresoever social media, theresoever the impetus to shape attention capital into a brand with pecuniary potential. The steps in this process are, first, the construction of a public persona (micro-celebrity) to generate attention capital, and second the purposive interaction with communicants with the goal of social and economic gain (Page 2012: 181). In the course of this, online identity transmogrifies into a branded commodity (Senft 2013: 346). The consequences are as follows: Affective labour becomes monetised; full platform access carries an entry price; and the brand becomes strategically positioned, on a global level, as a revenue source. If the first motivation behind fame is attention, the second acceptance, branding marks the third, and is a step into outright accumulation. In taking these steps, affirmative lifestyle gurus end up becoming part of the very system that they proclaim to abhor and reject.

Sites of affirmative perfectionism generally emphasise the ordinary characteristics of the lifestyle communicator. Life coaches are just regular guys or girls. Except they are not like your family or friends, and certainly not like stuffy, toffee-nosed professionals, who otherwise advise about lifestyle planning and management issues. For example, 'entrepreneur, writer, philanthropist and unshakeable optimist dedicated to helping you', Marie Forleo, describes herself as 'a born and raised Jersey girl' (Forleo 2018). This suggests an ordinary background. In fact, before taking an online training course that enabled her to become a life coach and motivational speaker, Forleo was a trading assistant on the floor of the New York stock exchange and went on to work for the elite magazines, *Gourmet* and *Mademoiselle*. This work *cv* surely puts a dampener on her contrived online image as a plain old 'Jersey Girl'. Her passion for 'seemingly unconnected things' suggests a wary outlook of specialised knowledge with its time-consuming accoutrements of deep study, long periods of training and careful, balanced adjudication and the sober process of making plausible connections. Instead, she privileges instinct, fun, gaming, eclecticism, and emotion in determining what is useful in lifestyle and intimate relations. Thus, she is upfront about being 'passionate' about 'writing, hip-hop, psychology, entrepreneurship, creativity, spirituality, fitness and philanthropy' without, of course, offering herself up as an expert in any one of them (Forleo 2018). As such, inchoate, seemingly confusing experience is presented as a strength, not a liability. Parenthetically, it fits with the times. Her site again, insists that it is located firmly outside the system. 'I coined the term "Multi-Passionate Entrepreneur,"' explains Forleo, 'because I just didn't (and never will) fit into a conventional box' (Forleo 2018). Contrarily, the lead products in her blogshop are an eight-week online business course called 'B-School' (advertised as 'the world's best online business school for modern entrepreneurs')' 'The Copy Cure', a copywriting course that 'connects from the heart and cuts through the noise having the power to sell anything'; and her 'bestselling book', 'Make Every Man Want You' (Forleo 2018). It is tricky to see how the strategy and programme of self-revelation and self-transformation for sale here, connects up with not fitting 'into a conventional box'. On the contrary, the goals of market success and sexual stereotyping would seem to be devotedly conformist. If there is any note of dissent about them it is that Forleo presents them as adjuncts of her micro-celebrity. The attention capital that she generates for herself through her platform, provides the associative glamour for her communicants to follow (and buy) the lifestyle strategies, activities and commodities advertised in her blog and blogshop.

Likewise, lifestyle influencer and self-proclaimed 'spirit junkie', Gabby Bernstein's platform is also heavily dependent upon achieving glamorous attention capital for herself as a means of attracting an audience (Bernstein 2018). Echoing Oprah's mission for happy living, her strapline is 'Become the happiest person you know' (Bernstein 2018). Again, the clear inference here is that most of her subscribers do not see themselves as happy, or at least believe that they deserve to be more happy. The victimhood motif is plainly insinuated. Her online bio describes Gabby as a *New York Times* 'bestselling author'; featured turn on Oprah Winfrey's *SuperSoul Sunday*; and named by *The New York Times* as 'a role model', and expert in Kundalini yoga and student in 'Transcendental Meditation, as taught by the *David Lynch Foundation*' (Bernstein 2018). It is noteworthy that the site's measure of substantive success is its recognition by institutional media. Bernstein's online shop offers a wide range of merchandise for sale including online courses on 'The Secret to Living a Better Life', 'Transform Fear into Faith', 'Finally Full', 'Turn on Your Inner Light' and 'The Art of Manifesting'. The particulars of what subscriber's need to affirm, and what exactly is missing in their lives, are liquid. Instead, the foreground is upon the traffic lights of being recognised, standing out, making social impact.

The Gabby Bernstein and Marie Forleo Web 2.0 blogshops, suggest product lines that stridently proclaim that anything is possible for those willing to throw their hat into the ring and take the chance of discovering their true self. Instead of deep, systematic thought, they offer the virtue of immediately energising oneself and following the rule of purposeful, liquid activism. The attention capital aspect of these lifestyle sites is a crucial factor in explaining their attraction. Lifestyle gurus and blogshops offer the experience of 'vicarious consumption' and 'emulation' (Abidin 2018). They offer consumption as an extension of empowerment. The tension, that they do not satisfactorily resolve, is that they perpetuate the commodification of the imagined audience while at the same time promising to free them in a journey of self-discovery and personal autonomy from the gremlins that are holding them back.

The ideology of affirmative perfectionism may be distilled notationally in the following five points:

1. A person-centred programme of self-help centred in drawing out, and articulating, the latent talents and capacities in the self in order to achieve acceptance, approval, social impact and self-validation.
2. A flexible, just-in-time approach to lifestyle management that encourages positive thinking about changing life conditions and challenges.
3. A perspective that makes a virtue of eclecticism in knowledge, practice and method and which is wary of professional privilege.
4. A programme that presents life skills pedagogy in ludic terms as play and, proof that serious things can be learned in fun ways.
5. A perspective that has virtually no interest in organised politics or social progress because the parameters of society are understood to be matters of self-discovery and alert, personal intervention.

Having identified lifestyle gurus with the cult of perfectionism, and differentiated between two versions of perfectionism (the 'assured' and 'affirmative' types), we are moving to the end of our study. In the welter of self-help material that we have considered the message of self-discovery is perhaps ascendant. The payload of nearly all lifestyle guru sites today is that self-discovery holds the strong chance of self-validation, acceptance and approval by others. It is the rosetta stone leading to well-being, contentment and social impact. But this positive gloss disguises the real experience of most of those who are drawn to lifestyle gurus: immediate, localised crisis; a bleak corrosion of confidence; a blockage in aspiration; and, at worst, a fear of powerless submission to an enveloping cloud of indignation, frustration and remorse. Lifestyle gurus offer solace, positive thinking and an escape route. What they feed off is something that all modern societies claim to spurn: low trust.

7

Living in a Low-Trust Society

Lifestyle gurus are part of the digitalisation of the service economy. Their profile in everyday life is the product of radically new conceptions of selfhood in modernity unbounded by the structural certainties of tradition with lifestyle advice sought at a greater volume (the unprecedented size of the world's population) and velocity (the unparalleled speed of data transmission and exchange) than in the past. Primary and secondary relationships, that have traditionally been the axis and mainstay of emotional support and self-validation, are now joined ubiquitously by tertiary relationships that offer individuals interaction with socially and spatially remote strangers. These figures are presented and, it seems, are accepted as role models and independent problem solvers. The exoticism of the stranger, in being conversant with knowledge and practice that is beyond the quotidian range of primary and secondary relationships, magnifies the power of their appeal (Simmel 1950). The labour of lifestyle gurus competes with, and increasingly supplants, much of the service formerly offered by certified counsellors, trainers and other professionals. In the long run, for economic reasons, much of this new service will, surely, itself be digitised by lifestyle guidance and advice sites curated and hosted by Artificial Intelligence. The just-in-time principle that lifestyle gurus advocate for others to follow in order to reach their dreams and be fulfilled, applies in the end, to themselves.

For the moment, lifestyle gurus are imperturbable in their sense of permanence. Their business success has been one of the standout features of the digitalisation of the third sector in the business economy. The internet enables them to sustain caseloads that are vastly beyond the capacity of regular helping and caring professionals. What arises from volume and velocity must, in turn, make a virtue of volume and velocity. Recall for a moment, that Joe Wicks' *Body Coach* site claims to have achieved over 100,000 'client transformations'. Given that he only graduated with a Sports Science degree from St Mary's University, Twickenham, in 2008, at the time of writing, his success rate averages out at a staggering 10,000 clients per year. It might be objected that there is no evidence to confirm that Wicks' 'client transformations' are equivalent in quality to those achieved by regular professionals. Be that as it may, from the perspective of potential subscribers, this is beside the point. It is Wicks who possesses the all important public profile. He has the popular social media accounts; he is the television presenter of the Channel 4 programme, *The Body Coach*; he is the author of the cookbook, *Lean in 15: 15 Minute Meals* (2015), which allegedly sold 900,000 copies; it is he who is featured in *The Daily Mail, The Times, Women's Health, Men's Fitness, Cosmoplitan, Grazia, E&S, Forever Sports*; and it is his site that has the ever-so-welcoming pop-up box, 'Any Questions? Chat Now' (Wicks 2018). Wicks' website goes to great pains to give the impression that it is open for business to anyone who has the courage to get ahead. In a world where it is taken for granted that nothing is free, the lifestyle programmes on *The Body Coach* site come with a price. Start-up programmes and up-dates require remuneration from subscribers. The traditional cash nexus between professionals and clients is scrupulously observed. But in other ways the emphasis is upon unconventionality, approachability, no-hierarchy and convenience. The whole business of monetary transactions is achieved as an exercise in mateship, as if everyone is in the same team, and that team is four square set against stuffy, aloof, condescending, elitist ways of behaving. In other words, much of the appeal of the site lies in marketing. Take, for example, Kardashian's lifestyle site, *Poosh*. In a section of the site entitled, 'Who You Are', the impression of friendship and intimacy is deliberately fostered: 'We get you, and we're here to give you all the sweet treats that your heart (and body) desire ... You want it all, and you want a place that provides a little bit of everything, without being lectured or preached to (you already have a parent/ partner/ child/ sibling – we feel you). Think of us as a really good friend ... but way less judgy' (Poosh 2019). Just as Oprah built a million-dollar empire by appearing accessible to the masses regardless of race, sex or creed, Kardashian presents her lifestyle site as a place of affirmation, acceptance and inclusivity. Lifestyle management is indeed metaphorically presented as an extension of sport. One needs to train, one needs to invest in one's performance, one needs to play the game, if one is to get a result – i.e. the achievement of approval, acceptance, social impact and self-validation.

As the previous chapters have indicated, a perusal of lifestyle guru sites swiftly reveals considerable variation in cultic formation. However, we have argued that, regardless of the variations in content and form of the belief systems and methods of application espoused in their programmes, today the sites typically express affirmative perfectionism as the ultimate goal of involvement. To think that you are found wanting in some respect, that you are obviously losing in an envy playground where others are winning, and that this may be directly, swiftly and decisively, corrected by means of a step-by-step programme of instruction that culminates in the acquisition of peak performance, is the lifestyle guru calling card. The invitation, which is understandably, awfully tempting in a liquid world where most things are ambivalent and uncertain, is to unlock the 'real' you so that you may present the best version of yourself to the world. This is evident in *The Body Coach* site. But it is a common denominator in lifestyle guru sites in general. If we briefly refer to a few supplementary examples, in Australia, Melissa Ambrosini is a self-styled life coach and motivational speaker. Her 'mission' is 'to help women create a vibrant, fulfilling life' (Derrick 2017). The strapline on the 'Bio' entry of her website commences by stating, 'I'm so glad you're here beautiful. Pour yourself a cuppa, get comfy, and let's get to know each other' (Ambrosini 2018). Again, the non-condescending, sisterly, team-talk, tone is striking, as it is with rival sites that we have considered before, such as Marie Forleo (Forleo 2018), Sue Stone (Stone 2018) and the other 'happiness', 'empowerment' and 'confidence' life coaches that we have considered in this book. There is no need to fix an appointment, there is no need to confess your embarrassing problems to an expert, there is no waiting room where you must grate-fully assemble with other patients seeking help. Online lifestyle servicing is simple, convenient, friendly, flexible, private and direct.

Ambrosini started her working life as a professional dancer, actress and television presenter. This outwardly glamorous lifestyle was not what it appeared to be. In reality she was often assailed with anxiety, panic attacks, depression, eating disorders and 'toxic' relationships. When this climaxed in a period of hospitalisation, it precipitated the Reset: 'a wake up call' that led to the decisive act (Derrick 2017). From the low crisis point, Ambrosini decided to turn her life around. Melissa studied holistic nutrition, yoga and, of course, life coaching. She made it her mission to educate women in the business of self-help and self-love. Her blog site magnanimously shares the lessons of her life experience with others (Derrick 2017). Thus, she developed a career as a self-appointed 'self-love' and 'spiritual' teacher. The prevailing message is simple and winning: to affirm yourself you must first love yourself. Her successful lifestyle book *Mastering Your Mean Girl*, sought to still the 'inner critic' and was aimed at all women who feel 'stuck', 'uninspired' and 'disillusioned' (Derrick 2017). Ambrosini uses the David and Goliath technique of setting her advice and mission against 'so much (professional) relationship advice' that is 'unrealistic', 'unhelpful' or 'just skates over the surface' (Derrick 2017). Her self-help advice manual, *Mastering Your Mean Girl*, advertises the book as a 'No BS guide to … becoming wildly WEALTHY, fabulously HEALTHY, and bursting with LOVE' (Ambrosini 2016 [emphasis in original]). On her website, her range of merchandise includes audio and book versions of *The Glow Kitchen* and *Business Bootcamp*. The on-site marketing material is revealing. The first promises a 'life changing, eating philosophy' that will result in 'sexy skin, humming hormones' and 'a lit-from-within-glow'; the second, offers 'exact step-by-step strategies' to grow your business from daydreams or a 'side project' into a 'seriously successful' venture. Ambrosini combines a pitch to those who have been victimised by the trials of life based upon her own disclosed biographical experience (not independently verified), with a golden rule book to get up on the road to wealth creation based upon what life in business has taught her. Emotionally speaking, it is as if an indifferent, haughty, uncaring world is finally receiving its comeuppance. By dint of this, she positions herself outside the system and propagates a mix of mysticism, designer picked science and folk knowledge fused with her own life experience that is purported to be deeper than professional-expert alternatives. The broad brush strokes of Ambrosini's documented life history of outward success, inner demons, a crisis event that prompts the Reset and then, the decisive act leading to health, wealth and fame, is familiar. It recurs repeatedly in the lifestyle wellness guru networks.

To refer, briefly, to another case: Gala Darling, a New Zealander living in New York, is the author of the successful book *Radical Self-Love: A Guide to Loving Yourself and Living Your Dreams* (Darling 2016). According to her online bio, the book is a venture to 'rewire' her brain after a decade long history of 'eating disorders' and 'depression'. Associatively, this life history provides her with the credentials to 'rewire' others. The tone adopted by her website suggests that it is only neighbourly of Gala to impart to others the secrets of self-validation and success that she has learned the hard way. For have they not delivered her from a world riddled with frustration and bogus promises to active achievement and serene fulfilment? Again, what comes through most cogently is the empathy that personal misfortune has given her, and the force of the desire to Reset her life and the lives of others, via the Decisive Act. Her 'mission' is to 'show women how magnificent they are, and to inspire them to step up and grab the life they've dreamed about with both hands' (Darling 2016). Talent and the essentials of attraction and impact are to be found within, it is simply a matter of accepting the key to open the lock. It is hard to think of a more succinct expression of the ideology of affirmative perfectionism – the inner self is already perfect, it just has to be 'discovered'. The fact that this process is presented as being achievable by everyone – since authenticity is believed to be found from within – is part of the broad appeal of today's lifestyle gurus. It is also implausible to consider Gala's approach as engaging others unless the specifics of her personal journey touch upon conditions of life that are generally distributed and deplored by the many.

Going Viral

Online technologies have an unprecedented multiplier effect in enabling lifestyle narratives to flourish (Page 2018). When a narrative 'goes viral' it achieves escape velocity, departing from the immediate locus of exchange, to attain exponential speed and global impact and influence. The stories shared on the web create a parallel universe that contrasts both with institutionalised channels of communication, expertise and custom. They consolidate far-flung interests to constitute an interplay of endlessly self-conceiving and supporting narratives that are commonly shared and extended. Stripped to its core components, an online shared viral narrative consists of (a) a telling; (b) a retelling (produced by multiple tellers), and (c) the gestation of agglomerated attitudes between communicators and communicants to become 'facts' (Page 2018: 197). In studies of Twitter, researchers submit that online narrative exchange is categorically different to soap-box oratory. Rather, communicators harness and extend online resources to finesse their narratives for a coherent, *imagined, global audience* that *precedes* their narrative but shapes the form that it takes (Marwick and boyd 2011: 115–16). The imagined audience is assumed to be *already* co-present on the internet, albeit residing in a latent state. The online narrative is designed to empower the audience by bringing them *into confidence* and rests on the assumption that the specific, local details of life experience that it recounts resonate meaningfully with general experience. To put it differently, the purpose of telling stories is to bring audiences into definition. That is, to permit them to exercise their natural right to be affirming and to discover their best self.

Affirmative behaviour necessarily presumes confronting the obstacles and interests that act as intolerable fetters on development. This regulates the narrative use of language, cultural referents and style. Further, it is assumed that communicants have common access to credited professional knowledge and folk norms about what is really going on in the world and how life with others really works. It also assumes that we need to listen to that little voice inside ourselves that repeatedly tells us that we are unique and special. Imagined audiences are pictured as 'bearing' lay knowledge from the experience of transacting with the frustrations and obstacles of, *inter alia*, the labour market, corporations, state bureaucracies, religious organisations, the institutionalised media, domineering personal relationships, and the various abstract philosophies of life that, when weighed in the balance, ultimately lack the power of persuasion. This is assumed to make them receptive to the business of taking successful, decisive acts and propagating lifestyle programmes that comprise the parallel universe of meaning that are understood to be outside (discredited) convention. Being complicit in unearthing an alternative level of authenticity that professional-expert relations cannot grasp, is an important component in all of this. It strips down psychological defence mechanisms and resistance and encourages online participants to believe that 'we are all in it together' but that those who have the courage to transform themselves can, with friendly, managed guidance, *from someone who has overcome the same problems*, do so. From the condition of general low trust, the individual can free themselves, if only they have the courage to press the escape button.

The transmission of shared stories has been rightly analysed as inspired by the desire to collaborate and expand participatory culture (Jenkins 1992; Bruns and Jacobs 2006). Crowdsourcing, in which an individual posts a problem online and others respond with suggested solutions, is an example. As a first step – but only as a first step – it makes sense to regard the phenomenon as part of the enabling economy and to credit the web as the technical means by which this can be realised. Lifestyle sites share know-how, the confirmation of raw life experience and offer digital access in order to enhance personal freedom and well-being (David 2017). The content and style of expression feeds upon folk resources. This is evident, not only in the language of trust and authenticity, but also in the disassociation of narrated 'facts' from any interest in, or commitment to, independent, objective processes and standards of verification. Folk traditions set high store on stories that are told with dramatic effect, verve and *panache*. This fully carries over into the stories told on social media sites. The more colourful, decisive and eye-catching online lifestyle content is, the greater its power to capture and hold attention. Balance and evidence play second fiddle to the display of bravura, affirmation and enthusiastic complicity.

This study signals the need to analyse critically the techniques lifestyle gurus use to achieve authority and influence online; namely, how they persuade others they are credible and trustworthy in the eyes of a lay public. Influencers habitually communicate as 'ordinary' internet users who deploy textual and visual narratives centering upon their 'everyday' personal lives and lifestyles (Abidin 2018). Influencers are conventionally thought of as an adjunct of social media. However, as we have established in this study, strictly speaking, neither its 'ordinary' aspects, nor its deployment of 'everyday' textual and visual narratives, focusing upon their personal lives and lifestyles, are novel or original. Whether they be conscious of it or not, influencers are part of a long Western history of lifestyle agents of awareness seeking to build positive consciousness of how to be with others and what to do in order to be regarded as successful by society. Today we use the term 'lifestyle guru' to categorise them. In earlier times they figured in society in the shape of a *congerie* of print-based advisers on etiquette, courtship, marriage, child-rearing, grooming, schooling, household management, sickness, realistic aspiration and well-being. Nineteenth and early twentieth-century lifestyle guides, such as Samuel Smiles, Catharine Beecher and Isabella Beeton, were certainly household names in bourgeois domiciles. As we have seen, the advice they imparted drew upon Scripture and lay knowledge, but it was dominated by the imprimatur of scientific knowledge and rational procedure. The doctrine of assured perfectionism that they imparted provided a benchmark for many lives in their day. The technology of the internet has not been the only factor in changing circumstances. The nature of low trust today, differs from that of its precedent in the nineteenth century. The lifestyle citizenship ethos has developed from what is seen as the *collapse* of conventional middle-class solutions to life problems. The dissatisfaction with organised politics and the revolt against the elites are symptoms of this. However, this is not to say that the lifestyle strategies and practices developed by lifestyle gurus and lifestyle citizenship have broken with class. In the emphasis upon individual solutions to personal and social problems, the reliance upon the value of the demonstration effect in cultivating good behaviour in others, the support for the metric of finance as the ultimate metric of success, we submit that lifestyle gurus and the ethos of lifestyle citizenship constitute a redefined continuation of middle-class value presumptions.

Today's lifestyle gurus generally have little time for Scripture. Additionally, they scorn many aspects of professional knowledge and elite thinking as cold, authoritarian hokum. Instead, they value immediacy and informality, the just-in-time exchange of emotion, natural, healing remedies and the affirmative embrace of volume and velocity over the dead weight of confinement and tradition. Assured perfectionism, with its unbending adherence to the Bible and science and its tenacious belief in a finite, total life-plan, is dismissed as philosophy worthy of a fossil. Its irrelevance to a world that moves rapidly on multiple levels is so obvious that it hardly needs to be stated. In positioning themselves outside the professional-expert courtroom, lifestyle gurus who promote affirmative perfectionism run the risk of being labelled as heretics. This, of course, is part of their appeal. They are definitively offering alternative remedies. But the consequences of going viral can be fatal. Consider the case of the young Pakistani micro-celebrity, Fouzia Azeem ('Qandeel Baloch'). She auditioned to be a finalist in the Pakistan's *American Idol* but was rejected on national television. A clip from the audition was posted on YouTube. It went viral, especially in Pakistan and India. To capitalise on online interest, Azeem posted risqué photographs and bedroom videos on Instagram, Twitter and Facebook. She may not have followed the principles of self-branding that we have considered in lifestyle guru sites in earlier chapters, but her espousal of lifestyle values was followed and emulated by a large audience. Azeem presented an alternative to received models and called upon followers to adopt a different life strategy which popularised native knowledge and techniques of gaming against professional, elite precedents. She used social media to broadcast this life strategy. This is why we feel it appropriate to consider it in our book.

Azeem referred to herself as 'Girl Power', as she danced, teased and flirted online. Among her famous catchphrases was, 'How I'm looking? Beautiful?' The media labelled her a sex symbol: 'Pakistan's Kim Kardashian'. The social attention that her online lifestyle postings fomented were financially rewarding. However, conservatives condemned her frank comments, revealing dress and salacious conduct as misbehaviour and a threat to society. It was held to be intentionally disreputable and shamed Muslim values of modesty, decorum and family life. One of her most infamous postings promised that she would strip naked online if Pakistan won an international cricket match with India. This never occurred because Pakistan lost the match. But conservatives regarded her undertaking to be both a threat to respectable order and atrociously immoral against cherished feminine values to boot. When controversial selfies showed her consorting in a hotel room with a senior cleric, Mufti Abdul Qavi, were posted on social media, it triggered a digital sensation. This escalated into a public scandal. Her 'mindset' and the values that she encouraged were widely and intensively deplored as a lifestyle role model for young Pakistani females. She was demonised and subject to a volley of hate mail and death threats. On 15 July 2016 she suffered a so-called 'honour killing', by asphyxiation, at the hands of her brother.

Azeem's case illustrates the potential risks and real hazards that arise when a micro-celebrity lifestyle site goes viral. Celebrity culture has evolved a network of cultural intermediaries situated between the celebrity and the audience. These consist of agents, managers, stylists, publicists, doctors and security staff. Their purpose is to manicure the public face of the celebrity to ensure smooth public consumption and add to the attraction of the brand. Micro-celebrities are not equipped with a buffer zone of cultural intermediaries. When they build and launch their sites, most stand alone before the audience. When they go viral they lack the means to manage and control social reactions in order to prevent them from becoming life threatening. By definition, going viral produces a multiplier effect. Micro-celebrities and their lifestyle sites are continually required to devise new ways and means of achieving approval, acceptance, social impact and self-validation. It is a market of transmission and exchange built upon unplanned disequilibrium, since demand always exceeds supply. Micro-celebrities are trapped by the desire to seek status and attention (Marwick 2013). Azeem was caught up in this vortex. The challenge that she laid down to conventional gender norms produced an accumulation of negative emotion centred upon her rather than the lifestyle she espoused. It was undoubtedly, the main reason why she was murdered, facilitated by the global exposure she received online. There are other end-points to the vortex of disequilibrium caused when a micro-celebrity and the associated lifestyle site go viral. These are worth briefly considering.

In the first instance, let us turn to the case of Jessica Ainscough. Ainscough was an Australian cancer patient and online editor of the teen publication, *Dolly*. At the age of 22, doctors diagnosed her with epithelioid sarcoma, a rare soft-tissue cancer that is slow-growing but difficult to eradicate. The cancer was located in her left arm and, according to Ainscough, she was advised by doctors that her only hope of survival would be to amputate her limb. She refused surgery, opting to take responsibility for her illness and steer her body into a condition in which it could 'heal itself' in line with the cultural ethos of healthism discussed in Chapter 4. She forsook her lifestyle of self-described 'late nights', 'cocktails' in favour of 'carrot juice, coffee enemas and meditation' (Science-Based Medicine 2018). She embraced the controversial Gerson therapy of 'optimum health', which involves drinking thirteen fresh organic vegetable juices and five coffee enemas per day in combination with adhering to an organic, whole-food, plant-based diet and consuming additional supplements. Her daily regime of therapy was exacting. In common with other lifestyle gurus, Ainscough documented her wellness journey on her blog and website, *The Wellness Warrior*. In her blog she often complained that it seemed like a full time job that left her exhausted. She describes a typical day of Gerson therapy thus:

> 7am: drag myself out of bed and meditate
> 7.30am: first coffee enema of the day
> 8am: breakfast (orange juice and oats with honey, banana, raisins and kiwi fruit)
> 9am: green juice
> 9.30am: carrot and apple juice
> 10am: carrot and apple juice, work on blog and other writing bits and pieces
> 11am: carrot juice, work on blog and other writing bits and pieces
> 12pm: green juice, coffee enema #2
> 1pm: carrot and apple juice, lunch (soup, salad, veggies, potato), watch a bit of Oprah while we eat
> 2pm: green juice, do more writing
> 3pm: carrot juice, yoga
> 4pm: carrot juice, take my dog for a walk
> 5pm: carrot and apple juice, meditate
> 6pm: carrot and apple juice, coffee enema #3
> 7pm: green juice, dinner (soup, salad, veggies, potato)
> 8pm: watch a bit of TV or read in bed
> 10pm: sleep (Science-Based Medicine 2018)

Ainscough rose to global prominence as the 'Wellness Warrior', a holistic health counsellor for the world to learn from and emulate. Her website was critical of conventional professional-expert medicine and remedies which, after all had, in her case, failed. Instead, she was an advocate of 'natural health'. Her goal was to empower people to take control of their health by adhering to the edicts of her lifestyle. The site operated not only as an online resource to proselytise healthy living, but also as a message board to document her progress as she battled with the illness. The message board component strengthened the belief among her audience that they were dealing not only with a friend, but a friend in need. Again, velocity and the just-in-time principle are integral to understanding the appeal and impact of the site. She believed, and taught, that her wellness regime and the Gerson therapy were effective. She felt better and her tumours seemed to go into remission. Sometimes her blog claimed to see them coming out of her skin and vanishing (Science-Based Medicine 2018). Sadly, she was deluded. It is not uncommon in the progress of certain types of cancer, like epithelioid sarcoma, for tumours to erode the skin and give the impression of disappearing. Ainscough died of the disease in 2015. With conventional treatment she might be alive today.

There is no evidence to prove that Gerson therapy has any curative yield to treat cancer. In fact, professional medical opinion suggests that the practice can be very harmful for people who are ill because the diet is restrictive and rejects conventional cancer treatments, such as chemotherapy (Cancer Research UK 2018). Nevertheless, Ainscough accumulated a significant web following and even when her cancer became terminal, she never renounced the Gerson protocol. It is impossible to ignore or discount the demonstration effect that this must have had among sections of her audience. As her site went viral she was unable to discard audience expectations about 'healthy healing'. She became trapped and becalmed around the expectations in herself and in her audience that her programme of treatment was unable to match. Her ideas about how to cope with, and cure, her cancer were widely influential. Even though towards the end of her life she blogged that she never claimed that Gerson therapy is a panacea that cured her cancer, her advocacy of the method, when her illness was stable, led many people to the opposite conclusion (Science-Based Medicine 2018). The probability is that many cancer sufferers who followed her advice about conventional medical treatments are now themselves dead. All of the evidence indicates that Ainscough acted from the best intentions. She was genuinely convinced that healthy eating, detoxifying the body and faithful adherence to the Gerson protocol, were more beneficial in addressing her condition than the conventional medical treatment offered by qualified professionals. However, in amplifying the popularity of these alternative treatments on her social media platform, she exerted an unexamined, moral influence over a credulous audience who felt her pain. The shared recognition of vulnerability establishes a *modus operandi* for lifestyle advice, hints and points of view to be exchanged without let or hindrance.

It is worth noting here that the contrast with professional empathy could not be more stark. Professional empathy is a salaried resource. It is designed and packaged to facilitate diagnosis and treatment that complies with professionally defined and independently accredited procedures and goals. The empathy that can be claimed by someone who is mortally ill or who has undergone a major life trauma and has benefited from 'natural healing' is of a separate order. Misfortune grants them the licence to talk to others about what direct, painful, but revealing experience, has supposedly taught them. Anecdotal evidence, based on their feelings rather than controlled clinical trials, makes them accessible and relatable, and forms the basis of their credibility. The good fortune of professionals is to receive payment for imparting knowledge and treatment from the healthy to those in need. It does not have the ring of sincerity that someone who has been there, who has looked at death in the mouth, or faced other blistering blows, can automatically command. Moreover, experts are taught to restrain emotional identification with the patient in favour of a therapeutic approach that professes the superior worth of objectivity, impartiality and neutrality. Against this, lifestyle gurus use emotional intelligence as the hook to land their audience. Instead of objectivity they offer empathy, instead of impartiality they offer complicity and instead of neutrality they offer partnership. It is a code of practice that proceeds on the basis that we are all in this together. As such, hierarchy is denigrated on *a priori* grounds.

Among the mourners at Ainscough's funeral was Belle Gibson. In June 2009 Gibson caught public attention after claiming she had been diagnosed with an incurable form of brain cancer, leaving her with only months left to live. Having defied all odds by surviving the terminal brain tumour, the self-described 'wellness guru' explained how she cured herself by rejecting conventional medicine in favour of a healthy lifestyle, encouraging other cancer sufferers to do the same. Gibson's story was documented on a blog, which became the basis for a bestselling app – *The Whole Pantry* – that she later developed into a book for Penguin: a 'wellness bible' featuring lifestyle advice and healthy recipes. Like Ainscough, Gibson's advocacy of well-being privileged diet and lifestyle in the fight against cancer (namely, omitting the common food villains – gluten, caffeine and dairy – from her diet). She was also a proponent of the anti-vaccination movement and an advocate of raw milk (unpasteurised milk), which is illegal in Australia because milk that has not been pasteurised to kill the bacteria increases people's risk of contracting serious illnesses. Through her public narrative of survival, she encouraged others to shun conventional medicine. In her book, Gibson recounted how, despite having tried chemotherapy and radiotherapy for two months, which left her 'knee deep in nausea and other side effects', she decided to heal herself through nutrition and holistic medicine:

> I pulled myself out of chemo and radiotherapy – my doctors freaked out, but they couldn't stop me ... I was empowering myself to save my own life, through nutrition, patience, determination and love – as well

as salt, vitamins and Ayurvedic treatments, cranioscal therapy, oxygen therapy, colonics and a whole lot of other treatments. (Gibson 2015: 2)

With hundreds and thousands of Instagram followers, a book published by Penguin and a successful app available on Apple, Gibson's message had public reach and influence. Her bestselling app was downloaded over 200,000 times in the first month of its release and was selected to feature in the new Apple Watch. Gibson's message extended beyond her niche community of followers and was given legitimacy by the mainstream media with Gibson awarded a *'Fun, Fearless Female Award'* by *Cosmopolitan Magazine* (nominated by the editor of the magazine and voted for by the public). In 2015, Gibson was exposed as a fraud. But not before developing an online persona as a trusted 'wellness guru' that generated significant wealth for her and influenced thousands of people.

In the aftermath of the scandal, there were various attempts to explain the motivation behind Gibson's actions: money, attention, reputation, and even a personality disorder – Munchausen's disease – that thrives on sympathy and manipulation (Feldman 2004). Beyond the psychology behind Gibson's lies, a more pressing question is to consider the cultural and technological conditions that enabled Gibson's persona to flourish? Gibson's rise to fame demonstrates the capacity for manipulation online. It is not that hoodwinking is new. Fraudsters have always existed, but prior to the rise of smartphones and social media, their influence was limited. Blogs and social media extend audience reach and the speed with which information is transmitted. This has serious social implications when applied to health and illness. Just as Gibson's downfall confirms the capacity to investigate and nullify false claims and bogus therapies on the internet. There is a rhythm here, a riff, that is repeated. The cases of both Ainscough and Gibson involved each of them rising to prominence as a consequence of a life-threatening crisis. Ainscough really did have cancer, whereas Gibson used the disease as a tool for personal aggrandisement and wealth creation. However, the online impact of both women was closely bound up with their stories of suffering, being ignored by experts and elites and deciding on a Reset and taking the Decisive Act to eventually become inspirational heroes and 'wellness gurus'. The part that 'life crisis' and 'the reset' of rehabilitation plays in the ascent of micro-celebrities and social media influencers is revealing. The cycle of disjuncture, comprehension and conjuncture forms the basis of most lifestyle platforms. It supplies them with a licence for apparently authentic empathy, which partly accounts for their ready, ecumenical appeal.

Detox Junction

In placing considered weight upon the importance of technology in supporting and enabling the volume and velocity that have helped lifestyle gurus to flourish, it is vital to refrain from slipping into a simplistic model of technological determinism. The internet has *not created* lifestyle gurus. Rather, it has provided the means for them to exploit and develop emotional wants and aspirational needs that are born and incubated in society on an unprecedented scale. A combination of social, cultural and economic factors have resulted in contemporary society exhibiting high levels of ambivalence and uncertainty about nearly everything. There are many dimensions along which this can be explored. To name but a few, environmental risk, professional malpractice, representational politics, obstacles to upward mobility, inter-personal strains and tensions, the impartiality of news media, health hazards deriving from diet and pollution, adulterated foodstuffs, over-population, mugging and assault, cloning, web fraud, contractions and insecurities in the job market and sexual harassment (Leader 2008). Since 9/11 the figurative corpus in Western culture in which fear, anxiety and uncertainty has been most chillingly expressed, is the terrorist. The terrorist, who can strike unexpectedly, and wreak death and mayhem without apparently, any thought of self-preservation, symbolises the fragility of social order and the absence of real control.

Zygmunt Bauman sought to capture some of this with his characterisation of modern times as 'liquid' (Bauman 2007). There are difficulties with the metaphor. Not the least of them is that it exaggerates the omnipresence of fluidity, and under-plays the significance of stabilising social forces that seek to squeeze out liquid form with uncompromising, iron-clad, primitive certainties. For example, religious fundamentalism, nativism and xenophobia (Rattansi 2017). If one takes a few steps back from Bauman, it is perfectly clear that it is impossible to speak of liquidity without considering solidity. Arguably, Bauman himself knew this only too well. His famous study of the Holocaust is a study of what happens when the maniacal, grotesque, irrational, pursuit of certainty is allowed free reign (Bauman 1989). Liquid and solid forms presuppose one another and, in fact, are always co-present. However, Bauman's contention that the metaphor of 'liquid times' currently has the upper hand is surely sound.

Those who flock to lifestyle gurus seek to find tertiary relationships that will provide personal security, companionship and the ability to succeed. In this book we have argued that at the heart of these relationships is the generation of attention capital that enables acceptance, approval, social impact and self-validation. The rise of lifestyle gurus online is an indicator that primary and secondary relationships are widely experienced as providing insufficient ontological grounding. The impression of not feeling at home with one's family and friends is habitual and common-place. The postwar ideology of the welfare state and consumer society as a sort of fail safe back stop mechanism to support the wayward vagaries of negative family life is no longer robust. Part of the appeal of today's lifestyle gurus, which feed from the perceived failures of the family to support members, is that the state in the current age is in no position to fill the breech. In this void, lifestyle gurus have emerged to employ a series of techniques (creating a compelling narrative and persona, self-disclosure and authenticity) to establish trust and intimacy with online audiences, turning online users into disciples and 'followers'.

The inadequacy of a strong sense of ontological security deriving from the defects of primary and secondary relationships and the perceived inadequacies of the state are not the only reasons why lifestyle gurus have a large and expanding market. The data deluge, from which they themselves originate and accumulate, carries powerful themes repre-senting the social, economic, political and environmental dimensions of the external world, as fraught with hazard and uncertainty. The internet has even brought new risks and hazards of its own. Cyberbullying, hate mail and clickbait are new digital dangers that can overwhelm anyone with a smart phone. Simultaneously, the internet has been criticised for offering new, maladaptive pathways for producing new types of self-persecution. The collective term that has been coined to cover these forms of digitally managed maladaptation is 'digital self harm'. The term refers to the anonymous online posting of data that is hurtful to oneself (Hinduja and Patchin 2017: 762). Digital self harm reveals something of the depth of anxiety, fear and uncertainty that permeates current times. Ambivalence and uncertainty in the home, find their parallel in the external ambivalence and uncertainty in society as a whole. It is easy to see how life in these conditions can appear to many to be toxic. Many of these concerns are not new, they are simply amplified by digital communication. The in-door to one's life provides no refuge, and the out-door opens up a disdainful, threatening world without respite. The data deluge is overwhelming. The sheer volume and velocity of data dealing with alarming subjects carries with it a social and psychological fear of sinking, flailing around, or being destroyed and disappearing. Needless to say, this is one reason why Bauman's metaphor of 'liquid times' is so suggestive and compelling.

In some of her blog posts, Ainscough referred to her pleasure and self-validation in 'de-toxifying' her body by means of her 'natural help' programme. In doing so, she was unwittingly grasping the nettle to expose the wider directional energy behind the lifestyle guru phenomenon. The sense of being born and raised in a toxic social and physical environment is so commonplace as to merit the description of being a general condition of contemporary life in the West. So far from offering an escape route towards safety and wholeness, experts and professionals are widely suspected of compounding the problem. For example, there is now a growing critical literature attacking medical practitioners for packaging psychological and bodily problems to meet the requirements of pharmaceutical corporations (Rose 2006; Leader 2008; Marshall 2010; Healy 2013). A new emphasis on surface conduct, manageable by tranquillisers and other prescription drugs, has replaced a deeper engagement with unconscious causes and social and economic factors in the aetiology of health and illness. In promulgating the beneficial effects of the Reset and the Decisive Act, lifestyle guru sites present themselves as junctions of detoxification. Permeated with a doctrine of affirmative perfectionism they maintain that they trade in gilt-edged, honest advice and helpful practical guidance that enables the audience and subscribers to take responsibility for themselves and achieve happy, positive outcomes. As we have seen, the retreat from experts and professionals is one consequence of this (Nichols 2017). The cash links between science and corporate interests has produced a wave of scepticism about the independence and objectivity of scientific endeavour and findings.

In some hands all of this has been shaped into the thesis that a new condition of 'post-truth' now prevails in everyday life (McIntyre 2018; Stenmark et al. 2018). The term refers to a condition in which the stated verity of facts presented by official institutional outlets in society is no longer automatically trusted. Citizens find it increasingly challenging to separate fact from the barrage of fiction (McNair 2017). Although references to the 'post-factual age' were made in media and communication research over three decades ago, several developments have brought the post-truth thesis to a head today (Ettema 1987). Traditional news sources are mistrusted for framing news, opinions and related data to advance particular social, political and economic interests (Castells 2009; Wolin 2010: 196, 284). This has been exacerbated by social media and the data deluge. A shift in the balance of power between news media and consumers has occurred from media personnel operating as 'gatekeepers', to citizens operating as the direct source and editors of news (Kovach and Rosenstiel 2011). One aspect of living with ambivalence, which has not received sufficient attention, is that those who, for whatever reason, are disinclined to stand on the side of iron-clad solidity or swim in liquid streams of post-truth and fake news, find themselves in no-man's land. The yearning for direction, security and meaning are capillaries for the popularity of lifestyle gurus.

The ideology of affirmative perfectionism that is currently dominant in online sites, situates lifestyle gurus on the other side of the post-truth condition. The life-plan programmes that they offer are based on the supposed authenticity of experience and the demonstrable utility of their programmes of lifestyle realignment. Set against the post-truth thesis this is a *non sequitor*. If truth in the world is phantom (because the world has succumbed to the implacable reign of post-truth), upon what basis can lifestyle gurus posit that the 'truths' in their programmes actually deliver anything of value? Hovering over all lifestyle guru websites is the incubus that what they purport to achieve for subscribers is factually spurious. Part of the difficulty lies in the broad beamed nature of the four goals of acceptance, approval, social impact and self-validation that the sites typically offer. These are all subsumed under the positive ideology of affirmative perfectionism. Finding your inner self and setting it free, replacing helplessness with authentic self-discovery and a 'can do' attitude and de-toxifying the body and mind from the harmful elements in primary and secondary relationships and society, *sui generis*, fits well with the times. However, this raises a question that has not been fully explored and answered in the literature. What exactly do the objectives of acceptance, approval, social impact and self-validation affirm? The right to be noticed and recognised as special is a common characteristic of the services offered by lifestyle gurus. But if the ordinary is automatically portrayed and celebrated as 'special', surely it vaporises the worth of discretion and judgement. Lifestyle programmes that race ahead on the principle that everyone has a right to be a heard, end in the din of over-praised mediocrity. When Ambrosini promises that followers of her programme with be 'wildly WEALTHY', 'fabulously HEALTHY' and 'bursting with LOVE' she lets capital letters stand in for truth (Ambrosini 2016).

Low-Trust Society

Lifestyle gurus exploit and develop the common discontent, disturbance anxieties and fears that derive from living with others in low-trust society. Ours is a society in which social integration is weak. The modern self is a city of fragments. There is good reason for this. Velocity and volume combine to make life fragmentary, insecure and unstable. Where general relations of trust are compromised by sharp social divisions and furtive, acquisitive, social interests, the highways and byways of social interaction are strewn with broken glass. The condition of low trust obtains. The freedom, equality, security and justice promised by Western democracy becomes reviewed sceptically. It is not worth the paper that it is written upon, because ordinary life experience recounts that these values are often evasive, furtive, or simply absent in society. Fundamentally, the democratic, plebiscitary system perpetually fails to deliver what it perpetually promises. The central political issue of the day, according to Sheldon Wolin, is 'the incompatibilities between the culture of everyday reality' and 'the virtual reality' upon which 'corporate capitalism thrives' (Wolin 2010: 268). The post-truth thesis says nothing more. The world that is presented to us through the qualitative and statistical analyses of corporations and state departments is a world that cannot be assumed to bear any tenable relationship to the qualities of social reality. This is the world audiences and subscribers to lifestyle guru sites inhabit. It is the world in which their frustrations, set backs and anxieties evolve. It is from this nadir that lifestyle gurus typically purport to soar.

Low-trust society is a veritable box of tricks. It prides itself upon sweeping away privilege and replacing it with equality of opportunity. But in reality it protects the advantaged. Between 2011 and 2014 the share of wealth of the top 10% in the USA increased from 72.8 to 74.6%. Over the same period, the middle 40% suffered a decline of nearly 2% (from 9.2% to 7.3%), while wealth in the bottom 50% almost halved, from 2.5% to 1.3% (Eng and Ornstein 2016: 619). Since 2007, in the Southern European countries, the real income of the bottom 10% has been falling between 12 and 28% annually (OECD 2017: 8). The effects of the Great Recession (2007) have been more severe and protracted than the economic contractions of 1974–1976 and 1980–1982 (Pontusson and Raess 2012: 13–14). In the first eighteen months after the recession US GDP declined by 4.1%; UK GDP fell by 6.3%; and US investment fell by 23.4% (Labonte 2010; Crocker 2015). The fall in real wages translates into a fall in macroeconomic demand. The shortfall in liquidity has been temporarily plugged by increasing the quantity of money and extending the credit economy. This has acted as a fig leaf to disguise macro-level defects in the structure of the Western economy and financial sector. The first to suffer were private debtors. It is estimated that in the USA home foreclosures tripled between 2006 and 2008, to almost 2.5 million (Mian et al. 2015). Governments' debt-to-GDP ratios have risen from 41% in 2008, to 74% in the USA; from 47% to 70% in the EU; and from 95% to 126% in Japan. Despite near zero interest rates in the USA and real interest rates of zero in the Eurozone, the evidence since 2008, is that the Western economic power bloc has been in a prolonged condition of 'sclerotic stagnation' (Summers 2016). The result of this is that social divisions escalate.

Over the last twenty years, in most OECD countries, income inequality has been escalating. This is especially pronounced in the Anglo-American bloc (Kuhn et al. 2014: 28). In the UK, households in the bottom 10% of the population have an average net income of £8,277. In the top 10%, net incomes are nine times greater (£83,897). In the USA, the top 0.1% of families have increased their share of wealth decade by decade. It expanded from 7% in 1978 to 22% in 2012 (Saez and Zucman 2016: 530). Over the same time-line wages have fallen. In the UK, between 1980 and 2011 wage share of output fell from 59.1% to 53.7%. In the USA and the Eurozone, government has displayed stubborn resistance to strengthen tax regimes against the richest in society. Instead, generally speaking, government policy has favoured enhanced austerity programmes with various degrees of intensity, and rewarded 'enterprise'. Lifestyle gurus need no persuading that these social and economic conditions have consequences for mental life, equanimity and well-being. To go into this fully would require writing a separate book. But we can refer to the essence of things by referring briefly to the work of Darian Leader. He quotes figures that demonstrate that depression is the single largest public health problem in Western society, affecting between 25 and 45 per cent of the adult population (with increasing rates in children and adolescents); in 1950 depression was estimated to affect only 0.5 per cent of the population (Leader 2008: 13). These findings are supported by the World Health Organisation (2018b), which notes that depression affects more than 300 million people worldwide, with mental health conditions on the rise globally.

Social media is rightly credited for offering productive and positive means of managing certain psychological, emotional and social needs (Livingstone 2008; De Ridder and Van Bauwel 2013). This needs to be firmly stated because lifestyle guru sites would not survive unless they staged a Reset that some subscribers find meaningful and tenable. In the leading lifestyle guru sites, it may be that this outcome reflects the sense of self-importance that subscribers gain from voyeuristic contact with the 'guru' as a celebrity, *qua* celebrity, rather than the practicable results of the programmes which they offer. This is a question that requires further research. Regardless of whether subscribers acquire sustenance from the glamour glow of contact with the lifestyle guru, or whether the lifestyle management steps imparted in the online programmes are a genuine escalator to negotiate the volume and velocity of life optimally, if the sites help some to cope with life's problems, challenges and apparent impasses, upon what possible grounds can they be decried? The question is appropriate because the tone in this book has evidently been critical. So how should it be answered?

Lifestyle gurus equip subscribers to succeed in societies where low-trust relations are dominant. Acceptance, approval, social impact and self-validation are packaged as solutions for people to do better in conditions where many are doing worse. Assured perfectionism was guilty of many failings. It was sanctimonious, inflexible, autocratic, pontifical and peremptory. Setting all of that to one side, it was also absolutely right to insist that individual progress is not enough. Self-progress must go hand-in-hand with social progress. The affirmative perfectionism of today's lifestyle guru sites have forgotten this lesson. They focus narrowly upon individual gain, and fail to see that preparing people to do well in a society that is in key respects regressing, merely compounds the general problem. Falling back on a demonstration effect to show the worth of their knowledge is self-deluding. Real social change requires mobilisation, organisation, protest and action. Defending the truth, cherishing the standards that deliver and protect the truth, ensuring that the physical environment is stable, and providing resources to help those who are in want, need and misery are not politically correct, liberal *desiderata*. They are, *sui generis*, social goods. Societies that fail to defend and nurture these qualities face profound social unrest, repeated jarring conflict and arguably extinction. The left behind, the marginal and those who cannot get ahead to develop the best version of themselves (despite their exhaustive efforts), will come to reject a system that has no reward for them, and only serves to protect cosseted elites. In turn, this risks flirting with the emergence of a New Caesarism in which the virtues of democracy are squashed beneath the feet of a tyrant who grandly promises a 'Reset' for the whole of society, and takes the decisive act, in the name of detoxifying the elite stable (Greenblat 2018). Lifestyle guru sites forge the very chains that their life management programmes profess to overcome.

If we may borrow a term coined by Leszek Kolakowski in another context to explain what we mean here. The programmes offered by online lifestyle gurus produce *embodied antinomy*: a step-by-step approach to detoxification, acceptance, approval, social compact and self-validation in societies of low trust, that is finally unable to implement what they bullishly purport to deliver (Kolakowski 2005: 1073). In subjecting the ideologies of assured and affirmative perfectionism to critical analysis, we do not wish to throw the baby out with the bathwater. Perfectionism, as such, is a perfectly reasonable ideal to follow, both in personal and collective life. It is a question of what kind of perfectionism is at stake. Stanley Cavell's discussion of this matter has been seminal (Cavell 1990, 1995, 2004). He submits that *moral perfectionism* requires individuals to take responsibilities for themselves and to change their lives if needed (Urbas 2010; Kovalainen 2017). It is a position that is heavily influenced by the writings of Henry Thoreau and Ralph Waldo Emerson on the moral responsibilities of the individual. As Polonius declares to Laertes in Shakespeare's *Hamlet* (Act 1, Scene 3), 'To thine own self be true.' This is the burden of what Thoreau and Emerson preach. Cavell takes this over and makes innovative suggestions to lever it into to a full blown theory of moral perfectionism. To begin with, he observes that all philosophy emerges, not from talk, but from a sense of loss (Cavell 1989: 114). It might be thought that the virtue of the philosophy that he advances is that it is designed to overcome loss. On the contrary, Cavell asks us to view loss as an unavoidable human condition. As such, it is a nonsense to suppose that it can be finally overcome. In a word, it is *permanent,* but of course, the details of the face that it sets to the world change. The more the action of moral perfection is directed to replace a sense of loss at the level of an individual life, the more it reveals the necessity to go further and deeper in seeking to nourish what might be meant by the transcendent self.

When all is said and done, Cavell's philosophy of moral perfectionism does not seek to impart fixed affirmative objectives or a set finite ends for individuals and societies to pursue. Rather it outlines a morality which exploits and develops a respect for self-transcendence beyond the impaired, low-trust relations of life as it is mundanely encountered and experienced (Roth 2010: 395; Gustaffson 2014: 101). It need hardly be added that Cavell sees this as a serious and sober undertaking. Those who take upon themselves the responsibility of striving to follow moral perfectionism do so with a view to furthering the self to achieve a higher state of being not merely for oneself, but in the name of social progress for all. This exalted objective requires the individual to confront and accept the need to change. The sake of the change is not, strictly speaking, to make oneself a better person. Rather, it is to take it upon oneself to reach for the realm of becoming more fully human by recognising that the low-trust relations in which one is enmeshed extend beyond the boundaries of the family, the community, the nation state, the power bloc to tack upon nothing less than the world in its entirety. This is not so much a question of taking a decisive act. Not a closing down of the self to gain self-momentum, but an opening up to selves that are separately, mysteriously located, is required. Selflessness is in the nature of this moral enterprise. For when one enters the realm of the fully human, the narrow sense of self, with its insatiable appetite for the rewards of self-interest, dissolves. It is replaced by a more complete sense of presence with others and in the world that we propose to refer to as 'species being'. However, it is a mistake to hold that once this realm is theoretically attained the churn of transcendence stops. In both the realm of species being and the standing walls of individual life, the idea of 'ultimate perfection' is a delusion (Cavell 2004: 3). Cavell asks his readers to approach moral perfectionism as a serious, ennobling quest that, however, must be unerringly understood to be a quest for a state beyond the self without end. The philosophy of moral perfectionism outlined here connects success with the ultimate loss of self, since in its fulfilment, all become one.

What follows immediately, from encountering Cavell's ideas, is that discontent and dissatisfaction are the lot of those on the road to moral perfection. For they are obliged not to flinch from what is lacking in themselves, or the conditions in the life around them that contribute to their sense of absence. But the goal is to get beyond the narrow interests of the self in order to become the more complete being that we hold in our imagination's eye. It would be wholly wrong to see Cavell as some sort of closet neo-liberal. Nevertheless, his philosophy of moral perfectionism clearly carries the birthmarks of the immediate surrounding social and ideological circumstances from which it hails. For example, in confronting and recognising loss and the need for change, the accent, in the first instance, is upon addressing the self. While it is the case that Cavell proceeds on the basis that there is a necessary set of relationships between the predicament of the individual and the condition of society, the articulation of these relationships is vague and under-developed. No part of his argument on moral perfectionism provides for the necessity for social conditions to be deliberated upon, inventoried and reformed, as preconditions for freeing up moral advance. He is not a revolutionary.

In other ways, his philosophy could not be at greater odds with the neo-liberal credo. To begin with, the cause of individual liberty is dismissed as a mirage. Herein, he reveals himself to be a fatalist. The challenge of human history is to see past the turrets and barricades of habitual order. The thrust of Cavell's philosophy is not to set individuals free, but to contribute to their dissolution.

Needless to say, the goal is not to instigate the cessation of human beings. Rather, it is to lift them from an atomised, conflicted existence in favour of reconciliation with species being wherein one become all. From this perspective the route maps of self-discovery and self-validation typically proffered by lifestyle guru sites are dead ends. Their goal is to lift the self from encumbered existence. In contrast, Cavell's goal is to lift the self from its primitive, cabined and confined sense of self itself. The spirit and worth of collectivism is unmistakable. Neo-liberalism maintains that there is nothing higher, or more worthy of a call to arms, than self-interest. Cavell discounts this as a fool's errand. Ultimately, self-interest alienates individuals from one another and produces a pay game of competitive self-advantage. Because of this, he holds that the cause of higher human existence lies in the direction of voluntarily, extinguishing the self and embracing the species nature that all hold in common. When Marie Forleo declares on her website that, 'The World *Needs* That Special Gift That Only You Have', and promises to show subscribers 'How You Can Get *Anything* You Want', she is articulating and legitimating the type of egoism that Cavell would have abhorred (Forleo 2018). Yet, it is Forleo's take on perfectionism that is in hegemonic ascendance on lifestyle guru websites. The affirmative is not necessarily in opposition with the moral. This only happens when egotistic affirmation is encouraged to be an end in itself. It is our contention that this is the general condition of today's lifestyle gurus. As such, we maintain that their proliferation, and prosperity, is likely to contribute to low trust rather than alleviate it. The paradox of lifestyle gurus is that in general, they are part of the trust problem that they purport to solve.

References

Abidin, C. (2018). *Internet Celebrity: Understanding Fame Online*. Bingley: Emerald.

Adorno, T. (1990). *Negative Dialectics*. London: Routledge.

___ (2008). *Lectures on Negative Dialectics*. Cambridge: Polity.

Advertising Standards Authority (2018). *Recognising online ads as ads*. [online] Asa.org.uk. Available at: https://www.asa.org.uk/news/recognising-online-ads-as-ads.html.

Agrawal, A. (2016). *How to connect with website visitors in an authentic way*. [online] Inc.com. Available at: https://www.inc.com/aj-agrawal/how-to-connect-with-website-visitors-in-an-authentic-way.html.

Aitkenhead, D. (2017). Sienna Miller: 'I feel relatively immune to bitchy criticism now'. [online] *Guardian*. Available at: https://www.theguardian.com/film/2017/mar/16/sienna-miller-i-feel-relatively-immune-to-bitchy-criticism-now.

Alexander, J. C. (2017). *The Drama of Social Life*. Cambridge: Polity.

Alexander, J. C., Giesen, B. and Mast, J. L., eds. (2006). *Social Performance: Symbolic Action, Cultural Pragmatics, and Ritual*. Cambridge: Cambridge University Press.

Allen, T. (2005). Clockwork nation: Modern time, moral perfectionism and American identity in Catharine Beecher and Henry Thoreau. *Journal of American Studies*, 39(1): 65–86.

Alter, A. (2017). *Irresistible: The Rise of Addictive Technology and the Business of Keeping us Hooked*. New York: Penguin.

Amalgamated Press Ltd. (1930). *The Marriage Book: For Husbands and Wives – and All Who Love Children*. London: Waverley Press.

Ambrosini, M. (2016). *Mastering Your Mean Girl*. New York: Penguin.

___ (2018). *Melissa Ambrosini – Bestselling Author and Host of The Melissa Ambrosini Show*. [online] Melissa Ambrosini. Available at: https://melissaambrosini.com/.

Assaraf, J. (2018). *Join us for the 7th Annual LIVE Brain-A-Thon*. [online] NeuroGym. Available at: http://johnassaraf.com/

Avrich, B. (2016). *Moguls, Monsters and Madmen: An Uncensored Life in Show Business ECW press* [DVD].

Baker, S. A. (2012). From the criminal crowd to the 'mediated crowd': The impact of social media on the 2011 English riots. *Safer Communities*, 11(1): 40–9.

____ (2014). *Social Tragedy: The Power of Myth, Ritual, and Emotion in the New Media Ecology*. New York: Palgrave Macmillan.

Baker, S. A. and Rojek, C. (2019). The Belle Gibson scandal: The rise of lifestyle gurus as micro-celebrities in low-trust societies. *Journal of Sociology*.

Baker, S. A. and Walsh, M. J. (2018). 'Good Morning Fitfam': Top posts, hashtags and gender display on Instagram. *New Media and Society*, 20(12): 4553–70.

Baker, S. A. and Walsh, M. J. (2019). You are what you Instagram: Clean eating and the symbolic representation of food. In D. Lupton and Z. Feldman, eds., *Digital Food Cultures*. London: Routledge.

Barker, G. (2014). *Pop into The Pantry app for a healthier lifestyle*. [online] The Sydney Morning Herald. Available at: https://www.smh.com.au/technology/pop-into-the-pantry-app-for-a-healthier-lifestyle-20140717-ztvos.html.

Baudelaire, C. (1986). *The Painter of Modern Life*. New York: De Capo Press.

Bauman, Z. (1989). *Modernity and the Holocaust*. Cambridge: Polity.

____ (2003). *Liquid Love: On the Frailty of Human Bonds*. Cambridge: Polity.

____ (2007). *Liquid Times: Living in an Age of Uncertainty*. Cambridge: Polity.

Beck, U. (1992). *Risk Society: Towards a New Modernity*. London: Sage.

____ (1994). The reinvention of politics: Towards a theory of reflexive modernization. In U. Beck, A. Giddens and S. Lash, ed., *Reflexive Modernization: Politics, Tradition and Aesthetics in the Modern Social Order*. Cambridge: Polity, pp. 1–55.

____ (2006). Living in the world risk society: A Hobhouse Memorial Public Lecture given on Wednesday 15 February 2006 at the London School of Economics. *Economy and Society*, 35(3): 329–45.

Beck, U. and Beck-Gernsheim, E. (1995). *The Normal Chaos of Love*. Cambridge: Polity.

Beecher, C. (1841). *A Treatise on Domestic Economy*. New York: Harper.

Beecher, H. K. (1955). The powerful placebo. *Journal of the American Medical Association*, 159(17): 1602–6.

Beetham, M. (2008). Good taste and sweet ordering: Dining with Mrs Beeton. *Victorian Literature and Culture*, 36(2): 391–406.

Beeton, I. (1861). *Mrs Beeton's Book of Household Management*. London: Chancellor Press.

Benford, R. and Gough, B. (2006). Defining and defending 'unhealthy' practices: A discourse analysis of chocolate 'addicts'' accounts. *Journal of Health Psychology*, 11(3): 427–40.

Benkler, Y. (2006). *Wealth of Networks*. New Haven: Yale University Press.

Bernstein, G. (2018). *Gabby Bernstein – #1 NYT Best Selling Author, Speaker and Spirit Junkie*. [online] Gabby Bernstein. Available at: https://gabbybernstein.com/.

Bingham, A. (2012). Newspaper problem pages and British sexual culture since 1918. *Media History*, 18(1): 51–63.

Bingham, A. and Conboy, M. (2015). *Tabloid Century: The Popular Press in Britain, 1896 to the Present*. Oxford: Peter Lang.

boyd, d. (2010). Social network sites as networked publics: Affordances, dynamics, and implications. In Z. Papacharissi, ed., *A Networked Self*. Routledge, pp. 47–66.

—— (2014). *It's Complicated: The Social Lives of Networked Teens*. Cambridge, MA: Yale University Press.

Branden, N. (1995). *The Six Pillars of Self-Esteem*. New York: Bantam Dell Publishing Group.

Brodesser-Akner, T. (2018). How goop's haters made Gywneth Paltrow's company worth $250 million. *The New York Times*. [online] Available at: https://www.nytimes.com/2018/07/25/magazine/big-business-gwyneth-paltrow-wellness.html.

Bruns, A. (2007). Produsage: A working definition. *Produsage.org*, 31.

Bruns, A. and Highfield, T. (2012). Blogs, Twitter, and breaking news: The produsage of citizen journalism. In R. A. Lind, ed., *Produsing Theory in a Digital World: The Intersection of Audiences and Production in Contemporary Theory*. New York: Peter Lang Publishing Inc., pp. 15–32.

Bruns, A. and Jacobs, J. (2006). *Uses of Blogs*. New York: Peter Lang.

Brunsdon, C. (2005). Feminism, postfeminism, Martha, Martha, and Nigella. *Cinema Journal*, 44(2): 110–16.

Bucher, T. and Helmond, A. (2018). The affordances of social media platforms. In J. Burgess, T. Poell and A. Marwick, eds., *The SAGE Handbook of Social Media*. London: SAGE Publications, pp. 233–53.

Byrne, R. (2006). *The Secret*. London: Simon & Schuster.

Calhoun, C. (2012). *The Roots of Radicalism*. Chicago: Chicago University Press.

Cancer Research UK (2018). *Gerson therapy | Cancer in general | Cancer Research UK*. [online] Cancerresearchuk.org. Available at: https://www.cancerresearchuk.org/about-cancer/cancer-in-general/treatment/complementary-alternative-therapies/individual-therapies/gerson.

Carbraugh, D. (1994). *Talking American: Cultural Discourses on Donohue*. Norwood, NJ: Ablex Publishing.

Carr, N. (2008). Is Google making us stupid? What the Internet is doing to our brains. *The Atlantic*. [online] Available at: https://www.theatlantic.com/magazine/archive/2008/07/is-google-making-us-stupid/306868/.

—— (2010). *The Shallows: How The Internet is Changing the Way we Think, Read and Remember*. Atlantic Books Ltd.

Carr, C., Evans, P. and Padarin, H. (2015). *Bubba Yum Yum, The Paleo Way for New Mums, Babies and Toddlers*. Self-published.

Castells, M. (2009). *Communication Power*. Oxford: Oxford University Press.

____ (2012). *Networks of Outrage and Hope*. Cambridge: Polity.

Caulfield, T. (2015). *Is Gwyneth Paltrow Wrong about Everything?: When Celebrity Culture and Science Clash*. Canada: Penguin.

Cavell, S. (1989). *This New Yet Unapproachable America: Lectures After Emerson After Wittgenstein*. Albuquerque: Living Batch Press.

____ (1990). *Conditions Handsome and Unhandsome: The Constitution Of Emersonian Perfectionism*. Chicago, Chicago University Press.

____ (1995). *Philosophical Passages: Wittgenstein, Emerson, Austin, Derrida*. Oxford: Blackwell.

____ (2004). *Cities of Words: Pedagogical Letters on a Register of Moral Life*. Cambridge, MA: Harvard University Press.

Chouliaraki, L. (2013). *The Ironic Spectator: Solidarity in the Age of Post-Humanitarianism*. John Wiley & Sons.

Cole, P. (2005). The structure of the print industry. In R. Keeble, ed., *Print Journalism: A Critical Introduction*. New York: Routledge, pp. 21–38.

Comte, A. (1998). *Comte: Early Political Writings*. Cambridge: Cambridge University Press.

Condé Nast. (2018). *Condé Nast and Goop Enter Multi-Platform Partnership Including Launching Goop in Print – Condé Nast*. [online] Available at: http://www.condenast.com/press/conde-nast-and-goop-enter-multi-platform-partnership-including-launching-goop-in-print/.

Confessore, N., Dance, G. J., Harris, R. and Hansen, M. (2018). The follower factory. *The New York Times*. [online] Available at: https://www.nytimes.com/interactive/2018/01/27/technology/social media-bots.html.

Contois, E. J. (2015). Guilt-free and sinfully delicious: A contemporary theology of weight loss dieting. *Fat Studies*, 4(2): 112–26.

Cooley, C. (1902). *Human Nature and Social Order*. New York: Pantianos Classics.

Couldry, N. 2002. Playing for celebrity: Big Brother as ritual event. *Television and New Media*, 3(3): 283–93.

Crary, J. (2014). *24/7: Late Capitalism and the Ends of Sleep*. London: Verso.

Crawford, R. (1980). Healthism and the medicalization of everyday life. *International Journal of Health Services*, 10(3): 365–88.

Crocker, G. (2015). Keynes, Piketty, and basic income. *Basic Income Studies*, 10(1): 91–113.

Darling, G. (2016). *Radical Self Love*. London: Hay House.

David, M. (2017). *Sharing: Crime Against Capitalism*. Cambridge: Polity.

Davies, C. E. (2004). Language and American 'good taste': Martha Stewart as mass-media role model. In J. Aitchison and D. M. Lewis, eds., *New Media Language*, Routledge, pp. 160–70.

Davis, K. (2007). *The Making of Our Bodies, Ourselves: How Feminism Travels Across Borders*. Durham, NC: Duke University Press.

Denise, J. (2016). Mommy blogger says blog consumed her life. *ABC News*. [online] Available at: https://www.youtube.com/watch?v=HHSsyt7Yxmg

De Ridder, S. and Van Bauwel, S. (2013). Commenting on pictures: Teens negotiating gender and sexualities on social networking sites. *Sexualities*, 16(5–6): 565–86.

Derrick, K. (2017). Are you ready to open wide with Melissa Ambrosini? – The Style Files | Active in Style. [online] Activeinstyle.com. Available at: https://www.activeinstyle.com/the-style-files/2017/12/22/5951/.

Donelly, B. and Toscano, N. (2017). *The Woman who Fooled the World*. London: Scribe UK.

Driver, E. (1989). *A Biography of Cookery Books Published in Britain 1875–1914*. London: Prospect.

Durkheim, E. ([1912] 2001). *The Elementary Forms of Religious Life*. Oxford: Oxford University Press.

Ehrenreich, B. (1989). *Fear of Failing: The Inner Life of the Middle Class*. New York: Harper Perennial

Elliott, P. (2014). *The Sociology of the Professions*. Basingstoke: Palgrave.

Eng, N. and Ornstein, A. (2016). Introduction: Reframing the inequality debate toward opportunity and mobility. *Journal of Social Issues*, 72(4): 619–28.

Ettema, J. S. (1987). Journalism in the 'post-factual age'. *Critical Studies in Mass Communication*, 4(1): 82–6

Evans, P., Gregg, C. and Padarin, H. (2015). *Bubba Yum Yum, The Paleo Way for New Mums, Babies and Toddlers*. C. Carr.

Feldman, M. D. (2004). *Playing Sick? Untangling the Web of Munchausen Syndrome*. London: Routledge.

Flaubert, G. ([1856] 2008). *Madame Bovary*. Oxford: Oxford University Press.

Forleo, M. (2018). *Marie Forleo – host of MarieTV, entrepreneur and philanthropist*. [online] Marieforleo.com. Available at: https://www.marieforleo.com/.

Foucault, M. (1977) *Discipline and Punish: The Birth of the Prison*. London: Allen Lane.

Fox, S. and Duggan, M. (2013). *Health Online 2013*. [online]. Pew Research Center: Internet, Science & Tech. Available at: http://www.pewinternet.org/2013/01/15/health-online-2013/.

Frances, S. (2018). *Stella Frances – Live the Life You Totally Love Living*. [online] Stellafrances.com. Available at: https://stellafrances.com/.

Frisby, D. (1985). *Fragments of Modernity*. Cambridge: Polity.

Fuchs, C. (2007). *Internet and Society: Social Theory in the Information Age*. London: Routledge.

___ (2014). *Social Media: A Critical Introduction*. London: Sage.

Furedi, F. (2003). *Therapy Culture: Cultivating Vulnerability in an Anxious Age*. London: Routledge.

____ (2013). *Authority: A Sociological History*. Cambridge: Cambridge University Press.

Fürsich, E. (2012). Lifestyle journalism as popular journalism: Strategies for evaluating its public role. *Journalism Practice*, 6(1): 12–25.

Gettelman, D. (2011). 'Those who idle over novels': Victorian critics and post-romantic readers. In B. Palmer and A. Buckland, ed., *A Return to the Common Reader: Print Culture and the Novel, 1850–1900*. Surrey: Ashgate, pp. 55–68.

Gibson, B. (2015). *The Whole Pantry*. London: Penguin.

Giddens, A. (1991). *Modernity and Self-identity: Self and Society in the Late Modern Age*. Cambridge: Polity.

____ (1992). *The Transformation of Intimacy*. Cambridge: Polity.

Gillin, P. (2008). New media, new influencers and implications for the public relations profession. *Journal of New Communications Research*, 2(2): 1–10.

Gilmore, J. H. and Pine, B. J. (2007). *Authenticity: What Consumers Really Want*. Cambridge, MA: Harvard Business Press.

Godwin, W. (1793). *Enquiry Concerning Political Justice: And its Influence on Morals and Happiness*. London: G.G.J. and J. Robinson.

____ (1842). *Political Justice*. London: J. Watson.

Goffman, E. (1959). *The Presentation of Self in Everyday Life*. London: Penguin.

Goldacre, B. (2009). *Bad Science*. London: Fourth Estate.

____ (2012). *Bad Pharma: How Medicine is Broken, and How We Can Fix It*. London: Fourth Estate.

Goldstein, K. (1940). *Human Nature in the Light of Psychopathology*. Cambridge, MA: Harvard University Press.

Golec, M. J. (2006). Martha Stewart: Living and the marketing of Emersonian perfectionism. *Home Cultures*, 3(1): 5–20.

Goop (2017). What's goop?: The story behind the brand | goop. *Goop*. [online] Available at: https://goop.com/whats-goop/.

____ 2018a). Postnatal depletion even 10 years later | Goop. *Goop*. [online] Available at: https://goop.com/wellness/health/postnatal-depletion-even-10-years-later/.

____ (2018b). G.P. and Sara Gottfried, M.D., on Perimenopause, menopause and hormone resets | Goop. *Goop*. [online] Available at: https://goop.com/wellness/health/gp-unpacks-perimenopause-hormone-remedies-with-sara-gottfried-m-d.

____ (2018c). Don't call it menopause: Embracing the change. [online] *Goop*. Available at: https://goop.com/wellness/health/dont-call-it-menopause-embracing-the-change/.

____ (2018d). Introducing Madame Ovary: A supplement regimen for your 40s and beyond | Goop. *Goop*. [online] Available at: https://goop.com/wellness/introducing-madame-ovary-a-supplement-regimen-for-your-40s-and-beyond/.

Gramsci, A. (1971). *Selections from the Prison Notebooks* (Vol. 294). London: Lawrence and Wishart.

Greenblatt, S. (2018). *Tyrant: Shakespeare on Power*. London: Bodley Head.

Gregg, M. (2009). Learning to (love) labour: Production cultures and the affective turn. *Communication and Critical/Cultural Studies*, 6(2): 209–14.

Griffin, R. (2019). Gwyneth Paltrow's Goop is cashing in on the world's booming wellness market. *Sydney Morning Herald*. [online] Available at: https://www.smh.com.au/lifestyle/health-and-wellness/gwyneth-paltrow-s-goop-is-cashing-in-on-the-world-s-booming-wellness-market-20190320-p515s9.html.

Grindstaff, L. (2008) *The Money Shot: Trash, Class, and the Making of TV Talk Shows*. Chicago: University of Chicago Press.

Grossman, L. (2006). You – Yes, You – Are TIME's Person of the Year. *Time Magazine*. [online] Available at: http://content.time.com/time/magazine/article/0,9171,1570810,00.html.

(The) *Guardian* (2018). Dear Mariella | Life and style | *Guardian*. [online] Available at: https://www.theguardian.com/lifeandstyle/series/dearmariella.

Gunter, J. (2018). Gwyneth Paltrow wants to monetise menopause. [online] Dr Jen Gunter. Available at: https://drjengunter.wordpress.com/2018/11/05/gwyneth-paltrow-wants-to-monetise-menopause/.

Gustaffson, M. (2014). 'What is Cavellian perfectionism?'. *Journal of Aesthetic Education*, 48(3): 99–110.

Haag, L. L. (1993). Oprah Winfrey: The construction of intimacy in the talk show setting. *Journal of Popular Culture*, 26(4): 115–22.

Haas, R. (2018). *World in Disarray*. London: Penguin.

Habermas, J. (1962). *The Structural Transformation of the Public Sphere: An Inquiry into a Category of Bourgeois Society*. Cambridge: Polity.

Haidt, J. (2012). *The Righteous Mind: Why Good People Are Divided by Politics and Religion*. New York: Pantheon.

Hall, C. (2016). Constance Hall. [online] Facebook.com. Available at: https://www.facebook.com/1019711431407015/posts/we-had-parent-sex-yesterday-you-know-what-parent-sex-is-its-that-35-minutes-you-/1061290347249123/.

Halmos, P. (1978). *The Personal and the Political: Social Work and Political Action*. London: Hutchinson.

Hanusch, F. ed., (2013). *Lifestyle Journalism*. New York: Routledge.

Haraway, D. (1994). A manifesto for cyborgs: Science, technology, and socialist feminism in the 1980s. In S. Seidman, ed., *The Postmodern Turn: New Perspectives on Social Theory*, Cambridge: Cambridge University Press, pp. 82–115.

Hardt, M. (1999). Affective labour. *Boundary 2*, 26(2): 89–100.

Hargittai, E. (2002). Second-level digital divide: Differences in people's online skills. *First Monday*, 7(4).

Hari, V. (2015). *The Food Babe Way*. New York: Little, Brown and Company.

____ (2018). *Food Babe*. [online] Food Babe. Available at: https://foodbabe.com/.

____ (2019). *Feeding You Lies: How to Unravel the Food Industry's Playbook and Reclaim Your Health*. Hay House.

Harpo Productions (2018). About *SuperSoul Sunday*. [online] Available at: http://www.oprah.com/app/super-soul-sunday.html.

Hawkins, P. and Shohet, R. (2012). *Supervision in the Helping Professions*. UK: McGraw-Hill Education.

Healy, D. (2013). *Pharmageddon*. Berkley: University of California Press.

Hearn, A. 2008. 'Meat, mask, burden'. Probing the contours of the branded 'self.' *Journal of Consumer Culture*, 8(2): 197–217.

Hemingway, E. ([1940] 1995). *For Whom the Bell Tolls*. New York: Scribner's.

Hill, N. ([1937] 2011). *Think and Grow Rich*. Hachette UK.

Hinduja, S. and Patchin, J. W. (2017). Cultivating youth resilience to prevent bullying and cyberbullying victimization. *Child Abuse and Neglect*, 73: 51–62.

Hochschild, A. R. (1979). Emotion work, feeling rules, and social structure. *American Journal of Sociology*, 85(3): 551–75.

____ (1983). *The Managed Heart*. Berkeley: University of California Press.

Honest Company (2018). *The Honest Company*. [online] Available at: https://www.honest.com/about-us/who-we-are.

Horton, D. and Wohl, R. (1956). Mass communication and para-social interaction: Observations on intimacy at a distance. *Psychiatry*, 19(3): 215–29.

Howe, J. (2006). The rise of crowdsourcing. *Wired Magazine*, 14(6): 1–4.

Hudson, S. and Hudson, D. (2006). Branded entertainment: a new advertising technique or product placement in disguise? *Journal of Marketing Management*, 22(5–6): 489–504.

Hutchby, I. (2001). Technologies, texts and affordances. *Sociology*, 35(2): 441–56.

Illouz, E. (1999). 'That shadowy realm of the interior': Oprah Winfrey and Hamlet's Glass. *International Journal of Cultural Studies*, 2(1): 109–31

____ (2003). *Oprah Winfrey and the Glamour of Misery: An Essay on Popular Culture*. Columbia University Press.

____ (2007). *Cold Intimacies: The Making of Emotional Capitalism*. Cambridge: Polity.

____ (2008). *Saving the Modern Soul: Therapy, Emotions, and the Culture of Self-Help*. University of California Press.

Instagram (2018). *@goop on Instagram: 'Here's to rebranding life after 40. Link in bio for our newest #goopwellness addition'*. [online] Available at: https://www.instagram.com/p/BphYgkvHJKB/.

James, W. (1890). *The Principles of Psychology*. Henry Holt and Company.

____ (1896). *The Will to Believe: And Other Essays in Popular Philosophy*. Longmans Green.

Jenkins, H. (1992). *Textual Poachers: Television Fans and Participatory Culture.* London: Routledge.

_____ (2006). *Fans, Bloggers, and Gamers: Exploring Participatory Culture.* Vancouver: NYU Press.

Junger, A. (2009). *Clean: The Revolutionary Program to Restore the Body's Natural Ability to Heal Itself.* New York: Harper Collins.

Kahneman, D. and Tversky, A. (2004). Conflict resolution: A cognitive perspective. In E. Shafir, ed., *Preference, belief, and similarity: Selected writings by Amos Tversky.* Cambridge, MA: MIT Press, pp. 729–46.

Kahneman, D., Lovallo, D. and Sibony, O. (2011). Before you make that big decision. *Harvard Business Review,* 89(6): 50–60.

Keane, J. (2009). *The Life and Death of Democracy.* London: Pocket Books.

Keen, A. (2008). *The Cult of the Amateur.* London: Nicholas Brealey.

Kenyon, C. (2016). Being authentic and consistent in your branding on social media. [online] YouTube. Available at: https://www.youtube.com/watch?v=A6ZWTfKPLPE

Khamis, S., Ang, L. and Welling, R. (2017). Self-branding,'micro-celebrity'and the rise of social media influencers. *Celebrity Studies,* 8(2): 191–208.

King, B. (2008). Stardom, celebrity and the para-confession. *Social Semiotics,* 18(2): 115–32.

Klein, N. (1999). *No Logo: Taking on the Brand Bullies.* New York: Picador.

Kolakowski, L. (2005). *Main Currents of Marxism.* New York: Norton.

Kovach, B. and Rosenstiel, T. (2011). *Blur: How to Know What's True in the Age of Information Overload.* Bloomsbury Publishing USA.

Kovalainen, H. A. (2010). Emersonian moral perfectionism. An alternative ethics – but in what sense?. *European Journal of Pragmatism and American Philosophy,* 2(II-2).

Kuhn, T., van Elsas, E., Hakhverdian, A. and van der Brug, W. (2014). An ever wider gap in an ever closer union: Rising inequalities and euroscepticism in 12 West European democracies, 1975–2009. *Socio-Economic Review,* 14(1): 27–45.

Labonte M. (2010). *The 2007–9 Recession: Similarities to and Differences from the Past.* Congressional Research Service CRS 7–5700. Washington, DC: Congressional Research Service.

LaFrance, A. (2014). In 1858, People said the Telegraph was 'too fast for the truth'. *The Atlantic.* [online] Available at: https://www.theatlantic.com/technology/archive/2014/07/in-1858-people-said-the-telegraph-was-too-fast-for-the-truth/375171/.

Langer, E. J. (1975). The illusion of control. *Journal of Personality and Social Psychology,* 32(2): 311–28.

Lasch, C. (1979). *The Culture of Narcissism: American Life in an Age of Diminishing Expectations.* New York: Warner books.

Lawrence, D. ([1928] 2006). *Lady Chatterley's Lover.* London: Penguin Books.

Leader, D. (2008). *The New Black*. London: Penguin.

Leavitt, S. (2002). *From Catharine Beecher to Martha Stewart: A cultural history of domestic advice*. University of North Carolina Press.

LeBesco, K. and Naccarato, P. (2008). Julia Child, Martha Stewart, and the rise of culinary capital. In K. LeBesco and P. Naccarato, eds., *Edible Ideologies: Representing Food and Meaning*. State University of New York Press, pp. 223–38.

Lehrer, J. (2010). Our cluttered minds. *The New York Times*. [online] Available at: https://www.nytimes.com/2010/06/06/books/review/Lehrer-t.html.

Lewis, T. (2008). *Smart living: Lifestyle Media and Popular Expertise*. Peter Lang.

Ling, R. (2010). The 'unboothed' phone: Goffman and the use of mobile communication. In M. Jacobsen, ed., *The Contemporary Goffman*. New York: Routledge, pp. 275–92.

Livingstone, S. (2004). The challenge of changing audiences. *European Journal of Communication*, 19(1): 75–86.

____ (2008). Taking risky opportunities in youthful content creation: Teenagers' use of social networking sites for intimacy, privacy and self-expression. *New Media and Society*, 10(3): 393–411.

____ (2011). Internet, children and youth. In M. Consalvo and C. Ess, eds., *The Handbook of Internet Studies*. Oxford: Blackwell, pp. 348–68.

Lofton, K. (2006). Practicing Oprah; Or, the prescriptive compulsion of a spiritual capitalism. *Journal of Popular Culture*, 39(4): 599–621.

____ (2011). *Oprah: The Gospel of an Icon*. University of California Press.

Lyotard, J. F. (1984). *The Postmodern Condition: A Report on Knowledge*. University of Minnesota Press.

McCartney, M. (2016). Clean eating and the cult of healthism. *British Medical Journal*, 354: 4095.

McGee, M. (2005). *Self-help, Inc.: Makeover Culture in American Life*. Oxford: Oxford University Press.

____ (2012). From makeover media to remaking culture: Four directions for the critical study of self-help culture. *Sociology Compass*, 6(9): 685–93.

McGonigal, J. (2016). *SuperBetter: A Revolutionary Approach To Getting Stronger, Happier, Braver and More Resilient*. New York: Harper Collins.

MacIntyre, A. (1981). *After Virtue: A Study in Moral Theory*. Indiana: University of Notre Dame Press.

McIntyre, L. (2018). *Post-Truth*. Cambridge, MA: MIT Press.

McNair, B. (2017). *Fake News: Falsehood, Fabrication and Fantasy in Journalism*. London: Routledge.

McNally, D. and Speak, K. D. (2002). *Be Your Own Brand*. Berrett-Koehler Publishers.

Malthus, T. (1798). *An Essay on the Principle of Population*. Oxford: Oxford University Press.

Marshall, B. L. (2010). Sexual medicine, sexual bodies and the 'pharmaceutical imagination'. *Science as Culture*, 18(2): 133–49.

Martin, B., Mattson, M. P. and Maudsley, S. (2006). Caloric restriction and intermittent fasting: Two potential diets for successful brain aging. *Ageing Research Reviews*, 5(3): 332–53.

Martin, G. (2017). *The Essential Social Media Marketing Handbook: A New Roadmap for Maximizing Your Brand, Influence, and Credibility*. Weiser.

Marvin, C. (1988). *When Old Technologies Were New: Thinking about Electric Communication in the Late Nineteenth Century*. Oxford: Oxford University Press.

Marwick, A. E. (2013). *Status Update: Celebrity, Publicity, and Branding in the Social Media Age*. Yale University Press.

____ (2015). You may know me from YouTube. In P. D. Marshall and S. Redmond, ed., *A Companion to Celebrity*. John Wiley & Sons, p.333.

Marwick, A. E. and boyd, d. (2011). I tweet honestly, I tweet passionately: Twitter users, context collapse, and the imagined audience. *New Media and Society*, 13(1): 114–33.

Maslow, A. H. (1950). Self-actualising people: A study of psychological health. *Personality*, Symposium 1, pp. 11–34.

____ (1954). *Motivation and Personality*. New York: Harper & Row.

Mason, A. and Meyers, M. (2001). Living with Martha Stewart media: Chosen domesticity in the experience of fans. *Journal of Communication*, 51(4): 801–23.

Mayes, C. (2015) *The Biopolitics of Lifestyle: Foucault, Ethics and Healthy Choices*. London: Routledge.

Mead, G. H. (1930). Cooley's contribution to American social thought. *American Journal of Sociology*, 35(5): 693–706.

____ (1934). *Mind, Self and Society*. Chicago: University of Chicago Press.

Mian, A., Sufi, A. and Trebbi, F. (2015). Foreclosures, house prices, and the real economy. *Journal of Finance*, 70(6): 2587–634.

Mill, J. S. ([1836] 1859). Civilization. In J. S. Mill, *Dissertations and Discussions, Political Philosophical, and Historical*. London: J.W. Parker, pp. 160–205.

Mills, E. (2018). *About – Deliciously Ella*. [online] DeliciouslyElla. Available at: https://deliciouslyella.com/about/.

Mobray, K. (2009). *The 10Ks of Personal Branding: Create a Better You*. iUniverse.

Montoya, P. and Vandehey, T. (2002). *The Brand Called You*. Nightingale Conant.

Morris, M. (2016). *William 1: England's Conqueror*. London: Penguin.

Nichols, T. (2017). *The Death of Expertise: The Campaign Against Established Knowledge and Why it Matters*. Oxford: Oxford University Press.

Norman, D. A. (1988). *The Psychology of Everyday Things*. New York: Basic Books.

OECD (2017). *Centre for Opportunity and Equality – Organisation for Economic*

Co-operation and Development. [online] Oecd. Available at: http://oecd/cope-divide-europe-2017.

Office for National Statistics (2017). *Internet Access – Households and Individuals: 2017.* [online] Office for National Statistics. Available at: https://www.ons.gov.uk/peoplepopulationandcommunity/householdcharacteristics/homeinternetandsocialmediausage/bulletins/internetaccesshouseholdsandindividuals/2017.

O'Neill, E. (2015). ESSENA O'NEILL – WHY I REALLY AM QUITTING SOCIAL MEDIA. [online] YouTube. Available at: https://www.youtube.com/watch?v=gmAbwTQvWX8.

Oprah Winfrey Network (2012). Why Oprah says we all lead spiritual lives. *Oprah's Life Class* [online] Available at: https://www.youtube.com/watch?v=wGu4HuMu0hs.

O'Reilly, T. (2005a). What Is Web 2.0: Design patterns and business models for the next generation of software. [Blog] *O'Reilly.* Available at: http://www.oreilly.com/pub/a/web2/archive/what-is-web-20.html?page=1.

____ (2005b). Web 2.0: Compact definition?. *Radar.* [online] Available at: http://radar.oreilly.com/2005/10/web-20-compact-definition.html.

Page, R. (2012). The linguistics of self-branding and micro-celebrity in Twitter: The role of hashtags. *Discourse and Communication,* 6(2): 181–201.

____ (2018). *Narratives Online: Shared Stories in Social Media.* Cambridge: Cambridge University Press.

Peale, N. V. (1952). *The Power of Positive Thinking.* New York: Prentice-Hall.

Pearson, G. (1983). *Hooligan: A History of Respectable Fears.* London: Basingstoke.

Peters, T. (1997). The brand called you. *Fast Company,* 10(10): 83–90.

Peterson, M. (2018). *Consultations – Don't Eat That.* [online] Don't Eat That. Available at: http://mikhailapeterson.com/consultations/.

Pew Research Center: Internet, Science & Tech. (2018a). *Demographics of Internet and Home Broadband Usage in the United States.* [online] Available at: http://www.pewinternet.org/fact-sheet/internet-broadband/.

____ (2018b). *Demographics of Social Media Users and Adoption in the United States.* [online] Available at: http://www.pewinternet.org/fact-sheet/social media/.

Plato ([1935] 2006). *The Republic: Books 6–10* (Vol. 276). Cambridge, MA: Harvard University Press.

Pontusson, J. and Raess, D. (2012). How (and why) is this time different? The politics of economic crisis in Western Europe and the United States. *Annual Review of Political Science,* 15: 13–33.

Poosh (2019). About. [online] Available at: https://poosh.com/about.

Population Reference Bureau (2018). *2017 World Population Data Sheet.* [online] Prb.org. Available at: https://www.prb.org/2017-world-population-data-sheet/.

Power, S. (2013). *'A Problem from Hell': America and the Age of Genocide*. Basic Books.

Raisborough, J. (2011). *Lifestyle Media and the Formation of the Self*. Basingstoke: Palgrave.

Rampersad, H. K. (2008). *Authentic Personal Branding*. Jakarta: PPM Publishing.

Rattansi, A. (2017). *Bauman and Contemporary Sociology*. Manchester: Manchester University Press.

Ratto, M. and Boler, M., eds. (2014). *DIY Citizenship: Critical Making and Social Media*. MIT Press.

Raun, T. (2018). Capitalising intimacy: New subcultural forms of micro-celebrity strategies and affective labour on YouTube. *Convergence*, 24(1): 99–113.

Rieff, P. (1966). *The Triumph of the Therapeutic: Uses of Faith after Freud*. New York: Harper & Row.

Ritzer, G. and Jurgenson, N. (2010). Production, consumption, prosumption: The nature of capitalism in the age of the digital 'prosumer'. *Journal of Consumer Culture*, 10(1): 13–36.

Roberts, K. (2005). *Lovemarks: The Future Beyond Brands*. PowerHouse Books.

Rogers, C. R. (1961). *On Becoming a Person: A Therapist's View of Psychology*. London: Constable.

Rojek, C. (2001). *Celebrity*. London: Reaktion.

____ (2012). *Fame Attack: The Inflation of Celebrity and its Consequences*. London: Bloomsbury.

____ (2016). *Presumed Intimacy: Parasocial Interaction in Media, Society and Celebrity Culture*. Cambridge: Polity.

Rose, N. (1989) *Governing the Soul: The Shaping of the Private Self*. London: Routledge.

____ (2001). The politics of life itself. *Theory, Culture and Society*, 18(6):1–30.

____ (2006). Disorders without borders: The expanding scope of psychiatric practice. *BioSocieties*, 1(4): 465–84.

____ (2010). *Inventing our Selves: Psychology, Power, and Personhood*. Cambridge: Cambridge University Press.

Rosen, J. (2006). The people formerly known as the audience. *PressThink: Ghost of Democracy in the Media Machine*. [online] Available at: http://archive.pressthink.org/2006/06/27/ppl_frmr.html.

Roth, K. (2010). Stanley Cavell on philosophy, loss, and perfectionism. *Educational Theory*, 60(4): 395–403.

Runciman, D. (2018). *How Democracy Ends*. London: Profile Books.

Saccone Joly, A. (2018*). About*. [online] Anna Saccone Joly. Available at: http://www.annasaccone.com/p/about.html.

Saez, E. and Zucman, G. (2016). Wealth inequality in the United States since 1913: Evidence from capitalised income tax data. *The Quarterly Journal of Economics*, 131(2): 519–78.

Schawbel, D. (2009). *Me 2.0: Build a Powerful Brand to Achieve Career Success.* Kaplan Books.

Science-Based Medicine (2018). *The Gerson Protocol, Cancer, and the Death of Jess Ainscough, a.k.a. 'The Wellness Warrior'.* [online] Available at: https://sciencebasedmedicine.org/the-gerson-protocol-and-the-death-of-jess-ainscough/.

Scrinis, G. (2008). On the ideology of nutritionism. *Gastronomica*, 8(1): 39–48.

Senft, T. M. (2008). *Camgirls: Celebrity and Community in the Age of Social Networks.* New York: Peter Lang.

____ (2013). Microcelebrity and the branded self. In J. Hartley and A. Burns, eds., *A Companion to New Media Dynamics.* New York: Wiley-Blackwell, pp. 346–54.

Sense about Science (2009). *Debunking Detox – Sense about Science.* [online] Senseaboutscience.org. Available at: https://senseaboutscience.org/activities/debunking-detox/.

Sharot, T. (2011). The optimism bias. *Current Biology*, 21(23), pp.R941–R945.

Sherriff, L. (2015). Teen Instagram Star Essena O'Neill reveals she restricted calories and staged photos to fake perfect life. *The Huffington Post.* [online] Available at: https://www.huffingtonpost.co.uk/2015/11/03/teen-instagram-star-essena-oneill-reveals-fake-perfect-life_n_8458840.html?guccounter=1&guce_referrer_us=aHR0cHM6Ly93d3cuZ29vZ2xlLmNvbS88&guce_referrer_cs=rJF5GyvRlQdAmPN8qVTNaw.

Shop.goop.com. (2018). *Psychic Vampire Repellent.* [online] Available at: https://shop.goop.com/shop/products/psychic-vampire-repellent.

Simmel, G. (1950). The stranger. In K. Wolff, ed., *The Sociology of Georg Simmel.* New York: Free Press, pp. 402–8.

____ ([1918] 2010). *The View of Life: Four Metaphysical Essays With Journal Aphorisms.* Chicago: University of Chicago Press.

Sinetar, M. (1989). *Do What You Love, The Money Will Follow: Discovering Your Right Livelihood.* Dell.

Smiles, S. (1859). *Self-help.* London: Penguin.

____ (1908). *Character.* London: John Murray.

Solon, O. (2017). Ex-Facebook president Sean Parker: Site made to exploit human 'vulnerability'. [online] *Guardian.* Available at: https://www.theguardian.com/technology/2017/nov/09/facebook-sean-parker-vulnerability-brain-psychology.

Spigel, L. (1989). The domestic economy of television viewing in postwar America. *Critical Studies in Media Communication*, 6(4): 337–54.

Springhall, J. (1977). *Youth, Empire, and Society: British Youth Movements, 1883–1940.* Taylor & Francis.

Statista (2017). *Global Instagram influencer market size from 2017 to 2019* (in billion US dollars). [online] Available at: https://www.statista.com/statistics/748630/global-instagram-influencer-market-value/.

____ 2018). *Number of monthly active Twitter users worldwide from 1st quarter 2010* to 4th quarter 2018 (in millions). [online] Available at: https://www.statista. com/statistics/282087/number-of-monthly-active-twitter-users/.

_____ (2019a). *Topic: Internet usage worldwide.* [online] www.statista.com. Available at: https://www.statista.com/topics/1145/internet-usage-worldwide/.

_____ (2019b). *Number of monthly active Facebook users worldwide as of 4th quarter 2018 (in millions).* [online] Available at: https://www.statista. com/statistics/264810/number-of-monthly-active-facebook-users-worldwide/.

_____ (2019c). *Most famous social network sites worldwide as of January 2019, ranked by number of active users (in millions).* [online] Available at: https://www.statista.com/statistics/272014/global-social-networks-ranked-by-number-of-users/.

Stenmark, M., Fuller, S. and Zackariasson, U. (2018). *Relativism and Post-Truth in Contemporary Society Possibilities and Challenges.* Palgrave Macmillan.

Stone, S. (2018). *Sue Stone – Welcome. [online] Suestone.com.* Available at: http://www.suestone.com/.

Summers, L. H. (2016). The age of secular stagnation: What it is and what to do about it. *Foreign Affairs,* 95: 2.

Tagg, J. (1988). *The Burden of Representation.* Basingstoke: Macmillan.

Tapscott, D. and Williams, A. D. (2008). *Wikinomics: How Mass Collaboration Changes Everything.* Penguin.

Taussig, M. T. (1992). *The Nervous System.* New York: Routledge.

Taylor, C. (1989). *Sources of the Self: The Making of the Modern Identity.* Harvard University Press.

Terranova, T. (2004). *Network Culture: Politics for the Information Age.* Pluto Press.

The Tig (2018). *Farewell, Darling | The Tig.* [online] Available at: http://thetig. com/; archive: https://web.archive.org/web/20170128130403/http://thetig.com/category/living/.

Thompson, E. P. (1967). Time, work-discipline, and industrial capitalism. *Past and Present,* 38(1): 56–97.

_____ (1993). *Customs in Common: Studies in Traditional Popular Culture.* London: Penguin.

Thompson, J. B. (2000). *Political Scandal: Power and Visability in the Media Age.* Cambridge: Polity.

Timberg, B. M. and Erler, R. J. (2010). *Television Talk: A History of the TV Talk Show.* University of Texas Press.

Toffler, A. (1980). *The Third Wave.* New York: Bantam Books.

Tort, G. (2018). SELFEE Social Media Nano-influencer Tracking and Reward System and Method. US Patent Application 15/831, 410.

Trammell, K. and Keshelashvili, A. (2005). Examining the new influencers: A self-presentation study of A-list blogs. *Journalism and Mass Communication Quarterly,* 82(4): 968–82.

Trunk, P. (2018). *Penelope Trunk*. [online] Penelopetrunk.com. Available at: https://penelopetrunk.com/.

Turkle, S. (2011). *Alone Together: Why We Expect More from Technology and Less from Each Other*. New York: Basic Books.

Turner, G. (2010). *Ordinary People and the Media: The Demotic Turn*. London: Sage.

___ (2013). *Understanding Celebrity*. London: Sage.

Urbas, J. (2010). Cavell's 'moral perfectionism' or Emerson's 'moral sentiment'? *European Journal of Pragmatism and American Philosophy*, 2 (II-2).

van Dijck, J. (2009). Users like you? Theorising agency in user-generated content. *Media, Culture and Society*, 31(1): 41–58.

van Krieken, R. (2012). *Celebrity Society*. London: Routledge.

Various (1930). *The Marriage Book*. London: Amalgamated Press.

Varlow, V. (2018). *Veronica Varlow – Love Witch Veronica Varlow conjures legendary love and a luscious life for YOU*. [online] Lovewitch.com. Available at: https://www.lovewitch.com/.

Vaynerchuk, G. (2009). *Crush it!: Why Now is the Time to Cash in on Your Passion*. HarperStudio.

___ (2018). *GaryVaynerchuk.com*. [online] Garyvaynerchuk.com. Available at: https://www.garyvaynerchuk.com/.

Warner, A. (2017). *The Angry Chef: Bad Science and the Truth About Healthy Eating*. London: Oneworld Publications.

Wayne, C. (2018). *Coach Corey Wayne*. [online] YouTube. Available at: https://www.youtube.com/user/coachcoreywayne/videos.

Weber, M. ([1905] 2013). *The Protestant Ethic and the Spirit of Capitalism*. Routledge.

___ (1968). *On Charisma and Institution Building*. Chicago: University of Chicago Press.

Wensley, R. (2004). Isabella Beeton: Management lessons from the kitchen. *Business Strategy Review*, 15(3): 66–72.

Wicks, J. (2015). *Lean in 15: 15 Minute Meals and Workouts to Keep You Lean and Healthy*. London: Pan Macmillan.

___ (2018). *Welcome / The Body Coach*. [online] Thebodycoach.com. Available at: https://www.thebodycoach.com/.

Wiener-Bronner, D. (2018). Oprah dumped a quarter of her Weight Watchers stake. [online] CNNMoney. Available at: https://money.cnn.com/2018/03/07/news/companies/oprah-weight-watchers-shares/index.html.

Wimbrey, J. (2018). [online] *Johnnywimbrey.com*. Available at: https://www.johnnywimbrey.com/.

Winfrey, O. (2018a). What Oprah knows for sure about authenticity. *Oprah.com* [online] Available at: http://www.oprah.com/inspiration/what-oprah-knows-for-sure-about-authenticity.

___ (2018b). Ask Oprah: How would you describe The Oprah Winfrey Show? *#WatchingOprah*. [online] Available at: https://www.youtube.com/watch?v=o6pXgmPMuzw.

___ (2019). Welcome to the New OprahMag.com! The Oprah Magazine [online] Available at: https://www.oprahmag.com/about/a23518270/oprah-welcome-video/.

Wolin, S. S. (2010). *Democracy Incorporated: Managed Democracy and the Specter of Inverted Totalitarianism*. Princeton: Princeton University Press.

Woodward, E. (2016). *Deliciously Ella Every Day*. London: Yellow Kite.

World Health Organization (2018a). *Constitution of WHO: principles*. [online] Available at: https://www.who.int/about/mission/en/.

___ (2018b). *Depression*. [online] Available at: https://www.who.int/news-room/fact-sheets/detail/depression.

Wouters, C. (2007). *Informalization: Manners and Emotions Since 1890*. London: Sage.

YouTube (2017). *Advice for Starting a YouTube Channel! | The Mom's View*. [online] Available at: https://www.youtube.com/watch?v=kCKKzigrj74.

Zarrella, D. (2009). *The Social Media Marketing Book*. O'Reilly Media.

Zoglin, R. (1988). Lady with a calling. *Time Magazine*, pp. 62–4.

Index